Test Item File

MARKETING

An Introduction

Gail Kirby
Santa Clara University

Test Item File

Fourth Edition

MARKETING
An Introduction

Philip Kotler
Gary Armstrong

Prentice Hall
Upper Saddle River New Jersey 07458

Project editor: Richard Bretan
Acquisitions editor: David Borkowsky
Associate editor: John Larkin
Manufacturing buyer: Arnold Vila

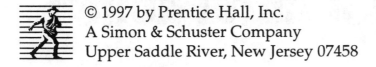

© 1997 by Prentice Hall, Inc.
A Simon & Schuster Company
Upper Saddle River, New Jersey 07458

Printed in the United States of America

10 9 8 7 6 5 4 3 2 1

ISBN 0-13-252909-2

Prentice-Hall International (UK) Limited, *London*
Prentice-Hall of Australia Pty. Limited, *Sydney*
Prentice-Hall Canada Inc., *Toronto*
Prentice-Hall Hispanoamericana, S.A., *Mexico*
Prentice-Hall of India Private Limited, *New Delhi*
Prentice-Hall of Japan, Inc., *Tokyo*
Simon & Schuster Asia Pte. Ltd., *Singapore*
Editora Prentice-Hall do Brasil, Ltda., *Rio de Janeiro*

CONTENTS

Prentice Hall Instructor Support
for Test Item Files

This printed Test Item File is just one part of Prentice Hall's comprehensive testing support service which also includes:

1. **Prentice Hall Custom Test.** This powerful computerized testing package is designed to operate on all platforms: DOS, Windows, and Macintosh. It offers full mouse support, complete question editing capabilities, random test generation, graphics and printing capabilities.

Prentice Hall Custom Test has a unique dual design: **Easytest** for the novice computer user, and **Fulltest** for those who wish to write their own questions or create their own graphics.

The built-in algorithmic module enables the instructor to create thousands of questions and answers from a single question template.

In addition to traditional printing capabilities, Prentice Hall Custom Test also offers the On-Line Testing System—the most efficient, time-saving examination aid on the market. With just a few keystrokes, the instructor can administer, correct, record, and return computerized exams over a variety of networks.

Prentice Hall Custom Test is designed to assist educators in the recording and processing of results from student exams and assignments. Much more than a computerized gradebook, it combines a powerful database with analytical capabilities so the instructor can generate a full set of statistics. There is no grading system more complete or easier to use.

Toll free technical support is offered to all users, and the Prentice Hall Custom Test is free. You may contact your local representative or call our Faculty Support Services department at 1-800-526-0485. Please identify the main text author and title.

2. For those instructors without access to a computer, we offer the popular **Prentice Hall Telephone Testing Service.** It's simple, fast, and efficient. Simply pick the questions you would like on your test from this bank and call our Simon & Schuster Testing Services at 1-800-550-1701; outside the U.S. and Canada call 612-550-1705.

Identify the main text and test questions you would like, as well as any special instructions. We will create the test (or multiple versions if you wish) and send you a master copy for duplication within 48 hours. This service is free to adopters for life of text use.

Chapter 1

1. The social and managerial process by which individuals and groups obtain what they need and want through creating and exchanging products and value with others is called:

   a) economics
   b) marketing
   c) sales
   d) demand analysis

   Answer: (b) Difficulty: 2 Page: 4

2. The term "marketing" is best understood as the process of:

   a) telling and selling.
   b) creating customer needs.
   c) making a sale.
   d) satisfying customer needs.

   Answer: (d) Difficulty: 1 Page: 4

3. Chrysler Corporation has recently announced that the firm will "completely align all aspects of its operations toward the goal of improving customer satisfaction." In order to accomplish this goal, Chrysler must become increasingly _____ - oriented.

   a) sales
   b) production
   c) marketing
   d) promotion

   Answer: (c) Difficulty: 3 Page: 4

4. A state of felt deprivation is called a(n):

   a) need.
   b) motive.
   c) want.
   d) desire.

   Answer: (a) Difficulty: 1 Page: 4

5. Basic needs such as those for food, clothing, shelter, and safety refer to:

   a) human needs.
   a) physical needs.
   b) social needs.
   d) individual needs.

   Answer: (b) Difficulty: 1 Page: 4

6. When individuals seek out friendship and group membership they are attempting to satisfy:

   a) human needs.
   b) physical needs.
   c) social needs.
   d) individual needs.

   Answer: (c) Difficulty: 1 Page: 4

7. The great majority of products on the market today are intended to:

   a) anticipate future desires.
   b) create new needs.
   c) satisfy existing wants.
   d) create psychological dependence.

   Answer: (c) Difficulty: 2 Page: 5

8. Human needs that are shaped by culture and individual personality are referred to as:

   a) human wants.
   b) new products.
   c) existing products.
   d) demands.

   Answer: (a) Difficulty: 1 Page: 5

9. All of the following are ways outstanding companies understand their customers except:

   a) Conduct consumer research about consumer likes and dislikes.
   b) Analyze customer inquiry, warranty, and service data.
   c) Observe customers using their own and competing products.
   d) Train salespeople regarding new product attributes.

   Answer: (d) Difficulty: 3 Page: 6

10. A _____ is anything that can be offered to a market to satisfy a need or want.

   a) product
   b) place
   c) service
   d) idea

   Answer: (a) Difficulty: 1 Page: 7

11. The Friendly Company has sold the same basic product since its entry into the marketplace. Each time the sales of its product has slipped, the firm has responded by cutting price and increasing promotion. In spite of its efforts, sales continued to decline, Friendly's "product-focused" response is evidence of:

    a) a profit-maximization philosophy.
    b) production myopia.
    c) maximization myopia.
    d) marketing myopia.

    Answer: (d)   Difficulty: 3 Page: 7

12. The tendency of some manufacturers to focus only on existing wants and lose sight of underlying customer needs is called:

    a) strategic selling
    b) marketing myopia
    c) production orientation
    d) demarketing

    Answer: (b)   Difficulty: 2 Page: 7

13. _____ depends on a product's perceived performance relative to the buyer's expectations.

    a) Customer value
    b) Customer satisfaction
    c) Quality
    d) TQM

    Answer: (b)   Difficulty: 1 Page: 8

14. The difference between the values that the customer gains from owning and using a product and the costs of obtaining the product is called:

    a) customer value
    b) customer satisfaction
    c) quality
    d) TQM

    Answer: (a) Difficulty: 1 Page: 8

15. One way to view delivered customer value is as:

    a) lost added value opportunity.
    b) customer value assessment.
    c) "profit" to the customer.
    d) unavoidable marketing costs.

    Answer: (c)   Difficulty: 3 Page: 8

16. _____ is an approach to improve the quality of products, services, and marketing process.

    a) Total customer satisfaction
    b) Total customer value
    c) Total quality management
    d) Return of quality

    Answer: (c)   Difficulty: 2 Page: 9

17. _____ is the act of obtaining a desired object from someone by offering something in return is called:

    a) Donation
    b) Exchange
    c) Sales
    d) Transaction

    Answer: (b)   Difficulty: 1 Page: 10

18. The shift in marketing from trying to maximize profit on individual transactions to maximizing mutually beneficial relationships with consumers and others is called:

    a) sales marketing.
    b) production marketing.
    c) societal marketing.
    d) relationship marketing.

    Answer: (d)   Difficulty: 2 Page: 12

19. Which of the following do marketers need to build long-term relationships with:

    a) valued customers
    b) distributors
    c) suppliers
    d) All of the above

    Answer: (d)   Difficulty: 1 Page: 12

20. Most basically, the goal of relationship marketing is to:

    a) deliver long-term value to customers
    b) build strong economic ties to customers.
    c) maximize the profit on each individual transaction.
    d) All of the above.

    Answer: (a)   Difficulty: 2 Page: 12

21. Which of the following best identifies how a company might build value and satisfaction by adding financial benefits?

    a) Ritz-Carlton Hotels employees treat customers as individuals.
    b) Saturn invited car owners to a "Saturn Homecoming".
    c) United Airlines offers frequent-flyer programs.
    d) FedEx offers its FedEx Ship program to many of its best customers.

    Answer: (c)   Difficulty: 3 Page: 12

22. The set of actual and potential buyers for a product is defined as a(n):

    a) sale.
    b) market.
    c) demand.
    d) population.

    Answer: (b)   Difficulty: 1 Page: 13

23. _____ means managing markets to bring about exchanges and relationships for the purpose of creating value and satisfying needs and wants.

    a) Marketing
    b) Selling
    c) Wholesaling
    d) Retailing

    Answer: (a)   Difficulty: 1 Page: 14

24. The analysis, planning, implementation, and control of programs designed to create, build, and maintain beneficial exchanges with target markets for the purpose of achieving organizational objectives is called:

    a) demand management
    b) sales management
    c) marketing management
    d) profitable customer relationships.

    Answer: (c)   Difficulty: 2 Page: 15

25. Another term for marketing management is:

    a) demarketing.
    b) value marketing.
    c) relationship marketing.
    d) demand management.

    Answer: (d)   Difficulty: 2 Page: 15

26. The aim of _____ is to reduce demand temporarily or permanently.

    a) societal marketing
    b) demarketing
    c) control marketing
    d) demand management

    Answer: (b)   Difficulty: 2 Page: 15

27. Faced with production cutbacks necessitated by the closing of its new nuclear plant, Hi-Voltage Electric has embarked upon a campaign to convince its customers to reduce their consumption of electrical energy. The firm's effort would be best described as:

    a) demarketing.
    b) remarketing.
    c) societal marketing.
    d) demand creation.

    Answer: (a)   Difficulty: 3 Page: 15

28. The _____ holds that consumers will favor products that are available and highly affordable.

    a) production concept
    b) product concept
    c) selling concept
    d) marketing concept

    Answer: (a)   Difficulty: 1 Page: 18

29. When demand for a product exceeds the supply, the most useful marketing management philosophy is typically which of the following?

    a) production concept.
    b) product concept.
    c) selling concept.
    d) marketing concept.

    Answer: (a)   Difficulty: 1 Page: 18

30. When the product's costs are too high for the market, which marketing management philosophy is appropriate for improving the company's position?

    a) production concept
    b) product concept
    c) selling concept
    d) marketing concept

    Answer: (a)   Difficulty: 1 Page: 18

31. The General Motors Corporation believes that marketing success results from production and distribution efficiency. The firm's marketing approach is based on the:

    a) production concept.
    b) product concept.
    c) selling concept
    d) marketing concept.

    Answer: (a)   Difficulty: 3   Page: 18

32. The _____ holds that consumers will favor products that offer the most quality, performance, and innovative features.

    a) production concept
    b) product concept
    c) selling concept
    d) marketing concept

    Answer: (b)   Difficulty: 1   Page: 18

33. Marketing myopia, or the tendency to focus too narrowly on one's business, is a risk of which marketing management philosophy?

    a) production concept
    b) product concept
    c) selling concept
    d) marketing concept

    Answer: (b)   Difficulty: 1   Page: 19

34. The Everlasting Company is experiencing all of the problems associated with marketing myopia. The firm is most likely practicing the _____ concept.

    a) production
    b) product
    c) selling
    d) marketing

    Answer: (b)   Difficulty: 3   Page: 19

35. The _____ holds that consumers will not buy enough of a company's products unless the company undertakes large-scale promotion effort.

    a) production concept
    b) product concept
    c) selling concept
    d) marketing concept

    Answer: (c)   Difficulty: 1   Page: 19

36. Which marketing management philosophy would a firm typically practice when marketing unsought goods?

    a) production concept
    b) product concept
    c) selling concept
    d) marketing concept

    Answer: (c)   Difficulty: 1 Page: 19

37. Which marketing management philosophy would a firm typically practice when they are faced with overcapacity?

    a) production concept
    b) product concept
    c) selling concept
    d) marketing concept

    Answer: (c)   Difficulty: 1 Page: 19

38. The _____ holds that achieving organizational goals depends on determining the needs and wants of target markets and delivering the desired satisfactions more effectively and efficiently than the competition.

    a) production concept
    b) product concept
    c) selling concept
    d) marketing concept

    Answer: (d)   Difficulty: 1 Page: 19

39. Which marketing management philosophy takes an inside-out approach?

    a) production concept
    b) product concept
    c) selling concept
    d) marketing concept

    Answer: (c)   Difficulty: 1 Page: 19

40. Which marketing management philosophy takes an outside-in approach?

    a) production concept
    b) product concept
    c) selling concept
    d) marketing concept

    Answer: (d)   Difficulty: 1 Page: 20

41. Which marketing management philosophy is based on making profits by creating long-term customer relationships based on customer value and satisfaction?

    a) product concept
    b) selling concept
    c) marketing concept
    d) societal marketing concept

    Answer: (c)   Difficulty: 1 Page: 20

42. The McDonald's Corporation devotes a great deal of time and effort to understanding the needs and wants of its present and potential customers. This marketing "intelligence" is used to create market offerings the firm believes will produce profits through the delivery of customer satisfactions. McDonald's practices the:

    a) selling concept.
    b) marketing concept.
    c) production concept.
    d) product concept.

    Answer: (b)   Difficulty: 3 Page: 20

43. The _____ holds that a company should determine the needs, wants, and interests of target markets and satisfy them in a way that improves individual and community well-being.

    a) production concept
    b) product concept
    c) marketing concept
    d) societal marketing concept

    Answer: (d)   Difficulty: 1 Page: 22

44. Under the societal marketing concept, a company will balance these considerations in setting their marketing policies except:

    a) company profits.
    b) consumer wants.
    c) society's interests.
    d) the competition's interests.

    Answer: (d)   Difficulty: 2 Page: 23

45. All of the following supports the societal marketing concept that questions whether the pure marketing concept is adequate except:

    a) environmental problems
    b) resource shortages
    c) population growth
    d) the changing world economy

    Answer: (d)   Difficulty: 1 Page: 22

46. The designing of social marketing campaigns to encourage energy conservation and concerns for the environment are characteristics of which new challenge to marketing?

    a) Rapid globalization.
    b) Growth of nonprofit marketing
    c) The changing world economy
    d) The call for social responsibility

    Answer: (b)   Difficulty: 2   Page: 25

47. According to John Naisbitt, author of *Megatrend* and *The Global Paradox*, "Telecommunications is the driving force that is simultaneously creating the huge global economy and making its parts smaller and more powerful." This statement reflects which new challenge to marketing?

    a) Rapid globalization.
    b) Growth of nonprofit marketing
    c) The changing world economy
    d) The information technology boom

    Answer: (d)   Difficulty: 2   Page: 26

48. The growing presence of "hybrid" products whose design, materials purchases, manufacturing, and marketing is taking place in several countries, is typical of which of the following?

    a) Rapid globalization.
    b) Growth of nonprofit marketing
    c) The changing world economy
    d) The call for social responsibility

    Answer: (a)   Difficulty: 2   Page: 27

49. The loss of buying power in the United States, even in the face of rising wages, is one characteristic of:

    a) Rapid globalization.
    b) Growth of nonprofit marketing
    c) The changing world economy
    d) The call for social responsibility

    Answer: (c)   Difficulty: 2   Page: 28

50. The fact that companies will be held to an increasingly higher standard of environmental responsibility in their marketing and manufacturing activities is one characteristic of:

    a) Rapid globalization.
    b) Growth of nonprofit marketing
    c) The changing world economy
    d) The call for social responsibility

    Answer: (d)   Difficulty: 2   Page: 30

TRUE/FALSE

51. Marketing is BEST understood in the broad sense of satisfying customer needs.

    Answer: True Difficulty: 1 Page: 4

52. A human need is a state of felt deprivation.

    Answer: True Difficulty: 1 Page: 4

53. A human want is a state of felt deprivation.

    Answer: False Difficulty: 2 Page: 4

54. Human wants are the form taken by human needs as they are shaped by culture and individual personality.

    Answer: True Difficulty: 2 Page: 5

55. Wants are described in terms of objects that will satisfy demands.

    Answer: False Difficulty: 2 Page: 5

56. Demands are wants backed by buying power.

    Answer: True Difficulty: 1 Page: 5

57. In designing marketing strategies it is important to understand customer needs, wants, and demand.

    Answer: True Difficulty: 2 Page: 6

58. At Motorola, top executives visit corporate customers at their offices to gain better insights into their wants.

    Answer: False Difficulty: 3 Page: 6

59. A product is any physical object that can be offered to market to satisfy a need or want.

    Answer: False Difficulty: 2 Page: 7

60. Most sellers focus their attention on the benefits produced by the products they offer.

    Answer: False Difficulty: 3 Page: 7

61. Goods and services are terms used to distinguish between physical products and intangible ones, respectively.

    Answer: True Difficulty: 2 Page: 7

62. Marketing myopia occurs when sellers are so taken with their products that they focus only on existing wants and lose sight of underlying needs.

    Answer: True Difficulty: 3 Page: 7

63. Customer satisfaction is the difference between the values that the customer gains from owning and using a product and the costs of obtaining the product.

    Answer: False Difficulty: 2 Page: 8

64. Customer value is the difference between the values that the customer gains from owning and using a product and the costs of obtaining the product.

    Answer: True Difficulty: 2 Page: 8

65. Customer satisfaction depends on a product's perceived performance in delivering value relative to a buyer's expectations.

    Answer: True Difficulty: 2 Page: 8

66. Although the customer-centered firm seeks to deliver high customer satisfaction relative to competitors, it does not try to maximize customer satisfaction.

    Answer: True Difficulty: 2 Page: 8

67. If a company wants to increase profits it can always increase customer satisfaction by lowering its price or increasing its service.

    Answer: False Difficulty: 3 Page: 9

68. Total quality management is an approach in which all the company's people are involved in improving the quality of products, services, and business processes.

    Answer: True Difficulty: 2 Page: 9

69. Exchange is the act of obtaining a desired object from someone by offering something in return.

    Answer: True Difficulty: 2 Page: 10

70. A transaction consists of a trade between two parties that involves at least one thing of value, agreed-upon conditions, a time of agreement, and a place of agreement.

    Answer: False Difficulty: 2 Page: 11

71. Relationship marketing is part of the larger idea of transaction marketing.

    Answer: False Difficulty: 2 Page: 12

72. Building good relationships and profitable transitions is the fundamental principle of relationship marketing.

    Answer: True Difficulty: 2 Page: 12

73. Relationship marketing means that marketers must focus on managing their customers as well as their products.

    Answer: True Difficulty: 2 Page: 13

74. A market is the set of all actual buyers of a product.

    Answer: False Difficulty: 2 Page: 13

75. The goal of marketing is to understand the needs and wants of specific markets and to serve as many markets as possible.

    Answer: False Difficulty: 3 Page: 14

76. Marketing is the process of managing markets to bring about exchanges and relationships for the purpose of creating value and satisfying needs and wants.

    Answer: True Difficulty: 2 Page: 14

77. Demarketing is to reduce or shift demand temporarily or permanently.

    Answer: True Difficulty: 1 Page: 15

78. Although related, demand marketing and marketing management are very different activities.

    Answer: False Difficulty: 2 Page: 15

79. Marketing today focuses on attracting new customers and making the sale.

    Answer: False Difficulty: 1 Page: 15

80. Companies today are going all out to retain current customers and build lasting customer relationships.

    Answer: True Difficulty: 2 Page: 15

81. The production concept is not a useful marketing management philosophy for making business decisions in situations where demand exceeds supply.

    Answer: False Difficulty: 2 Page: 18

82. Consumers will favor products that offer the most quality, performance, and innovative features is a central idea of the product concept.

    Answer: True Difficulty: 2 Page: 18

83. All manufacturers believe that if you build a better mousetrap, the world will beat a path to their door.

    Answer: False Difficulty: 2 Page: 18

84. Overcoming the reluctance of consumers to purchase enough of a product is a characteristic of the product concept.

    Answer: False Difficulty: 2 Page: 19

85. The selling concept is typically practiced with unsought goods and services.

    Answer: True Difficulty: 2 Page: 19

86. Achieving organizational goals depends on determining the needs and wants of target markets better than the competition is the goal of the marketing concept.

    Answer: True Difficulty: 2 Page: 19

87. The selling concept takes an "inside-out" perspective toward the exchange process.

    Answer: True Difficulty: 2 Page: 19

88. The marketing concept takes an "outside-in" perspective toward the exchange process.

    Answer: True Difficulty: 2 Page: 20

89. The societal marketing concept holds that the organization should determine the needs, wants, and interests of target markets.

    Answer: True Difficulty: 2 Page: 22

90. The pure marketing concept is adequate in an age of environmental problems, resource shortages, rapid population growth, worldwide economic stress, and neglected social services.

    Answer: False Difficulty: 2 Page: 22

91. The changing world economy is the primary reason for the emergence of "hybrid products", where design, material purchases, manufacture, and marketing may all take place in different countries.

    Answer: False Difficulty: 2 Page: 27

ESSAY

92. Define marketing and discuss its role in the economy.

    Answer:
    Marketing is a social and managerial process by which individuals and groups obtain what they need and want through creating and exchanging products and value with others. Marketing's importance has increased as a result of the development of a more affluent society and more intense competition. Economic roles include meeting needs, wants, and demand; creating products, creating value and satisfaction; facilitating exchanges, transactions, and mutually beneficial relationships; developing markets, meeting societal needs, increasing consumer choice, and providing fair profits.

    Difficulty: 3 Page: 4

93. Discuss how needs and wants differ. Does the marketer "create" either, or both, of these desires?

    Answer:
    Needs are best described as felt deprivations. At the extreme, the deprivation of physical requirements can cause discomfort or death. Psychological needs for belongingness, affection, and expression also exist--they are a basic part of human make-up.
       Wants are alternative means of satisfying needs. Acceptable wants are shaped by culture and the individual's personality. The marketer cannot alter needs or wants--it can only seek to stimulate a need by bringing it to the conscious consideration of the consumer and attempt to persuade the consumer that its particular offering is the best means of satisfying his or her desires.

    Difficulty: 3 Page: 5

94. What is a "product"? Why do marketers define product so broadly?

    Answer:
    Products consist of all attributes--both tangible and intangible--capable of providing want satisfaction. The key, of course, is satisfaction. The marketer is essentially selling satisfaction--the product is simply the vehicle by which that satisfaction is supplied. By defining product broadly, the marketer can focus on the fact that satisfaction is the real offering and can seek that combination of tangible and intangible attributes that will deliver the greatest total satisfaction for the consumer.

    Difficulty: 3 Page: 7

95. Define "demarketing". Under what circumstances might this form of demand management be required?

    Answer:
    Demarketing is the attempt to find ways to reduce demand for a product on a temporary or permanent basis. Typically, demarketing is a short-term response to overfull demand. The firm may seek to reduce demand to manageable levels by raising prices, reducing promotion, or rationing supply until production can catch up with demand. Occasionally, demarketing may be used in an attempt to permanently limit the demand of certain products that may be considered hazardous or socially unacceptable. Finally, a firm may deliberately demarket a product that it intends to remove from the market in the future.

    Difficulty: 3 Page: 15

96. Compare the five marketing management philosophies.

    Answer:
    Production concept: consumers favor products that are available and highly affordable.
    Product concept: consumers favor products that offer most value, performance, innovative features.
    Selling concept: consumers will not normally buy enough products on their own
    Marketing concept: determining the needs and want of target markets and delivering the desired satisfactions more effectively and efficiently than competitors do.
    Societal marketing concept: organizations must determine the needs, wants, and interest of target markets and deliver the desired satisfactions more effectively and efficiently than competitors in a way that maintains or improves the consumer's and society's well-being.

    Difficulty: 3 Page: 18-23

97. The Coca-Cola Company is a highly responsible corporation producing fine soft drinks that satisfy consumer tastes; yet Coke has little nutritional value, can harm people's teeth, contains caffeine and adds to the litter problem with disposable bottles and cans. Discuss the marketing management philosophy that focuses on these issues.

Answer:
The marketing management philosophy that focuses on these issues is the societal marketing concept. The societal marketing concept calls upon marketers to balance three considerations in setting their marketing policies: company profits, consumer wants, and society's interests. Although companies base marketing decisions on short-run profits, they began to recognize the importance of balancing consumer wants and society's interests.

Difficulty: 3 Page: 23

98. Discuss the relationship between value, satisfaction, and quality.

Answer:
Customer value is the difference between the values the customer gains from owning and using a product and the costs of obtaining it. Satisfaction depends on a product's perceived performance in delivering value relative to the buyer's expectations. Quality, especially in the form of TQM, is a company's commitment to constant improvement. Satisfaction comes from delighting and surprising customers with more quality, which heightens their perceived sense of value. Such practices are the formula for long-term success.

Difficulty: 3 Page: 8-9

99. Discuss the nine premises regarding quality improvement.

Answer:
1. Quality is in the eyes of the customer. 2. Quality must be reflected not just in the company's products, but in every company activity. 3. Quality requires total employee commitment. 4. Quality requires high-quality partners. 5. A quality program cannot save a poor product. 6. Quality can always be improved. 7. Quality improvement sometimes requires quantum leaps. 8. Quality does not cost more. 9. Quality is necessary but may not be sufficient.

Difficulty: 3 Page: 10-11

100. Identify and discuss the major forces now changing the marketing landscape and challenging marketing strategy.

Answer:
A growth in nonprofit marketing to meet new needs. Rapid globalization marked by geographic dispersion of purchasing, manufacturing, and marketing activities. A changing world economy marked by a decline in a real buying power and the increase in two-income households in the U.S. Increased demand for social responsibility including more ethical business practices and more attention to the environmental consequences of business decisions. A new marketing landscape chacterized by extremely rapid change.

Difficulty: 3 Page: 24-31

Chapter 2

1. The task of selecting an overall company strategy for long-run survival and growth is called:

   a) annual planning.
   b) marketing strategy.
   c) long-range planning.
   d) strategic planning.

   Answer: (d)   Difficulty: 1 Page: 37

2. The process of developing and maintaining a strategic fit between the organization's goals and capabilities and its changing marketing opportunities is called:

   a) annual planning.
   b) strategic planning.
   c) marketing planning.
   d) long-range planning.

   Answer: (b)   Difficulty: 1 Page: 37

3. Which of the following is true regarding formal planning for large types of companies:

   a) Encourages management to think ahead systematically.
   b) Forces the company to sharpen its objectives and policies.
   c) Provides clearer performance standards for control.
   d) All of the above

   Answer: (d)   Difficulty: 3 Page: 37

4. APPLE Corporation has just revised a five-year plan that includes the firm's long-term objectives, the major marketing strategies that will be used to attain them, and the necessary resources required. The document produced from their work is called the:

   a) annual plan.
   b) long-range plan.
   c) capital budget.
   d) strategic plan.

   Answer: (d)   Difficulty: 2 Page: 37

5. Marketing planning occurs at which of the following company levels:

   a) The business-unit level
   b) The product level
   c) The market level
   d) All of the above.

   Answer: (d)   Difficulty: 3 Page: 38

6. The statement of the organization's purpose that acts like an "invisible hand" in guiding people in the organization to action is called:

   a) the strategic plan
   b) the mission statement
   c) the company objectives and goals
   d) the business portfolio

   Answer: (b)   Difficulty: 2   Page: 38

7. When management asks the simple-sounding questions "What is our business?", "What do customers value?" and "What should our business be?", the answers are typically found in which of the following?

   a) the strategic plan
   b) the mission statement
   c) the company objectives and goals
   d) the business portfolio

   Answer: (b)   Difficulty: 2   Page: 38

8. A market-oriented mission statement defines the business in terms of satisfying basic customer needs. Thus, AT&T is in the:

   a) telephone business.
   b) computer business.
   c) communications business.
   d) technology business.

   Answer: (c)   Difficulty: 2   Page: 38

9. The first step in the strategic planning process requires the firm to:

   a) set company objectives and goals.
   b) define the firm's mission.
   c) design the business portfolio.
   d) identify strategic business units.

   Answer: (b)   Difficulty: 1   Page: 38

10. Ideally, the best company mission statements should be:

    a) business oriented.
    b) market oriented.
    c) product oriented.
    d) production oriented.

    Answer: (b)   Difficulty: 1   Page: 38

11. Mission statements should be all of the following except:

    a) be realistic.
    b) be specific.
    c) be motivating.
    d) be profit oriented.

    Answer: (d)   Difficulty: 2 Page: 40

12. When setting company objectives and goals, which of the following is true?

    a) Marketing strategies must be developed to support marketing objectives.
    b) Increasing dollars spent on market research will increase profits.
    c) Profits can be improved by reducing costs.
    d) All of the above

    Answer: (a) Difficulty: 2 Page: 40

13. The collection of businesses that make up the company are described in the:

    a) business portfolio.
    b) business plan.
    c) strategic plan.
    d) planning portfolio.

    Answer: (a)   Difficulty: 1 Page: 40

14. A tool by which management identifies and evaluates various businesses that make up the company is called:

    a) strategic planning.
    b) market share analysis.
    c) strategic business unit analysis.
    d) business portfolio analysis.

    Answer: (d)   Difficulty: 2 Page: 41

15. In most standard portfolio-analysis methods, the SBUs are evaluated on the basis of:

    a) company resources and management skills.
    b) market attractiveness and industry strength.
    c) sales potential and competitive costs.
    d) market size and distribution requirements.

    Answer: (b)   Difficulty: 2 Page: 41

16. Under the BCG growth-share matrix, the market growth rate provides a measure of:

    a) market attractiveness.
    b) relative market share.
    c) company market strength.
    d) product profitability.

    Answer: (a)   Difficulty: 1 Page: 41

17. Under the BCG growth-share matrix, relative market share provides a measure of:

    a) market attractiveness.
    b) company market strength.
    c) relative profitability.
    d) product profitability.

    Answer: (b)   Difficulty: 1 Page: 41

18. Under the BCG growth-share matrix, high-growth, high-share businesses or products are called:

    a) cash cows.
    b) dogs.
    c) question marks.
    d) stars.

    Answer: (d)   Difficulty: 1 Page: 41

19. Under the BCG growth-share matrix, low-growth, high-share businesses or products are called:

    a) cash cows.
    b) dogs.
    c) question marks.
    d) stars.

    Answer: (a)   Difficulty: 1 Page: 41

20. Under the BCG growth-share matrix, high-growth, low-share businesses or products are called:

    a) cash cows.
    b) dogs.
    c) question marks.
    d) stars.

    Answer: (c)   Difficulty: 1 Page: 42

21. Under the BCG growth-share matrix, low-growth, low-share businesses or products are called:

    a) cash cows.
    b) dogs.
    c) question marks.
    d) stars.

    Answer: (b)   Difficulty: 1 Page: 42

22. The Levi Strauss Company plans to introduce a new SBU. The introduction will be financed by funds generated by Levi's:

    a) stars.
    b) question marks.
    c) cash cows.
    d) dogs.

    Answer: (c)   Difficulty: 2 Page: 41

23. According to the BCG growth-share matrix, which type of SBU needs heavy investment to finance their rapid growth?

    a) cash cows.
    b) dogs.
    c) question marks.
    d) stars.

    Answer: (d)   Difficulty: 1 Page: 41

24. According to the BCG growth-share matrix, which type of SBU produces a lot of cash to support other SBUs in need of investment?

    a) cash cows.
    b) dogs.
    c) question marks.
    d) stars.

    Answer: (a)   Difficulty: 1 Page: 41

25. According to the BCG growth-share matrix, which type of SBU requires a lot of cash to hold their share?

    a) cash cows.
    b) dogs.
    c) question marks.
    d) stars.

    Answer: (c)   Difficulty: 1 Page: 42

26. According to the BCG growth-share matrix, which type of SBU generates enough cash to maintain itself, but does not appear to be a source of extra profits?

    a) cash cows.
    b) dogs.
    c) question marks.
    d) stars.

    Answer: (b)   Difficulty: 1 Page: 42

27. A decision by the company to increase the allocation of resources placed in the SBU to expand its share in the market is called a _____ strategy.

    a) build
    b) harvest
    c) hold
    d) divest

    Answer: (a)   Difficulty: 1 Page: 42

28. A decision by the company to maintain the SBU at its current level of market share is called a _____ strategy.

    a) build
    b) harvest
    c) hold
    d) divest

    Answer: (c)   Difficulty: 1 Page: 42

29. A decision to phase out the SBU and use the resources elsewhere in the company is called a _____ strategy.

    a) build
    b) harvest
    c) hold
    d) divest

    Answer: (d)   Difficulty: 1 Page: 42

30. A decision to milk the SBU of its short-term cash regardless of the long-term effect is called a _____ strategy.

    a) build
    b) harvest
    c) hold
    d) divest

    Answer: (b)   Difficulty: 1 Page: 42

31. The GIANT Corporation is reviewing its SBU portfolio. Of particular concern is a recently-acquired business which management considers to be a dog. GIANT's management freely admits that it lacks expertise in the troubled SBUs industry and expects it to become increasingly unprofitable in the future. The best solution to this problem is:

    a) harvest the SBU
    b) divest the SBU
    c) hold the SBU
    d) invest more in the SBU

    Answer: (b)   Difficulty: 3 Page: 42

32. Although matrix approaches are widely used, management should guard against the tendency to use the results of such analyses to:

    a) assist management to understand the company's overall situation.
    b) justify entry into unrelated businesses that they do not know how to manage.
    c) enhance their understanding of how each SBU contributes to the organization.
    d) assist in assigning resources to various SBUs.

    Answer: (b)   Difficulty: 2 Page: 42

33. Which of the following is a limitation of the BCG strategic planning method?

    a) The BCG approach is difficult and time consuming.
    b) The BCG approach is costly to implement.
    c) The BCG approach focuses on current businesses and provides little advice for future planning.
    d) All of the above.

    Answer: (d)   Difficulty: 2 Page: 43

34. Under the product/market expansion, the strategy of making more sales to present customers without changing products in any way is called:

    a) market penetration.
    b) market development.
    c) product development.
    d) diversification.

    Answer: (a)   Difficulty: 1 Page: 43

35. Under the product/market expansion, the strategy of finding new markets for its current products is called:

    a) market penetration.
    b) market development.
    c) product development.
    d) diversification.

    Answer: (b)   Difficulty: 1 Page: 44

36. Under the product/market expansion, the strategy of offering new products to current markets is called:

    a) market penetration.
    b) market development.
    c) product development.
    d) diversification.

    Answer: (c)   Difficulty: 1 Page: 44

37. Under the product/market expansion, the strategy of entering new markets with new products is called:

    a) market penetration.
    b) market development.
    c) product development.
    d) diversification.

    Answer: (d)   Difficulty: 1 Page: 44

38. Levi Strauss management wants to increase jean purchases among its existing customers. Management has decided that this goal can be best accomplished by cutting the price of its product and increasing the advertising support provided for it. Levi Strauss is following the strategy of:

    a) market development.
    b) product development.
    c) market penetration.
    d) diversification.

    Answer: (c)   Difficulty: 3 Page: 44

39. Levi Strauss just recently launched new advertising campaigns to boost its jeans sales in female and Hispanic markets. Levi Strauss is following the strategy of:

    a) market development.
    b) product development.
    c) market penetration.
    d) diversification.

    Answer: (a)   Difficulty: 3 Page: 44

40. Levi Strauss introduced its Dockers line of casual clothing in order to obtain more business from current customers. Levi Strauss is following the strategy of:

    a) market development.
    b) product development.
    c) market penetration.
    d) diversification.

    Answer: (b)   Difficulty: 3 Page: 44

41. If Levi Strauss decides to enter the exercise apparel market, a market in which it currently has no presence, it would be pursuing which growth strategy?

    a) market development.
    b) product development.
    c) market penetration.
    d) diversification.

    Answer: (d)   Difficulty: 3 Page: 44

42. Marketing plays a key role in the company's strategic planning by:

    a) providing a guiding philosophy of serving customer needs.
    b) providing inputs to strategic planners to identify market opportunities.
    c) designing strategies for business units to reach their objectives.
    d) All of the above.

    Answer: (d)   Difficulty: 3 Page: 45

43. In competing for target consumer to serve, a company must complete a three-step process better than its competitors. Which of the following is not a step in this process?

    a) market segmentation
    b) market targeting
    c) market positioning
    d) demand measurement and forecasting.

    Answer: (d)   Difficulty: 3 Page: 49

44. The process of dividing a market into distinct groups of buyers with different needs, characteristics or behaviors is called:

    a) market segmentation.
    b) market targeting.
    c) market positioning.
    d) demand forecasting.

    Answer: (a)   Difficulty: 1 Page: 49

45. A _____ consists of consumers who respond in a similar way to a given set of market efforts.

    a) market niche
    b) market target
    c) market segment
    d) market position

    Answer: (c)   Difficulty: 1 Page: 49

46. The set of controllable tactical marketing tools that the firm blends to produce the response it wants in the target market are referred to as the:

    a) segmentation mix.
    b) marketing mix.
    c) penetration mix.
    d) targeting mix.

    Answer: (b)   Difficulty: 2 Page: 39

47. The "4 Ps" of marketing refer to all of the following except:

    a) Place
    b) Price
    c) Person
    d) Product

    Answer: (c)   Difficulty: 1 Page: 53

48. The marketing function that analyzes the company's strengths and weaknesses while considering its opportunities and threats is called:

    a) marketing analysis.
    b) marketing planning.
    c) marketing implementation.
    d) marketing control.

    Answer: (a)   Difficulty: 2 Page: 54

49. A.B. Smith, an independent consultant, has been hired to evaluate Pepsi-Cola's strengths and weaknesses as well as its current and possible marketing actions to determine which opportunities it can best pursue. A.B. Smith's assignment would be best described as:

    a) marketing planning.
    b) marketing implementation.
    c) marketing analysis.
    d) marketing control.

    Answer: (c)   Difficulty: 3 Page: 54

50. Marketing _____ involves deciding on marketing strategies that will help the firm attain its overall strategic objectives.

    a) analysis
    b) planning
    c) implementation
    d) control

    Answer: (b)   Difficulty: 1 Page: 55

51. Turning marketing plans into specific day-to-day, month-to-month activities is the concern of which marketing management function?

    a) marketing analysis
    b) marketing planning
    c) marketing implementation
    d) marketing control

    Answer: (c)   Difficulty: 1 Page: 58

52. A major marketing tool used to obtain a comprehensive, systematic, independent and periodic examination of a company's environment, objectives, strategies, and activities is called:

    a) marketing analysis.
    b) marketing control.
    c) marketing audit.
    d) marketing planning.

    Answer: (c)   Difficulty: 1 Page: 63

TRUE/FALSE

53. Strategic planning is the process of developing and maintaining a strategic fit between the organization's goals and capabilities and its changing marketing opportunities.

    Answer: True   Difficulty: 2 Page: 37

54. Most companies operate with formal strategic plans.

    Answer: False   Difficulty: 2 Page: 37

55. Strategic planning relies on developing a clear company mission, supporting objectives, a sound business portfolio, and coordinate functional strategies.

    Answer: True   Difficulty: 2 Page: 37

56. When the marketing environment becomes increasingly dynamic, marketing planning becomes less useful.

    Answer: False   Difficulty: 2 Page: 37

57. Marketing planning only occurs at the business-unit level.

    Answer: False   Difficulty: 2 Page: 38

58. The first step in the strategic planning process requires the firm to set company objectives and goals.

    Answer: False   Difficulty: 2 Page: 38

59. The firm's mission statement defines the organization's purpose --- what it wants to accomplish in the larger environment.

    Answer: True   Difficulty: 2 Page: 38

60. A clear strategic plan acts as an "invisible hand" that guides people in the organization.

    Answer: False   Difficulty: 2 Page: 38

61. A market-oriented mission statement defines the business in product or technological terms.

    Answer: False   Difficulty: 2 Page: 38

62. According to a market-oriented mission statement, AT&T is in the communication business.

    Answer: True   Difficulty: 2 Page: 38

63. Management should remember to make its mission statement broad.

    Answer: False   Difficulty: 1 Page: 39

64. A company's mission statement should not be stated as making more sales or profits.

    Answer: True   Difficulty: 2 Page: 40

65. A business portfolio is a collection of businesses and products that make up the company.

    Answer: True   Difficulty: 1 Page: 40

66. The best business portfolio is the one that best fits the company's strengths and weaknesses to opportunities in the environment.

    Answer: True   Difficulty: 1 Page: 40

67. By definition, an SBU can be a company division or even a product line but it cannot be a single product or brand itself.

    Answer: False   Difficulty: 1 Page: 41

68. The Boston Consulting Group approach plots SBUs in terms of industry attractiveness and business strength.

    Answer: False   Difficulty: 1 Page: 41

69. Under the Boston Consulting Group approach, stars are low-growth, high-share businesses or products that produce a lot of cash that the company uses to pay its bills and to support other SBUs that need investment.

    Answer: False   Difficulty: 2 Page: 41

70. In the Boston Consulting Group approach to portfolio planning, cash cows are vital to provide income needed to finance the firm's stars, question marks, and dogs.

    Answer: True   Difficulty: 2 Page: 41

71. A firm which has all of its products in the "star" or "cash cow" category has no need to develop new products.

    Answer: False   Difficulty: 2 Page: 42

72. Under the Boston Consulting Group approach, once the SBU has been classified, the company can harvest the SBU by selling it or phasing it out and using the resources elsewhere.

    Answer: False   Difficulty: 1 Page: 42

73. Under a divesting strategy, a firm seeks to increase the short-term cash flow realized from an SBU by investing little or nothing in it regardless of the long-term effect.

    Answer: False   Difficulty: 2 Page: 42

74. One problem with matrix approaches is that they focus on current businesses but provide little advice for future planning.

    Answer: True   Difficulty: 2 Page: 43

75. Roughly, 75 percent of the Fortune 500 companies practice some form of portfolio planning.

    Answer: True   Difficulty: 2 Page: 43

76. The product-market expansion grid is especially useful for identifying growth opportunities.

    Answer: True   Difficulty: 2 Page: 43

77. Market penetration refers to the strategy of creating new products to serve new markets.

    Answer: False   Difficulty: 2 Page: 44

78. A firm which cuts the price of its product, increases advertising, expands distribution, and improves in-store display is seeking to achieve deeper market penetration.

    Answer: True   Difficulty: 3 Page: 44

79. An a result of the declining birth rate, Gerber Baby Food began to explore the possibility of selling its products to the growing senior citizen market. This effort is best described as an example of a diversification growth strategy.

    Answer: False   Difficulty: 2 Page: 44

80. Levi Strauss could offer new lines and new brands of casual clothing to appeal to different users under a product development strategy.

    Answer: True   Difficulty: 2 Page: 44

81. Under a diversification strategy, a firm creates or buys businesses that are entirely outside of its current products and markets.

    Answer: True   Difficulty: 2 Page: 44

82. The company's strategic plan establishes what kinds of businesses the company will be in and its objectives for each.

    Answer: True   Difficulty: 2   Page: 45

83. Marketing alone can produce superior value for customers.

    Answer: False   Difficulty: 1   Page: 45

84. Marketing plays an integrative role to help ensure that all departments work toward maintaining company profits.

    Answer: False   Difficulty: 2   Page: 45

85. Today companies are "partnering" with the other members of the marketing system to improve the performance of the entire customer value delivery system.

    Answer: True   Difficulty: 2   Page: 46

86. The first step in the marketing process involves selecting the target markets.

    Answer: False   Difficulty: 1   Page: 48

87. Market Research Inc., is seeking to identify factors that are capable of classifying customers into groups with different needs, characteristics, or behavior. The firm is attempting to employ market segmentation.

    Answer: True   Difficulty: 3   Page: 49

88. The process of dividing a market into distinct groups of buyers with similar needs, characteristics, or behavior who might require different products or marketing mixes is called marketing segmentation.

    Answer: False   Difficulty: 2   Page: 49

89. Market positioning involves evaluating each market segment's attractiveness and selecting one or more segments to enter.

    Answer: False   Difficulty: 2   Page: 50

90. The marketing mix is the set of controllable tactical marketing tools and uncontrollable consumer reactions to their use.

    Answer: False   Difficulty: 2   Page: 52

91. The "4 Ps" of marketing include product, price, place, and person.

    Answer: False   Difficulty: 1   Page: 53

92. Managing the marketing effort involves four marketing management functions: analysis, planning, implementation and control.

    Answer: True   Difficulty: 1   Page: 54

93. Marketing analysis is the process that turns marketing plans into marketing actions in order to accomplish strategic marketing objectives.

    Answer: False   Difficulty: 2   Page: 58

94. Marketing control involves evaluating the results of strategies and plans and taking corrective action to ensure that objectives are attained.

    Answer: True   Difficulty: 2   Page: 60

ESSAY

95. Describe the strategic planning process. Identify the four steps of strategic planning.

    Answer:
    Strategic planning is defined as the process of developing and maintaining a strategic fit between the organization's goals and capabilities and its changing marketing opportunities. Strategic planning "forces" a firm to carefully and systematically consider its environmental situations, objectives, opportunities, and resources. The four steps in the strategic planning process include: 1. Defining the company mission; 2. Setting the company objectives and goals; 3. Designing the business portfolio; 4. Planning, marketing and other functional strategies.

    Difficulty: 3   Page: 37

96. Describe the Boston Consulting Group portfolio-planning method. Include a diagram (label correctly) in your discussion.

    Answer:
    The BCG approach evaluates SBU according to the growth-share matrix. On the vertical axis, market growth rate provides a measure of market attractiveness. On the horizontal axis, relative market share serves as a measure of company strength in the market. Four types of SBUs can be distinguished: Stars: high-growth, high-share businesses; Cash Cows: low-growth, high-share businesses; Question Markets: low-share business units in high-growth markets; Dogs: low-growth, low-share businesses.

    Difficulty: 3   Page: 42

97. Describe the product/market expansion grid. Use a diagram and identify the different types of growth opportunities.

    Answer:
    The product/market expansion grid is used to identify and evaluate future businesses and products for consideration. There are four growth opportunities. 1. Market penetration strategies may be employed if the firm desires to increase usage by current customers and/or attract new customers to its brands. Generally, such a strategy would indicate price cuts, advertising increases, distribution increases, and/or shelf placement enhancements. 2. Market development strategies evaluate the possibility of identifying and developing new demographic, institutional, or geographical markets for current products. 3. Under product development strategies, the firm investigates the feasibility of introducing new or modified products into current markets. 4. Diversification seeks to identify new businesses that the firm could feasibly enter.

    Difficulty: 3   Page: 43

98. What is market segmentation? How does this practice relate to market targeting and market positioning?

    Answer:
    Market segmentation is the practice of classifying customers into recognizable groups on the basis of differing needs, characteristics, or behavior. This task is typically a prerequisite to marketing targeting--the firm selects from those segments identified as the segment(s) it feels it can serve most effectively and profitably. Once a target segment has been selected, the firm must determine the position it would like to fill in that segment. Successful positioning requires a clear understanding of the needs, characteristics, and behavior of the target-segment. The firm's offering must be perceived as uniquely appropriate to some salient interests of the target group. Successful target market selections and positioning are dependent upon the precision with which market segmentation is carried out.

    Difficulty: 3 Page: 49

99. Identify the sections of a marketing plan. Discuss the strategic function of each section and what each section contains.

    Answer:
    Marketing plans have eight sections. The executive summary provides a brief overview of the proposed plan. Current marketing situation presents relevant background data on the market, product, competition, and distribution. Threats and opportunity analysis identifies the main threats and opportunities that might impact the product. Objectives and issues defines the company's objectives for the product in the areas of sales, market share, and profit, and the issues that will affect these objectives. Marketing strategy presents the broad marketing approach that will be used to achieve the plan's objectives. Action programs specifies what will done, who will do it, when it will be done, and how much it will cost. Budgets give profit and loss statements. Controls measures plan progress.

    Difficulty: 3 Page: 55

100. Identify and describe the marketing process.

    Answer:
    The marketing process consists of four basic steps: 1. analyzing marketing opportunities; 2. selecting target markets; 3. developing the marketing mix; and 4. managing the marketing effort.

    Difficulty: 2 Page: 48

Chapter 3

1. A company's _____ consists of the actors and forces outside marketing that affect marketing management's ability to develop and maintain successful relationships with its target customers.

   a) microenvironment
   b) macroenvironment
   c) marketing environment
   d) public environment.

   Answer: (c)   Difficulty: 1 Page: 71

2. The _____ consists of the forces close to the company that affect its ability to serve its customers.

   a) marketing environment
   b) macroenvironment
   c) microenvironment
   d) public environment.

   Answer: (c)   Difficulty: 2 Page: 71

3. The _____ consists of the larger societal forces that affect the marketing environment.

   a) company environment
   b) macroenvironment
   c) microenvironment
   d) public environment.

   Answer: (b)   Difficulty: 2 Page: 71

4. The Kellogg's Corporation watches the moves made by its major competitors very closely. Kellogg's competitors are part of the firm's:

   a) marketing environment.
   b) publics.
   c) macroenvironment.
   d) microenvironment.

   Answer: (d)   Difficulty: 3 Page: 71

5. Which of the following is not part of the firm's microenvironment?

   a) marketing channel firms
   b) suppliers
   c) customer markets
   d) cultural channels

   Answer: (d)   Difficulty: 1 Page: 71

6. Which of the following is not part of the firm's macroenvironment?

   a) cultural forces
   b) competitor forces
   c) environmental forces
   d) natural forces

   Answer: (b)   Difficulty: 1 Page: 71

7. Marketing managers work closely with other departments such as finance, research and development, purchasing, manufacturing and accounting. The departments are part of which element of the microenvironment?

   a) The company.
   b) The suppliers.
   c) Marketing intermediaries.
   d) The publics.

   Answer: (a)   Difficulty: 1 Page: 72

8. All of the following statements regarding suppliers are true except:

   a) Suppliers are part of the "value delivery system."
   b) Supplier developments rarely affect marketing.
   c) Marketing managers must monitor key input prices.
   d) Rising supply costs may force price increases.

   Answer: (b)   Difficulty: 2 Page: 72

9. _____ help the company to promote, sell, and distribute its goods to final buyers.

   a) Marketing intermediaries
   b) Suppliers
   c) Publics
   d) Physical distribution firms

   Answer: (a)   Difficulty: 2 Page: 73

10. Which of the following is not considered a marketing intermediary?

   a) Physical distribution firms
   b) Marketing service agencies
   c) Financial intermediaries
   d) Suppliers

   Answer: (d)   Difficulty: 2 Page: 73

11. _____ help the company find customers to make sales to them.

   a) Physical distribution firms.
   b) Marketing services agencies.
   c) Financial intermediaries.
   d) Resellers

   Answer: (d)   Difficulty: 1 Page: 73

12. Firms that help the company stock and move goods from their points of origin to their destinations are called:

    a) Physical distribution firms.
    b) Marketing services agencies.
    c) Financial intermediaries
    d) Resellers

    Answer: (a)   Difficulty: 2 Page: 73

13. Firms that provide the resources needed by the company to produce its goods and services are called:

    a) Physical distribution firms.
    b) Marketing services agencies.
    c) Financial intermediaries
    d) Resellers

    Answer: (c)   Difficulty: 2 Page: 73

14. A marketing research firm is considered to be which of the following?

    a) Physical distribution firms.
    b) Marketing services agencies.
    c) Financial intermediaries
    d) Resellers

    Answer: (b)   Difficulty: 2 Page: 73

15. Advertising agencies are considered which of the following marketing intermediaries?

    a) Physical distribution firms.
    b) Marketing services agencies.
    c) Financial intermediaries
    d) Resellers

    Answer: (b)   Difficulty: 2 Page: 73

16. Insurance companies are one kind of:

    a) Physical distribution firms.
    b) Marketing services agencies.
    c) Financial intermediaries
    d) Resellers

    Answer: (c)   Difficulty: 2 Page: 73

17. The type of customer market that consists of individuals and households that buy goods and services for personal consumption are part of the:

    a) consumer market.
    b) business market.
    c) government market.
    d) reseller market.

    Answer: (a)   Difficulty: 1 Page: 74

18. The type of customer market that buys goods and services for further processing is a:

    a) consumer market.
    b) business market.
    c) government market.
    d) reseller market.

    Answer: (b)   Difficulty: 1   Page: 74

19. Firms that buy and sell goods and services for a profit are called:

    a) consumer market.
    b) business market.
    c) government market.
    d) reseller market.

    Answer: (d)   Difficulty: 1   Page: 74

20. Firms that buy goods and services in other countries is an example of which type of customer market?

    a) consumer market.
    b) business market.
    c) government market.
    d) international market.

    Answer: (d)   Difficulty: 1   Page: 74

21. A _____ is any group that has an actual or potential interest in or impact on an organization's ability to achieve its objectives.

    a) customer
    b) competition
    c) public
    d) supplier

    Answer: (c)   Difficulty: 1   Page: 75

22. An organization that communicates an editorial opinion is usually considered to be part of which of the following?

    a) Financial publics
    b) Media publics
    c) Government publics
    d) Citizen-action publics

    Answer: (b)   Difficulty: 2   Page: 75

23. Environmental groups are one kind of the following?

    a) Government publics
    b) Local publics
    c) General publics
    d) Citizen-action publics

    Answer: (d)   Difficulty: 2   Page: 75

24. Neighborhood residents and community organizations belong to which of the following?

    a) Internal publics
    b) Local publics
    c) General publics
    d) Citizen-action publics

    Answer: (b)   Difficulty: 2 Page: 75

25. The Schwinn Bicycle Corporation routinely encourages its corporate officers to participate in community fund drives and make significant contributions to local charities. These actions are primarily aimed at the firm's:

    a) general public.
    b) citizen action publics.
    c) government publics.
    d) media publics.

    Answer: (a)   Difficulty: 3 Page: 75

26. The study of human populations in terms of size, density, location, age, gender, race, occupation, and other statistics is called:

    a) Demography
    b) Geography
    c) Sociology
    d) Psychology

    Answer: (a)   Difficulty: 1 Page: 76

27. The single most important demographic trend in the United States is:

    a) the world population is growing at an explosive rate.
    b) the changing age structure of the U.S. population.
    c) the changing American family.
    d) the geographic shifts in population.

    Answer: (b)   Difficulty: 2 Page: 77

28. The fact that people are marrying later and having fewer children are examples of:

    a) better educated and more white-collar population.
    b) the changing age structure of the U.S. population.
    c) the changing American family.
    d) the geographic shifts in population.

    Answer: (c)   Difficulty: 2 Page: 80

29. Over the past two decades, the U.S. population has shifted toward the Sun Belt states is indicative of:

    a) better educated and more white-collar population.
    b) the changing age structure of the U.S. population.
    c) the changing American family.
    d) the geographic shifts in population.

    Answer: (d)   Difficulty: 2 Page: 80

30. The massive exodus from the cities to the suburbs is one example of:

    a) better educated and more white-collar population.
    b) the changing age structure of the U.S. population.
    c) the changing American family.
    d) the geographic shifts in population.

    Answer: (d)   Difficulty: 2 Page: 80

31. Executives at the Universal Television Network have been reviewing current demographic trends with some concern. Which of the following trends is most likely to signal a decline in television viewing?

    a) better educated and more white-collar population.
    b) the changing age structure of the U.S. population.
    c) the changing American family.
    d) the geographic shifts in population.

    Answer: (a)   Difficulty: 2 Page: 81

32. The fact that the United States has become a "salad bowl" where various cultures have mixed yet retain their unique differences indicates which major trend:

    a) better educated and more white-collar population.
    b) increase ethnic and racial diversity
    c) the changing American family.
    d) the geographic shifts in population.

    Answer: (b)   Difficulty: 2 Page: 81

33. The _____ consists of factors that affect consumer purchasing power and spending patterns.

    a) demographic environment
    b) economic environment
    c) cultural environment
    d) political environment

    Answer: (b)   Difficulty: 2 Page: 82

34. During the economic downturn, the watchword for many marketers is:

    a) "income distribution."
    b) "value marketing."
    c) "squeezed consumer."
    d) "more for less."

    Answer: (c) Difficulty: 2 Page: 83

35. According to Engel's laws, as family income rises:

    a) the percentage spent on food rises.
    b) the percentage spent on housing increases.
    c) the percentage spent on savings remains constant.
    d) the percentage spent on other categories increases.

    Answer: (d) Difficulty: 2 Page: 84

36. The _____ involves the natural resources that are needed as inputs by marketers or that are affected by marketing activities.

    a) demographic market
    b) economic market
    c) natural market
    d) technological market

    Answer: (c) Difficulty: 1 Page: 85

37. Which of the following is not a trend in the natural environment that would concern marketers?

    a) shortages of raw materials
    b) increased cost of energy
    c) increased pollution
    d) increased regulation

    Answer: (d) Difficulty: 2 Page: 85

38. 3M runs a Pollution Prevention Pays program that has led to a substantial reduction in pollution and associated costs. 3M's program is a response to which trend in the natural environment?

    a) shortages of raw materials
    b) increased cost of energy
    c) increased pollution
    d) increased regulation

    Answer: (c) Difficulty: 2 Page: 85

39. The green movement is a response to which trend occurring in the natural environment?

    a) shortages of raw materials
    b) increased cost of energy
    c) increased pollution
    d) increased regulation

    Answer: (c)   Difficulty: 2 Page: 85

40. Marketers should watch which of the following trends in the technological environment?

    a) Fast pace of technological change.
    b) High R&D budgets
    c) Increased regulation
    d) All of the above.

    Answer: (d)   Difficulty: 2 Page: 88

41. The _____ consists of laws, government agencies, and pressure groups that influence and limit various organizations and individuals in a given society.

    a) demographic environment
    b) economic environment
    c) cultural environment
    d) political environment

    Answer: (d)   Difficulty: 2 Page: 88

42. What forces in a company's macroenvironment would dictate whether or not an environmentally dangerous product would be taken off the shelves?

    a) natural forces
    b) economic forces
    c) political forces
    d) technological forces

    Answer: (c)   Difficulty: 2 Page: 71

43. Laws that prevent companies from neutralizing competition reflect which reason for the existence of legislation affecting business?

    a) To protect companies from each other.
    b) To protect consumers from unfair business practices.
    c) To protect the interests of society.
    d) To protect businesses from unfair consumer demands.

    Answer: (a)   Difficulty: 2 Page: 89

44. Enlighten companies encourage their managers to look beyond what the regulatory system allows and to simply "do the right thing" reflects which trend in the political environment?

    a) The increased emphasis on ethics and social responsible actions.
    b) Legislation regulating business.
    c) Changing government agency enforcement.
    d) All of the above.

    Answer: (a)   Difficulty: 2 Page: 92

45. The _____ is made up of institutions and other forces that affect a society's basic values, perceptions, preferences, and behaviors.

    a) demographic environment
    b) political environment
    c) cultural environment
    d) economic environment

    Answer: (c)   Difficulty: 2 Page: 93

46. Values that are passed on from parents to children and are reinforced by schools, churches, business, and government are called:

    a) core beliefs.
    b) secondary beliefs.
    c) cultural beliefs.
    d) secondary cultural beliefs.

    Answer: (a)   Difficulty: 2 Page: 93

47. The fact that family-planning marketers have a far better chance of persuading Americans that people should get married later than they should not get married at all is an example of:

    a) core beliefs.
    b) secondary beliefs.
    c) cultural beliefs.
    d) secondary cultural beliefs.

    Answer: (b)   Difficulty: 2 Page: 93

48. Yankelovich marketing research firm tracks many U.S. cultural values in order to explain:

    a) shifts in core beliefs.
    b) shifts in secondary beliefs.
    c) shifts in secondary cultural values.
    d) shifts in cultural values.

    Answer: (c)   Difficulty: 2 Page: 93

49. Shifts in secondary cultural values can be expressed through which of the following?

    a) People's view of themselves.
    b) People's view of others.
    c) People's view of organizations.
    d) All of the above.

    Answer: (d)   Difficulty: 2 Page: 96

50. Firms that take aggressive actions to affect the publics and forces in their marketing environment are embodying a(n):

    a) selling concept perspective.
    b) marketing concept perspective.
    c) marketing management perspective.
    d) environmental management perspective.

    Answer: (d)   Difficulty: 1 Page: 97

TRUE/FALSE

51. A company's marketing environment consists of the actors and forces outside marketing that affect marketing management's ability to develop and maintain successful relationships with its target customers.

    Answer: True   Difficulty: 2 Page: 71

52. The marketing environment requires constant monitoring since it offers significant threats.

    Answer: False   Difficulty: 2 Page: 71

53. The firm's marketing environment offers both opportunities and threats, and the company must use its marketing research and marketing intelligence systems to watch the changing environment.

    Answer: True   Difficulty: 2 Page: 71

54. The macroenvironment consists of forces close to the company that affect its ability to service its customers.

    Answer: False   Difficulty: 2 Page: 71

55. The firm's microenvironment is composed of the demographic, economic, natural, technological, political, and cultural forces that affect its ability to serve its customers.

    Answer: False   Difficulty: 2 Page: 71

56. The macroenvironment consists of the larger societal forces that affect the whole microenvironment.

    Answer: True   Difficulty: 2 Page: 71

57. The purchasing department focuses on the problems of designing safe and attractive products.

    Answer: False   Difficulty: 2   Page: 72

58. Under the marketing concept, all of the company's functions must "think profit," and they should work in harmony to provide superior customer value and satisfaction.

    Answer: False   Difficulty: 2   Page: 72

59. Suppliers are an important link in the company's overall customer "value delivery system."

    Answer: True   Difficulty: 2   Page: 72

60. Marketing managers must watch supply availability since supply shortages or delays, labor strikes, and other events can cost sales in the short run.

    Answer: True   Difficulty: 2   Page: 72

61. Marketing intermediaries are firms that help the company promote, sell, and distribute its goods to final buyers.

    Answer: True   Difficulty: 2   Page: 73

62. Marketing services agencies are firms that help the company stock and move goods from their points of origin to their destinations.

    Answer: False   Difficulty: 2   Page: 73

63. Insurance companies are one type of marketing intermediary.

    Answer: True   Difficulty: 2   Page: 73

64. Banks and credit companies are considered suppliers while insurance agencies are considered marketing intermediaries.

    Answer: False   Difficulty: 2   Page: 73

65. Only firms depend on financial intermediaries to finance their transactions.

    Answer: False   Difficulty: 2   Page: 74

66. Customer markets are considered part of the company's microenvironment.

    Answer: True   Difficulty: 2   Page: 74

67. Business markets are considered part of the company's macroenvironment.

    Answer: False   Difficulty: 2   Page: 74

68. Typically, both large firms with dominant positions in an industry and small firms use the same competitive marketing strategy.

    Answer: False   Difficulty: 2   Page: 74

69. A public is any group that has an actual or potential interest in or impact on an organization's ability to achieve its objectives.

    Answer: True   Difficulty: 2   Page: 75

70. A company's internal publics include banks, investment houses, stockholders.

    Answer: False   Difficulty: 2   Page: 75

71. Chevron, one of the largest petroleum companies in the world, recently produced the advertising campaign "We Care." This promotion was developed to communicate to the media public their concern for the natural environment.

    Answer: False   Difficulty: 2   Page: 75

72. The GAP Corporation regularly provides press releases describing the firm's new fashions and community activities. The firm is attempting to obtain more and better coverage by "courting" its citizen-action publics.

    Answer: True   Difficulty: 2   Page: 75

73. Demography is the study of human populations in terms of size, density, location, age, gender, race, occupation, and other statistics.

    Answer: True   Difficulty: 2   Page: 76

74. The single most important demographic trend in the United States is the changing age structure of the population.

    Answer: True   Difficulty: 2   Page: 77

75. The baby boom refers to the growth in population that occurred between World War II and lasted until the early 1970s.

    Answer: False   Difficulty: 2   Page: 77

76. Among the changes in the American Family is the fact that people are marrying later and having fewer children.

    Answer: True   Difficulty: 2   Page: 80

77. Marketers of tires, automobiles, insurance, travel, and financial services are now directing their advertising to working women.

    Answer: True   Difficulty: 2   Page: 80

78. While the number of working women has increased, demographics reveals that the number of non-family households has held steady over the last few years.

    Answer: False   Difficulty: 2   Page: 80

79. Over the past two decades, the U.S. population has shifted toward the Midwest and Northeast states.

    Answer: False   Difficulty: 2   Page: 80

80. Among the major shifts in population in the United States is the trend of movement from the cities to the suburbs.

    Answer: True   Difficulty: 2   Page: 80

81. Better educated consumers watch more television than the population at large.

    Answer: False   Difficulty: 2   Page: 81

82. The increase in demand for quality products, books, magazines, and travel opportunities reflects the trend of a better educated population.

    Answer: True   Difficulty: 2   Page: 81

83. Although many racial and ethnic groups live in the United States, the culture acts as a kind of "melting pot" to create a more or less single homogeneous market.

    Answer: False   Difficulty: 2   Page: 81

84. The economic environment consists of factors that affect consumer purchasing power and spending patterns.

    Answer: True   Difficulty: 2   Page: 82

85. Value marketing has become the watchword for many marketers during the free-spending and high expectations of the 1990s.

    Answer: False   Difficulty: 2   Page: 83

86. According to Engle's laws, as family income rises, the percentage spent on food declines, and the percentage spent on savings increases.

    Answer: True   Difficulty: 2   Page: 84

87. The natural environment involves the natural resources that are needed as inputs by marketers or that are affected by marketing activities.

    Answer: True   Difficulty: 2   Page: 84

88. Trends in the natural environment include, shortages of raw materials, decreased cost of energy, increased pollution, government intervention in natural resource management.

    Answer: False   Difficulty: 2   Page: 86

89. The technological environment is the most dramatic force now shaping today's marketplace.

Answer: True   Difficulty: 2 Page: 86

90. As a result of high cost of developing and introducing new technologies, many companies are making minor product improvements instead of gambling on new products.

Answer: True   Difficulty: 2 Page: 88

91. The political environment consists of laws, government agencies, and pressure groups that influence and limit various organizations and individuals in a given society.

Answer: True   Difficulty: 2 Page: 88

92. The cultural environment is made up of institutions and other forces that affect a society's basic values, perceptions, preferences, and behaviors.

Answer: True   Difficulty: 2 Page: 93

93. Belief in marriage is a core belief while the belief that people should wait until thirty to marry is not.

Answer: True   Difficulty: 2 Page: 93

ESSAY

94. Describe the environmental forces that affect the company's ability to serve its customers.

Answer:
The marketing environment consists of all the actors and forces that affect the company's ability to transact effectively with the target market. The company's marketing environment can be divided into microenvironment and macroenvironment. The microenvironment consists of the company, marketing intermediaries, customers, competitors, and publics. The macroenvironment consists of demographic, economic, natural, technological, political, and cultural forces.

Difficulty: 3 Page: 71

95. Identify the major reasons why the population explosion is of major concern to governments and various groups throughout the world. What implications does the population explosion have for business?

Answer:
First, the earth's finite resources can support only so many people, particularly at the living standards to which many countries aspire. Second, the greatest population growth occurs in countries and communities that can least afford it. The less-developed countries often find it difficult to feed, clothe, and educate their growing populations. Implications for business means growing market opportunities.

Difficulty: 3 Page: 76

96. Compare and contrast the "baby boomers" and the "Generation Xers." Describe how marketing managers can serve both of these important markets profitably.

Answer:
Baby boomers account for a third of the population and make up 40 percent of the work force. The older boomers are now in their fifties, while the youngest are in their thirties. The boomers have shifted their focus from the outside world to the insider world. Marketers have paid the most attention to the more educated, mobile and wealthy segments.
Generation Xers represent 40 million consumers. They have experienced increasing divorce rates and higher employment rates. They are more skeptical, cynical about frivolous marketing pitches. Xers buy lots of products, such as sweaters, boots, cosmetics, electronics. However, their cynicism makes them more savvy and wary shoppers. Traditionally they have been overlooked by companies.

Difficulty: 3 Page: 78-79

97. Explain the effect of changes in the demographic and economic environments on marketing management decisions.

Answer:
Changes in the demographic environment that affect marketing decisions are the changing age structure of the U.S. population, the changing American family, geographic shifts in population, a better educated and more white collar work force, and increasing ethnic and racial diversity. Economic trends include changes in income and income distribution and changes in consumer spending patterns.

Difficulty: 3 Page: 76-84

98. Identify the major trends in the firm's natural and technological environments.

Answer:
Trends in the natural environment include shortages of raw materials, increased cost of energy, increased pollution, and government intervention in natural resource management. Trends in the technological environment include the fast pace of technological change, high R&D budgets, concentration on minor improvements and increased regulation.

Difficulty: 3 Page: 84-88

99. Explain the key changes that occur in the political and cultural environments.

Answer:
Changes in the political environment include legislation regulating business, changing government agency enforcement, the growth of public interest groups, and increased emphasis on ethics and socially responsible actions. Changes in the cultural environment include the persistence of cultural values, shifts in secondary cultural values, and people's views of themselves, others, organizations, society, nature, and the universe.

Difficulty: 3 Page: 88-97

Chapter 4

1. A _____ consists of people, equipment, and procedures to gather, sort, analyze, evaluate, and distribute needed, timely, and accurate information to marketing decision makers.

    a) management information system
    b) marketing information system
    c) decision information system
    d) management information plan

    Answer: (b)   Difficulty: 2 Page: 108

2. In assessing marketing information needs, the company needs to consider which of the following:

    a) what information managers would like to have.
    b) what information managers really need.
    c) what information is feasible to offer.
    d) All of the above.

    Answer: (d)   Difficulty: 2 Page: 108

3. The marketing management at New Idea Corporation are deciding whether to invest a significant amount of funds to acquire additional demographic statistics that may be of use in sales forecasting. The managers should:

    a) rely on internal records only
    b) use only such "free" sources of market data as Bureau of Census.
    c) weigh carefully the costs of obtaining additional information against the benefits resulting from its use.
    d) buy any information that may be relevant to the product

    Answer: (c)   Difficulty: 3 Page: 109

4. When developing information for the marketing manager, information is typically not obtained from:

    a) internal company records
    b) marketing intelligence
    c) marketing research
    d) distributing information

    Answer: (d)   Difficulty: 2 Page: 109

5. _____ consists of information gathered from sources within the company to evaluate marketing performance and to identify marketing problems and opportunities.

    a) Internal records information
    b) Marketing intelligence
    c) Marketing research
    d) Competitor analysis

    Answer: (a)   Difficulty: 2 Page: 109

6. The company's accounting department is a source of information for which element of the marketing information system?

   a) Salesforce reports
   b) Marketing research
   c) Internal company records
   d) Marketing intelligence

   Answer: (c)   Difficulty: 2 Page: 109

7. The sales force reports on reseller reactions and competitor activities is a source of information for which element of the marketing information system?

   a) Marketing research
   b) Customer database records
   c) Internal company records
   d) Marketing intelligence

   Answer: (c)   Difficulty: 2 Page: 109

8. Internal company records can be used for all of the following except:

   a) targeting segments of existing customers for special product and service offers.
   b) reduces the amount of time spent filling out reports.
   c) analyzing daily sales performance.
   d) obtaining information on market share.

   Answer: (d) Difficulty: 2 Page: 110

9. Internal company records provide marketing managers important marketing data because:

   a) they are fastest and easiest to use.
   b) they contain complete marketing information.
   c) they are more reliable than other sources.
   d) none of the above.

   Answer: (a)   Difficulty: 2 Page: 110

10. Which of the following is a common problem facing marketers when using information gathered from internal company records?

    a) Internal records may be incomplete for making marketing decisions.
    b) Internal records are reported in the wrong form for making marketing decisions.
    c) Keeping track of internal records is often difficult.
    d) All of the above.

    Answer: (d)   Difficulty: 2 Page: 110

11. _____ is everyday information about developments in the marketing environment that helps managers prepare and adjust marketing plans.

   a) Internal records
   b) Marketing intelligence
   c) Marketing research
   d) Observational research

   Answer: (b)   Difficulty: 2 Page: 110

12. The marketing information system that would typically set up an office and staff to collect and scan major publications, summarizing important news, and sending new bulletins to marketing managers is called:

   a) Internal records
   b) Marketing intelligence
   c) Marketing research
   d) Observational research

   Answer: (b)   Difficulty: 2 Page: 110

13. The ABC Company is deciding whether to enter the market for widgets. In order to make that decision, the ABC marketing manager needs information on the retail prices charged by potential competitors. Which of the following databases contains that information?

   a) Nielsen Marketing Research
   b) Adtrack
   c) The Electronic Yellow Pages
   d) Donnelly Demographics

   Answer: (a)   Difficulty: 2 Page: 110

14. _____ is the systematic design, collection, analysis, and reporting of data and findings relevant to a specific marketing situation facing an organization.

   a) Survey research
   b) Marketing research
   c) Consumer research
   d) Observational research

   Answer: (b)   Difficulty: 2 Page: 111

15. Marketing research is used to:

   a) identify and define marketing opportunities.
   b) generate refine, and evaluate marketing actions.
   c) improve understanding of the marketing process.
   d) all of the above.

   Answer: (d)   Difficulty: 2 Page: 111

16. Many marketing managers have direct access to the information network through personal computers. From any location managers are now able to obtain which of the following information?

    a) Analyze the information using statistical packages and models
    b) Prepare reports on a word processor or desktop publishing system
    c) Communicate with others in the network through electronic communications.
    d) All of the above.

    Answer: (d)   Difficulty: 2 Page: 114

17. Which of the following is not a step in the marketing research process?

    a) Defining the problem and research objective.
    b) Developing and implementing the research plan.
    c) Interpreting and reporting the findings.
    d) All of the above are part of the marketing research process.

    Answer: (d)   Difficulty: 1 Page: 115

18. Typically, researchers agree that the hardest step in the research process is:

    a) defining the problem and research objective.
    b) developing the research plan.
    c) implementing the research plan
    d) interpreting and reporting the findings.

    Answer: (a)   Difficulty: 1 Page: 115

19. The Coca-Cola Company made a much publicized mistake with its introduction of "new Coke" in 1985. This blunder can be attributed to:

    a) no marketing research was conducted.
    b) changing consumer tastes.
    c) an aggressive marketing campaign by Pepsi.
    d) marketing research was too narrowly focused.

    Answer: (d)   Difficulty: 2 Page: 115

20. The type of marketing research used to gather preliminary information that will help to better define problems and suggest hypotheses is called:

    a) exploratory research.
    b) descriptive research.
    c) causal research.
    d) investigative research.

    Answer: (a)   Difficulty: 1 Page: 116

21. The High-Tech Corporation knows that it has some marketing problems, but has no clear "feel" for their specific nature. Before taking any other action, the firm should conduct:

    a) descriptive research.
    b) exploratory research.
    c) causal research.
    d) situational research.

    Answer: (b)   Difficulty: 3 Page: 116

22. The type of marketing research used to describe things such as the market potential for a product is called:

    a) exploratory research.
    b) descriptive research.
    c) causal research.
    d) investigative research.

    Answer: (a)   Difficulty: 1 Page: 116

23. Tysons Corner shopping mall is interested in how the mall can better serve its customers. The mall is planning to conduct market research to measure consumer attitudes by demographic groups. The type of marketing research that would be most useful to the managers at the mall is called:

    a) exploratory research.
    b) descriptive research.
    c) causal research.
    d) investigative research.

    Answer: (b)   Difficulty: 1 Page: 116

24. The type of marketing research used to test hypotheses about cause-and-effect relationships is called:

    a) exploratory research.
    b) descriptive research.
    c) causal research.
    d) investigative research.

    Answer: (a)   Difficulty: 1 Page: 116

25. When the local shopping mall conducts an experiment to determine the impact of a price decrease on lower-level parking, the type of marketing research employed is called:

    a) exploratory research.
    b) descriptive research.
    c) causal research.
    d) investigative research.

    Answer: (b)   Difficulty: 1 Page: 116

26. Which step in the research process Spells out the specific research approaches, contact methods, sampling plans, and instruments that researchers will use to gather new data?

    a) Defining the problem and research objectives.
    b) Developing the research plan.
    c) Implementing the research plan.
    d) Interpreting and reporting the findings.

    Answer: (b)   Difficulty: 2 Page: 117

27. Which step in the marketing research process calls for determining the specific information needed?

    a) Defining the problem and research objectives.
    b) Developing the research plan.
    c) Implementing the research plan.
    d) Interpreting and reporting the findings.

    Answer: (b)   Difficulty: 2 Page: 118

28. _____ consists of information that already exists somewhere, having been collected for another purpose.

    a) Marketing data
    b) Primary data
    c) Secondary data
    d) Library data

    Answer: (c)   Difficulty: 1 Page: 118

29. _____ consists of information collected for the specific purpose at hand.

    a) Marketing data
    b) Primary data
    c) Secondary data
    d) Library data

    Answer: (b) Difficulty: 1 Page: 118

30. In relation to its usefulness to a current marketing research project, which of the following statements about secondary data is not true?

    a) Secondary data comes from internal and external sources.
    b) Secondary data is obtained less quickly than primary data.
    c) Secondary data is obtained at a lower cost than primary data.
    d) Secondary data can provide certain kinds of data that an individual company cannot collect on its own.

    Answer: (b)   Difficulty: 2 Page: 120

31. Secondary data provides a good starting point for research because it:

   a) helps define problems and research objectives.
   b) always fits project needs.
   c) is objectively collected and reported.
   d) is consistently accurate.

   Answer: (a)   Difficulty: 2 Page: 120

32. Problems associated with secondary data include:

   a) relevancy.
   b) accuracy.
   c) currency.
   d) All of the above.

   Answer: (d)   Difficulty: 2 Page: 120

33. Researchers check secondary data to make sure it was objectively collected and reported to ensure that it is:

   a) relevant.
   b) accurate.
   c) current.
   d) impartial.

   Answer: (d)   Difficulty: 1 Page: 120

34. Researchers make sure that the secondary data is up to date enough for the research problem to ensure that it is:

   a) relevant.
   b) accurate.
   c) current.
   d) impartial.

   Answer: (c)   Difficulty: 1 Page: 120

35. Researchers make sure that the secondary data was reliably collected and reported for the research problem to ensure that it is:

   a) relevant.
   b) accurate.
   c) current.
   d) impartial.

   Answer: (b)   Difficulty: 1 Page: 120

36. Researchers make sure that the secondary data fits the research projects needs to ensure that it is:

    a) relevant.
    b) accurate.
    c) current.
    d) impartial.

    Answer: (a)   Difficulty: 1 Page: 120

37. _____ is the gathering of primary data by observing relevant people, actions, and situations.

    a) Observational research
    b) Survey research
    c) Experimental research
    d) Market research

    Answer: (a)   Difficulty: 2 Page: 120

38. Measuring eye movements, pulse rates and other physical reactions is an example of which type of primary research method?

    a) Observational research
    b) Survey research
    c) Experimental research
    d) Market research

    Answer: (a)   Difficulty: 2 Page: 120

39. The gathering of primary data by asking people questions about their knowledge, attitudes, preferences, and buying behavior is called:

    a) Observational research
    b) Survey research
    c) Experimental research
    d) Market research

    Answer: (b)   Difficulty: 2 Page: 121

40. Which of the following are potential problems of survey research?

    a) People are unable to answer survey questions because they cannot remember or have never thought about what they do and why.
    b) People may be unwilling to respond to unknown interviewers or about things they consider private.
    c) Respondents may answer questions even though they do not know the answer in order to appear smarter or more informed.
    d) All of the above.

    Answer: (d)   Difficulty: 2 Page: 121

41. The primary data collection method that is best suited for gathering causal information is called:

    a) Observational research
    b) Survey research
    c) Experimental research
    d) Market research

    Answer: (c)   Difficulty: 2 Page: 122

42. Whether information is collected by mail, telephone, personal interview, or computer falls under which part of developing the marketing plan?

    a) Determining the research approach.
    b) Selecting the contact method.
    c) Choosing a sampling plan.
    d) Constructing a research instrument.

    Answer: b   Difficulty: 2 Page: 123

43. All of the following are advantages of mail questionnaires except:

    a) large amount of information can be collected at a low cost per respondent.
    b) that mail questionnaires are very flexible.
    b) respondents may give more honest answers.
    c) no interviewer is involved to bias the respondent's.

    Answer: (b)   Difficulty: 2 Page: 123

44. Which of the following is an advantage of mail questionnaires?

    a) Mail questionnaires are very flexible.
    b) The researcher cannot adapt the questionnaire based upon earlier answer.
    c) Response rates are typically higher than other survey methods.
    d) Mail questionnaires can be used to collect large amounts of information.

    Answer: (d)   Difficulty: 2 Page: 124

45. _____ is the best method of gathering information quickly.

    a) Mail questionnaires
    b) Telephone interviewing
    c) Personal interviewing
    d) Group interviewing

    Answer: (b)   Difficulty: 1 Page: 124

46. Which of the following is an advantage of telephone interviewing?

    a) It provides flexibility.
    b) It is the best method for gathering information quickly.
    c) It allows interviewers to explain questions that are not understood.
    d) All of the above are advantages.

    Answer: (d)   Difficulty: 2 Page: 124

47. Which of the following is a disadvantage of telephone interviewing?

    a) Cost per respondent is higher than mail questionnaires.
    b) People may not want to discuss personal questions with an interviewer.
    c) Telephone interviewing introduces interviewer bias.
    d) All of the above are disadvantages.

    Answer: (d)   Difficulty: 2 Page: 124

48. _____consists of six to ten people to gather for few hours with a trained moderator to talk about a product, service, or organization.

    a) Mail questionnaires
    b) Telephone interviewing
    c) Personal interviewing
    d) Group interviewing

    Answer: (d)   Difficulty: 1 Page: 124

49. The survey research contact method used to obtain greater insights into the thoughts and feelings of present and potential purchasers of a product is:

    a) mail questionnaires
    b) telephone interviewing
    c) personal interviewing
    d) group interviewing

    Answer: (c)   Difficulty: 1 Page: 124

50. The major drawbacks to personal interviewing include:

    a) costs and sampling problems.
    b) lack of flexibility.
    c) the fact that it takes too long to conduct the interviews.
    d) the fact that only a limited amount of information can be gathered.

    Answer: (b)   Difficulty: 2 Page: 124

51. _____ interviewing has become one of the major marketing research tools for gaining insight into consumer thoughts and feelings.

    a) mail questionnaires
    b) telephone interviewing
    c) personal interviewing
    d) focus-group interviewing

    Answer: (d)   Difficulty: 1 Page: 125

52. A _____ is a segment of the population selected to represent the population as a whole.

    a) unit
    b) sample
    c) section
    d) group

    Answer: (b)   Difficulty: 1 Page: 127

53. When using a _____, each population member has a known chance of being included in the sample.

    a) probability sample
    b) nonprobability sample
    c) cluster sample
    d) statistical sample

    Answer: (a)   Difficulty: 1 Page: 127

54. Phil Thomas is directing his firm's latest marketing research project. Phil has instructed his staff to find and interview 25 individuals in each of 15 prescribed categories. The firm is using a:

    a) judgement sample.
    b) quota sample.
    c) convenience sample.
    d) cluster sample.

    Answer: (b)   Difficulty: 1 Page: 127

55. Choosing a research instrument is part of which step in the marketing research process?

    a) Defining the problem and the research objectives.
    b) Developing the research plan.
    c) Implementing the research plan.
    d) Interpreting and reporting the findings.

    Answer: (b)   Difficulty: 2 Page: 127

56. Submitting a written proposal is part of which step in the marketing research process?

    a) Defining the problem and the research objectives.
    b) Developing the research plan.
    c) Implementing the research plan.
    d) Interpreting and reporting the findings.

    Answer: (b)   Difficulty: 2 Page: 129

57. Collecting, processing, and analyzing the information is part of which step in the marketing research process?

    a) Defining the problem and the research objectives.
    b) Developing the research plan.
    c) Implementing the research plan.
    d) Interpreting and reporting the findings.

    Answer: (c)   Difficulty: 2 Page: 129

58. When conducting marketing research in international markets, which of the following is a problem?

    a) Reaching respondents
    b) Translating a questionnaire.
    c) Language
    d) All of the above are problems.

    Answer: (d)   Difficulty: 2 Page: 132

TRUE/FALSE

59. An MIS system consists of people, equipment, and procedures to gather, sort, analyze, evaluate, and distribute needed, timely, and accurate information to marketing decision makers.

    Answer: True   Difficulty: 1 Page: 108

60. A good MIS system balances the information managers would like to have against what they really need and is feasible to offer.

    Answer: True   Difficulty: 1 Page: 108

61. In practice, a good MIS system can supply all the information that managers request.

    Answer: False   Difficulty: 2 Page: 108

62. Internal records consist of information gathered from sources within the company to evaluate marketing performance and to detect marketing problems and opportunities.

    Answer: True   Difficulty: 2 Page: 109

63. In the marketing information system, internal records falls under the category of developing information.

    Answer: True   Difficulty: 2 Page: 109

64. Manufacturing reports on production schedules, shipments, and inventories falls under the category of marketing intelligence.

    Answer: False   Difficulty: 2 Page: 109

65. Internal records can be accessed more quickly and cheaply than other information sources.

    Answer: True   Difficulty: 2   Page: 110

66. Marketing intelligence is special information about the marketing environment, usually developed secretly.

    Answer: False   Difficulty: 2   Page: 110

67. Marketing intelligence is everyday information about developments in the marketing environment.

    Answer: True   Difficulty: 2   Page: 110

68. Marketing research is the systematic design, collection, analysis, and reporting of data and findings relevant to a specific marketing situation facing the organization.

    Answer: True   Difficulty: 2   Page: 111

69. Companies rely primarily on outside suppliers for marketing intelligence information.

    Answer: False   Difficulty: 2   Page: 111

70. Defining the problem and the research objectives is often the hardest step in the research process.

    Answer: True   Difficulty: 2   Page: 115

71. The Coca-Cola Company defined its research problem too narrowly when it introduced New Coke.

    Answer: True   Difficulty: 2   Page: 115

72. The objective of causal research is to gather preliminary information that will help define the problem and suggest hypotheses.

    Answer: False Difficulty: 2   Page: 116

73. Prior to the initiation of a formal marketing research project, exploratory research should be conducted to aid in defining the problem and to suggest hypotheses.

    Answer: True   Difficulty: 2   Page: 116

74. Descriptive research describes things such as the demographic characteristics of a target market.

    Answer: True   Difficulty: 2   Page: 116

75. Causal research tests hypotheses about cause-and-effect relationships.

    Answer: True   Difficulty: 2   Page: 116

76. Secondary data consists of information that already exists somewhere, having been collected for another purpose.

    Answer: True   Difficulty: 2 Page: 118

77. Primary data consists of information collected for the specific purpose at hand.

    Answer: True   Difficulty: 2 Page: 118

78. Primary data usually can be obtained more quickly and at a lower cost than secondary data.

    Answer: False   Difficulty: 2 Page: 118

79. The researcher must evaluate secondary data to make certain that it is relevant, accurate, current, and impartial.

    Answer: True   Difficulty: 2 Page: 120

80. Observational research is the gathering of primary data by observing relevant people, actions, and situations.

    Answer: True   Difficulty: 2 Page: 120

81. Survey research is the most widely used method for primary data collection.

    Answer: True   Difficulty: 2 Page: 121

82. Survey research is the approach best suited for gathering descriptive information.

    Answer: True   Difficulty: 2 Page: 121

83. Single-source data systems that electronically monitor both consumers' purchases and consumers' exposure to various marketing activities is an example of survey research.

    Answer: False   Difficulty: 2 Page: 121

84. Experimental research is best suited for gathering causal information.

    Answer: True   Difficulty: 2 Page: 122

85. Mail questionnaires are the most flexible method of contacting respondents because the respondent can take as much time as they want to answer the questionnaire.

    Answer: False   Difficulty: 2 Page: 123

86. Mail questionnaires can be used to collect large amounts of information at a low cost per respondent.

    Answer: True   Difficulty: 2 Page: 123

87. Telephone interviewing is the best method for gathering information quickly.

    Answer: True   Difficulty: 2   Page: 124

88. Telephone interviewing runs little risk of interviewer bias since the respondent cannot actually see the interviewer.

    Answer: False   Difficulty: 2   Page: 124

89. Group interviewing is quite flexible, but, unfortunately, cannot be used to collect large amounts of data.

    Answer: False   Difficulty: 2   Page: 124

90. A marketing research project designed to provide insights into consumers' thoughts and feelings would likely include focus group interviews.

    Answer: True   Difficulty: 2   Page: 125

91. A sample is a segment of the population selected to represent the population as a whole.

    Answer: True   Difficulty: 1   Page: 127

92. A convenience sample is a type of probability sample where the researcher selects the easiest population members from which to obtain information.

    Answer: False   Difficulty: 1   Page: 127

93. A sample random sample is a type of probability sample where every member of the population has a known and equal chance of selection.

    Answer: True   Difficulty: 1   Page: 127

94. In marketing research, the questionnaire is the only research instrument suitable for collecting primary data.

    Answer: False   Difficulty: 2   Page: 127

95. The process of collecting, processing, and analyzing the information occurs during the implementation of the research plan.

    Answer: True   Difficulty: 2   Page: 129

96. Although there are many problems when conducting international marketing research, finding good secondary data is seldom one of them.

    Answer: False   Difficulty: 2   Page: 131

97. Most consumers feel positively about marketing research and believe that it serves a useful purpose.

    Answer: True   Difficulty: 2   Page: 134

98. Few advertisers openly rig their research designs or blatantly misrepresent the findings; most abuses tend to be subtle "stretches."

    Answer: True   Difficulty: 2 Page: 134

ESSAY

99. Explain the importance of information to the company.

    Answer:
    Marketing managers need timely, reliable, and relevant information in order to make decisions that will enhance the company's ability to compete successfully. Information is important but must be balanced between managers' needs and what is feasible to offer. Too much information can overwhelm managers, too little information can lead to poor decisions.

    Difficulty: 3 Page: 108

100. Describe the four steps in the marketing research process.

    Answer:
    The four steps in the marketing research process are 1) Defining the problem and the research objectives; 2) Developing the research plan; 3) Implementing the research plan; and, 4) Interpreting and reporting the findings.

    Difficulty: 3 Page: 115

101. Identify the different kinds of information a company might use.

    Answer:
    A company might use secondary data information or primary data information. Secondary data consists of information that already exists somewhere, having been collected for another purpose. Primary data consists of information collected for the specific purpose at hand.

    Difficulty: 3 Page: 118

102. Briefly contrast exploratory, descriptive, and causal research. Describe the role each may play in the resolution of a complex marketing problem.

    Answer:
    Exploratory research is used to gather preliminary information that will help to better define the problem and suggest hypotheses. This type of research is often used to guide the research process through the solution of a complex marketing problem. Exploratory research may be followed by either descriptive or causal research. Descriptive research is used to present items of interest to the marketer--frequently categorized on the basis of demographics or consumer attitudes. Causal research is used to test hypotheses about cause-and-effect relationships.

    Difficulty: 3 Page: 116

103. Compare the advantages and disadvantages of the different methods of collection information.

Answer:
1) Mail questionnaires- Advantages: collect large amounts of information, low costs, more honest, no interviewer bias. Disadvantages: not flexible, low response rates, long time to complete, lack of sample control.
2) Telephone interviewing- Advantages: best for quick collection, flexible, sample control, response rates. Disadvantages: cost higher than mail, interviewer bias.
3) Personal- Individual or Group- Advantages: flexible, focus. Disadvantages: costs, speed of data collection, and interviewer bias.

Difficulty: 3 Page: 124

104. Through marketing research, companies learn more about consumers' needs, resulting in more satisfying products and services. However, the misuses of marketing research can also harm or annoy consumers. Describe the two major public policy and ethics issues in marketing research.

Answer: (1) Intrusions on consumer privacy: (2) Misuse of research findings.

Difficulty: 3 Page: 134

Chapter 5

1. _____ refers to the buying behavior of final consumers.

   a) Consumer buying behavior
   b) Reseller buying behavior
   c) Business buying behavior
   d) Consumer's value chain

   Answer: (a)   Difficulty: 1   Page: 141

2. All the individuals who buy or acquire goods and services for personal consumption belong to the:

   a) business market.
   b) consumer market.
   c) target market.
   d) reseller market.

   Answer: (b)   Difficulty: 1   Page: 141

3. In studying consumers, the central question for marketers is:

   a) How do consumers respond to different advertising appeals?
   b) How will consumers respond to different product features?
   c) How do consumers respond to various marketing efforts that the company might use?
   d) All of the above.

   Answer: (c)   Difficulty: 2   Page: 141

4. The set of basic values, perceptions, wants, and behaviors learned by a member of society from family and other important institutions is called:

   a) social class.
   b) subculture.
   c) social factors.
   d) culture.

   Answer: (d)   Difficulty: 2   Page: 143

5. _____ is the most basic cause of a person's wants and behavior.

   a) Culture
   b) Subculture
   c) Social class
   d) Family

   Answer: (a)   Difficulty: 1   Page: 143

6. Marketers are always trying to spot _____ in order to discover new products that might be wanted.

   a) subcultural shifts
   b) cultural shifts
   c) social roles
   d) membership groups

   Answer: (b)   Difficulty: 2 Page: 143

7. Groups of people with shared value systems based on common life experiences and situations are called:

   a) cliques.
   b) social classes.
   c) subcultures.
   d) cultures.

   Answer: (c)   Difficulty: 1 Page: 143

8. Nationalities, religions, racial groups, and geographic regions can all form the basis for:

   a) lifestyle segmentation.
   b) social classes.
   c) subcultures.
   d) cultures.

   Answer: (c)   Difficulty: 1 Page: 143

9. The MFB Corporation specializes in orthopedic walking shoes for elderly consumers. The firm's chosen market segment could be described as a:

   a) culture.
   b) social class.
   c) social clique.
   d) subculture.

   Answer: (d)   Difficulty: 3 Page: 145

10. All of the following are important subculture groups except:

   a) Hispanic consumers
   b) African American consumers
   c) Mature consumers
   d) All of the above.

   Answer: (d)   Difficulty: 1 Page: 145

11. Relatively permanent and ordered divisions in a society whose members share similar values, interests, and behaviors are called:

    a) social classes.
    b) subcultures.
    c) cultures.
    d) reference groups.

    Answer: (a)   Difficulty: 1 Page: 146

12. A combination of occupation, income, education, wealth, and other variables are used to determine:

    a) culture.
    b) subculture.
    c) social class.
    d) groups.

    Answer: (c) Difficulty: 1 Page: 146

13. Marketers are interested in social class because:

    a) people within a given social class tend to exhibit similar buying behavior.
    b) social classes are fixed and rigid in the United States.
    c) people cannot move from one social class to another.
    d) All of the above.

    Answer: (a)   Difficulty: 2 Page: 146

14. Which of the following statements about social class is not true?

    a) Social classes show distinct product and brand preferences.
    b) The links between social classes are not fixed or rigid.
    c) It is solely determined by income.
    d) It is measured as a combination of occupation, income, education and other variables.

    Answer: (c)   Difficulty: 1 Page: 129

15. The Elite Corporation primarily targets professionals and "career" oriented persons in its marketing efforts. The firm's target market is centered in the _____ class.

    a) lower upper
    b) upper middle
    c) middle
    d) upper upper

    Answer: (b)   Difficulty: 3 Page: 147

16. Groups that have a direct influence and to which a person belongs are called:

    a) reference groups.
    b) membership groups.
    c) social groups.
    d) personal groups.

    Answer: (b)   Difficulty: 1 Page: 146

17. Organizations like religious groups, professional associations, and trade unions with which a person has more formal and less regular interaction are called:

    a) reference groups.
    b) membership groups.
    c) social groups.
    d) secondary groups.

    Answer: (d)   Difficulty: 2 Page: 148

18. Groups that serve as direct or indirect points of comparison in forming a person's attitudes or behavior are called:

    a) reference groups.
    b) membership groups.
    c) professional groups.
    d) secondary groups.

    Answer: (a)   Difficulty: 1 Page: 148

19. People within a reference group who, because of special skills, knowledge, personality traits, or other characteristics, exert influence on others are called:

    a) family leader.
    b) opinion leaders.
    c) social class leaders.
    d) focus group leaders.

    Answer: (b)   Difficulty: 1 Page: 148

20. The most important consumer buying organization in society is called:

    a) family members.
    b) opinion leaders.
    c) aspirational groups.
    d) reference groups.

    Answer: (a)   Difficulty: 1 Page: 148

21. Which, if any, of the following is not one of the personal factors of buyers that influences their purchase decisions?

    a) Occupation
    b) Age and Life-cycle state
    c) Lifestyle
    d) All of the above are personal factors.

    Answer: (d)   Difficulty: 2 Page: 150

22. A person's pattern of living as expressed in his or her activities, interests, and opinions is/are called:

    a) life-cycle stage.
    b) economic situation.
    c) lifestyle
    d) social class.

    Answer: (c)   Difficulty: 2 Page: 150

23. The technique of measuring lifestyles and developing lifestyle classifications is called:

    a) geographic.
    b) demographics.
    c) psychographic.
    d) econometrics.

    Answer: (c)   Difficulty: 2 Page: 150

24. The IfSo Corporation is interested in measuring the lifestyles of its present and potential customers. Which of the following techniques is the firm most likely to use?

    a) sociometric
    b) psychographic
    c) econometrics
    d) psychometrics

    Answer: (b)   Difficulty: 3 Page: 150

25. The most widely used lifestyle classification is the _____ typology.

    a) SRI
    b) VALS
    c) AIO
    d) social class

    Answer: (b)   Difficulty: 1 Page: 150

26. Marketers use AIO dimensions to measure which of the following personal factors affecting purchase decision-making?

    a) Age and life-cycle stage
    b) Occupation
    c) Economic situation
    d) Lifestyle

    Answer: (d)   Difficulty: 2 Page: 150

27. _____ buyers base their purchases on the actions and opinions of others.

    a) Status-oriented
    b) Action-oriented
    c) Self-oriented
    d) Principle-oriented

    Answer: (a)   Difficulty: 1 Page: 151

28. _____ buyers are driven by their desire for activity, variety, and risk taking.

    a) Status-oriented
    b) Action-oriented
    c) Self-oriented
    d) Principle-oriented

    Answer: (b)   Difficulty: 1 Page: 151

29. The unique psychological characteristics that lead to relatively consistent and lasting responses to one's own environment is called:

    a) psychographic.
    b) demographics.
    c) lifestyle.
    d) personality.

    Answer: (d)   Difficulty: 1 Page: 152

30. The statement "we are what we have" refers to:

    a) a person's self-concept.
    b) a person's buying behavior.
    c) the lifecycle concept.
    d) a person's psychographic.

    Answer: (a)   Difficulty: 2 Page: 152

31. All of the following are psychological factors affecting a person's buying choices except:

    a) Motivation
    b) Perception
    c) Learning
    d) All of the above are major psychological factors.

    Answer: (d)   Difficulty: 2 Page: 153

32. A _____ is a need that is sufficiently pressing to direct the person to seek satisfaction.

    a) motive
    b) desire
    c) perception
    d) demand

    Answer: (a)   Difficulty: 1 Page: 153

33. The theory of motivation that assumes people are largely unconscious about the real psychological forces shaping their behavior was developed by:

    a) Freud.
    b) Maslow.
    c) Kotler & Armstrong.
    d) Aristotle.

    Answer: (a)   Difficulty: 2 Page: 153

34. The theory of motivation that views needs as hierarchically ordered from lower ones to higher ones was developed by:

    a) Freud.
    b) Maslow.
    c) Kotler & Armstrong.
    d) Aristotle.

    Answer: (b)   Difficulty: 2 Page: 153

35. According to Maslow's hierarchy of needs, a starving person is seeking to satisfy which level of need?

    a) Psychological
    b) Safety
    c) Social
    d) Esteem

    Answer: (a)   Difficulty: 2 Page: 156

36. According to Maslow's hierarchy of needs, the need to be thought well of by others is which kind of need?

    a) Psychological
    b) Safety
    c) Social
    d) Esteem

    Answer: (c)   Difficulty: 2 Page: 156

37. The process by which people select, organize, and interpret information to form a meaningful picture of the world is called:

    a) attitude.
    b) consumption.
    c) perception.
    d) motivation.

    Answer: (c)   Difficulty: 1 Page: 157

38. People can form different perceptions of the same stimulus because of three perceptual processes. Which of the following is not one of those processes?

    a) Selective attention
    b) Selective distortion
    c) Selective retention
    d) Selective exposure

    Answer: (d)   Difficulty: 1 Page: 157

39. The tendency of people to adapt information to personal meanings is called:

    a) selective retention.
    b) selective distortion.
    c) selective interpretation.
    d) selective imaging.

    Answer: (b)   Difficulty: 1 Page: 157

40. Pat Dobbs, a "confirmed Republican," has just listened to a speech by the Democratic candidate for President. His interpretation of the speech will probably be quite different from that intended by the candidate as a result of selective:

    a) retention.
    b) exposure.
    c) imaging.
    d) distortion.

    Answer: (d)   Difficulty: 3 Page: 157

41. Changes in an individual's behavior arising from experience is called:

    a) perception.
    b) learning.
    c) stimulus.
    d) selective retention.

    Answer: (b)   Difficulty: 1   Page: 157

42. Which, if any, of the following are components of learning theory?

    a) Drives
    b) Stimuli
    c) Cues
    d) All of the above

    Answer: (d)   Difficulty: 1   Page: 157

43. A drive becomes a motive when it is directed toward a particular:

    a) attitude.
    b) stimulus object.
    c) belief.
    d) idea.

    Answer: (b)   Difficulty: 2   Page: 157

44. A/an _____ is a descriptive thought that a person has about something.

    a) attitude
    b) idea
    c) belief
    d) cognition

    Answer: (c)   Difficulty: 1   Page: 158

45. A/an _____ describes a person's relatively consistent evaluations, feelings, and tendencies regarding an object or idea.

    a) attitude
    b) idea
    c) belief
    d) cognition

    Answer: (a)   Difficulty: 1   Page: 159

46. All of the following are stages in the buyer decision process except:

    a) awareness.
    b) information search.
    b) evaluation of alternatives.
    c) purchase decision.

    Answer: (a)   Difficulty: 1   Page: 161

47. A buyer senses a difference between his or her actual state and some desired state in which of the following stages of the buyer decision process?

    a) Information search.
    b) Evaluation of alternatives.
    c) Need recognition.
    d) Purchase decision

    Answer: (c)   Difficulty: 2 Page: 161

48. The stage of the buyer decision process in which the consumer looks for material about a product is called:

    a) Information search.
    b) Evaluation of alternatives.
    c) Need recognition.
    d) Purchase decision

    Answer: (a)   Difficulty: 2 Page: 162

49. The consumer can obtain information from all of the following sources except:

    a) personal sources
    b) commercial sources
    c) public sources
    d) All of the above are sources

    Answer: (d)   Difficulty: 2 Page: 163

50. How the consumer processes information to arrive at brand choices occurs during which stage of the buyer decision process?

    a) Information search.
    b) Evaluation of alternatives.
    c) Need recognition.
    d) Purchase decision

    Answer: (b)   Difficulty: 2 Page: 163

51. The feelings of satisfaction or dissatisfaction following a purchase are part of the consumer's:

    a) need recognition.
    b) information search.
    c) evaluation of alternatives.
    d) postpurchase behavior.

    Answer: (d)   Difficulty: 1 Page: 164

52. Consumers frequently notice more cars of the make and model they just purchased after their purchase than they did before their purchase. This phenomenon is most closely related to:

    a) purchase expectations.
    b) cognitive dissonance.
    c) disappointment.
    d) alternative evaluations.

    Answer: (b)   Difficulty: 1   Page: 165

53. Regarding customer satisfaction, which of the following statements is true?

    a) Dissatisfied customers tend to behave much like satisfied customers.
    b) Bad word of mouth travels farther and faster than good word of mouth.
    c) Dissatisfied customers tell fewer people about their experience than do satisfied customers.
    d) Dissatisfied customers complain to the company in large numbers.

    Answer: (b)   Difficulty: 3   Page: 165

54. The mental process through which an individual passes from first hearing about an innovation to final adoption is called:

    a) the learning process.
    b) the purchase.
    c) the cognitive process
    d) the adoption process.

    Answer: (d)   Difficulty: 2   Page: 168

55. The decision by an individual to become a regular user of the product is called:

    a) Adoption
    b) Purchase
    c) Conversion
    d) Consumption

    Answer: (a)   Difficulty: 1   Page: 168

56. In which of the following stages of the adoption process is the consumer stimulated to seek information about the new product?

    a) awareness
    b) interest
    c) trial
    d) evaluation

    Answer: (b)   Difficulty: 1   Page: 168

57. The Tastee Food Company routinely distributes samples of its new products. The firm is attempting to ease the consumer through which of the following stages of the adoption process?

   a) awareness
   b) interest
   c) trial
   d) adoption

   Answer: (c)   Difficulty: 3 Page: 168

58. The adopter classification suggests that an innovating firm should research the characteristics of _____ and _____ and should direct marketing efforts toward them.

   a) early adopters and early majority
   b) innovators and laggards
   c) early adopters and late majority
   d) innovators and early adopters.

   Answer: (d)   Difficulty: 3 Page: 169

59. Which of the following adopter categories are most likely to be opinion leaders?

   a) innovators
   b) late adopters
   c) early majority
   d) early adopters

   Answer: (d)   Difficulty: 2 Page: 169

60. Skepticism is the major characteristic of the:

   a) late majority.
   b) innovator.
   c) early majority.
   d) early adopter.

   Answer: (a)   Difficulty: 2 Page: 169

61. The degree to which the innovation appears superior to existing products is called:

   a) relative advantage.
   b) compatibility.
   c) complexity.
   d) divisibility.

   Answer: (a)   Difficulty: 1 Page: 170

62. The degree to which the innovation fits the values and experiences of potential consumers is called:

   a) relative advantage.
   b) compatibility.
   c) complexity.
   d) divisibility.

   Answer: (b)   Difficulty: 1   Page: 170

63. The degree to which the innovation is difficult to understand or use is called:

   a) relative advantage.
   b) compatibility.
   c) complexity.
   d) divisibility.

   Answer: (c)   Difficulty: 1   Page: 170

64. The degree to which the innovation may be tried on a limited basis is called:

   a) relative advantage.
   b) compatibility.
   c) complexity.
   d) divisibility.

   Answer: (d)   Difficulty: 1   Page: 171

65. The degree to which the results of using the innovation can be observed or described is called:

   a) communicability.
   b) compatibility.
   c) complexity.
   d) divisibility.

   Answer: (a)   Difficulty: 1   Page: 171

TRUE/FALSE

66. The consumer market is composed of individuals and households who purchase goods or services for personal consumption.

   Answer: True   Difficulty: 1   Page: 141

67. Consumer buying behavior refers to the buying behavior of households who buy goods and services for personal consumption.

   Answer: False   Difficulty: 1   Page: 141

68. Consumers around the world purchase a variety of goods and services even though they are similar in age, income, education level and tastes.

   Answer: False   Difficulty: 2   Page: 141

69. The central question for marketers is: How do consumers respond to various marketing efforts that the company might use?

    Answer: True   Difficulty: 2 Page: 141

70. The buyer's black box consists of three basic parts: the buyer's characteristics, the buyer's decision process and the buyer's rate of adoption.

    Answer: False   Difficulty: 1 Page: 142

71. Culture is the most basic cause of a person's wants and behavior.

    Answer: True   Difficulty: 1 Page: 143

72. Marketers are always trying to spot cultural shifts in order to discover new products that might be wanted.

    Answer: True   Difficulty: 2 Page: 143

73. Cultures are groups of people with shared value systems based on common life experiences and situations.

    Answer: False   Difficulty: 2 Page: 143

74. Culture, like other purchase influences, changes over time.

    Answer: True   Difficulty: 1 Page: 143

75. Social class is determined exclusively by level of income.

    Answer: False   Difficulty: 2 Page: 146

76. Social classes are society's relatively permanent and ordered divisions whose members share similar values, interests, and behaviors.

    Answer: True   Difficulty: 2 Page: 146

77. Groups with whom a person has regular but informal interaction are called primary groups.

    Answer: True   Difficulty: 2 Page: 146

78. Opinion leaders are of importance to marketers seeking to utilize reference group influence to promote their products.

    Answer: True   Difficulty: 2 Page: 148

79. The importance of group influence is similar across products and brands.

    Answer: False   Difficulty: 2 Page: 148

80. Reference groups serve as direct or indirect points of comparison in forming a person's attitudes or behavior.

    Answer: True   Difficulty: 2   Page: 148

81. Secondary groups have formal and less regular interaction than do primary groups.

    Answer: True   Difficulty: 2   Page: 148

82. Status is the general esteem given by society to someone fulfilling their role.

    Answer: True   Difficulty: 2   Page: 149

83. A role consists of the activities that people are expected to perform according to the persons around them.

    Answer: True   Difficulty: 1   Page: 149

84. The family life-cycle refers to the stages through which families might pass as they mature over time.

    Answer: True   Difficulty: 1   Page: 149

85. Lifestyle is a person's pattern of living as expressed in his or her activities, interests, and opinions.

    Answer: True   Difficulty: 1   Page: 150

86. According to Freud, people are largely unconscious about the real psychological forces shaping their behavior.

    Answer: True   Difficulty: 2   Page: 153

87. According to Maslow, esteem needs must be satisfied before social needs are met.

    Answer: False   Difficulty: 1   Page: 156

88. Perception could be described as the process by which a person gives meaning to stimuli.

    Answer: True   Difficulty: 2   Page: 156

89. Selective distortion means that marketers must try to understand the mind-sets of consumers and how they will affect interpretations of advertising and sales information.

    Answer: True   Difficulty: 2   Page: 157

90. Selective attention is the tendency for people to adapt information to personal meanings.

    Answer: False   Difficulty: 3   Page: 157

91. A belief describes a person's relatively consistent evaluations, feelings, and tendencies regarding an object or idea.

    Answer: False   Difficulty: 1   Page: 159

92. Attitudes are difficult to change.

    Answer: True   Difficulty: 1   Page: 160

93. The buying process begins long before the purchase is made and ends when the purchase is actually made.

    Answer: False   Difficulty: 2   Page: 161

94. When the buyer senses a difference between his other actual state and some desired state, the buyer is in the information search stage of the buyer decision process.

    Answer: False   Difficulty: 2   Page: 161

95. When the consumer is aroused to search for more information, the consumer is in the information search stage of the buyer decision process.

    Answer: True   Difficulty: 2   Page: 162

96. In terms of information search, consumers can obtain information from personal and public sources but rarely from actual experience.

    Answer: False   Difficulty: 2   Page: 163

97. As more information is obtained during the information search, the consumer typically becomes confused and finds less differences between available brands.

    Answer: False   Difficulty: 2   Page: 163

98. Marketers should study buyers since they typically evaluate brand alternatives similarly.

    Answer: False   Difficulty: 1   Page: 164

99. Another term for postpurchase conflict is cognitive dissonance.

    Answer: True   Difficulty: 1   Page: 165

ESSAY

100. Define the consumer market. Describe the elements of a simple model of buying behavior.

    Answer:
    The consumer market is made up of all the individuals and households who buy or acquire goods and services for personal consumption. A simple model of consumer behavior consists of the four Ps: product, price, place, and promotion. Other stimuli include major forces and events in the buyer's environment: economic, technological, political, and cultural. All these inputs enter the buyer's black box, where they are turned into a set of observable buyer response: product choice, brand choice, dealer choice, purchase timing, and purchase amount.

    Difficulty: 3   Page: 142

101. Describe the importance of culture, subculture and social class influences on consumer buying behavior.

Answer:
Culture is the most basic cause of a person's wants and behavior. Subcultures are smaller groups of people with shared value systems based on common life experiences. Social classes are relatively permanent and ordered divisions in a society whose members share similar values, interests, and behaviors.

Difficulty: 3 Page: 143-146

102. Motivation research relies upon Freudian Theory to probe the subconscious motives of a small sample of consumers. Critique the validity of this marketing tool.

Answer:
Motivation research has several weaknesses. First, it is Freudian in approach. If Freudian Theory is flawed--and many theorists hold that it is--the validity of marketing research is suspect. The approach is highly subjective--researchers may "contaminate" even valid findings by the interjection of their own viewpoints. Sample sizes are typically quite small--and drawn from population centers near necessary research centers. Those technical problems undermine the validity of attempting to project findings to the total population. In fact, motivation research is rarely accepted as infallible today.

Difficulty: 3 Page: 153

103. Describe Maslow's theory of motivation. Include a diagram in your discussion.

Answer:
Maslow's theory sought to explain why people are driven by particular needs at particular times. Maslow's theory states that human needs are arranged in a hierarchy, from the most pressing to the least pressing. In order of importance, they are physiological needs, social needs, esteem needs, and self-actualization needs. A person tries to satisfy the most important need first.

Difficulty: 3 Page: 156

104. Identify and discuss the stages in the buyer decision process. Apply the stages to a product that you recently purchased that cost more than $50.

Answer:
There are five stages in the buyer decision process. 1) Need recognition: consumer recognizes a problem or need. 2) Information search: the consumer is aroused to search for more information. 3) Evaluation of Alternatives: the consumer uses information to evaluate alternative brands in the choice set. 4) Purchase decision: the consumer actually buys the product. 5) Postpurchase behavior: the consumer takes further action after the purchase based on their satisfaction or dissatisfaction.

Difficulty: 3 Page: 161-166

105. Explain why it is not "smart" to promise more than the product can deliver in order to get a sale. What steps can a marketer take to enhance postpurchase satisfaction?

Answer:
"Over-selling" the product accomplishes nothing but the raising of consumer expectations to unreasonable levels. When these prepurchase expectations are not met, the consumer will experience severe cognitive dissonance. Not only will they not purchase again, they will tell others of their experience--the marketer will lose multiple future sales. In some instances, irate consumers may relate their problems to the media, governmental agencies, or consumer groups--with disastrous results. True, cognitive dissonance may never be eliminated--but it can be minimized. The marketer should seek to understand the desires of the target market, create an offering that can provide desired satisfactions effectively, promote the product honestly, and stand by the product after the sale.

Difficulty: 3 Page: 165

106. Identify and discuss the stages in adoption process for new products.

Answer:
New product adoption process has five stages which include awareness, interest, evaluation, trial, adoption.

Difficulty: 2 Page: 168

107. Discuss the individual differences in innovativeness.

Answer:
People differ greatly in their readiness to try new products. There are five adopter groups each with differing values: innovators, early adopters, early majority, late majority, laggards.

Difficulty: 2 Page: 169

108. Opinion leaders exist in all social classes. Would you expect opinion leaders to have more influence within their own class or upon the class above or below their class? Why?

Answer:
Opinion leaders typically have the greatest influence horizontally--within their own class. This results from the fact that the members of their own class are more likely to know, or know of, them and to perceive the opinion leaders as similar to themselves in such important areas as income, education, and type of occupation. The greater the amount of perceived similarity, the greater the amount of social influence.

Difficulty: 3 Page: 148

Chapter 6

1. All the organizations that buy goods and services to use in the production of other products and services that are sold, rented or supplied to others is called:

   a) consumer market.
   b) business market.
   c) international market.
   d) public market.

   Answer: (b)   Difficulty: 1   Page: 179

2. The decision-making process by which business buyers establish the need for purchased products and services and identify, evaluate, and choose among alternative brands and suppliers is called:

   a) business buying.
   b) consumer buying.
   c) government buying.
   d) reseller buying.

   Answer: (a)   Difficulty: 1   Page: 179

3. The USA Steel Company sells steel to automobile manufacturers who utilize their product to produce a variety of cars and trucks. USA Steel sells to the:

   a) consumer market.
   b) business market.
   c) government market.
   d) reseller market.

   Answer: (b)   Difficulty: 2   Page: 179

4. Retailing and wholesaling firms that acquire goods for the purpose of reselling or renting them to others at a profit are part of the:

   a) consumer market.
   b) reseller market.
   c) government market.
   d) business market.

   Answer: (d)   Difficulty: 1   Page: 179

5. The characteristics of the business market that distinguish it from the consumer market include:

   a) market structure and demand.
   b) the nature of the buying unit.
   c) types of decisions and the decision process involved.
   d) all of the above.

   Answer: (d)   Difficulty: 1   Page: 179

6. All of the following are differences in market structure and demand between consumer and business markets except:

   a) business markets contain fewer but larger buyers.
   b) business markets have derived demand.
   c) business markets are more geographically concentrated.
   d) business markets have more elastic demand.

   Answer: (d)   Difficulty: 2 Page: 180

7. A small percentage increase in the consumer demand can cause _____ in business demand.

   a) large decreases
   b) large increases
   c) small decreases
   d) small decreases

   Answer: (b)   Difficulty: 2 Page: 180

8. In business markets, buying decisions are often more complex than in consumer markets. This is one example of which of the following characteristic differences between consumer and business markets?

   a) Market structure and demand
   b) Nature of the buying unit
   c) Types of decisions and decision process
   d) All of the above.

   Answer: (c)   Difficulty: 2 Page: 181

9. Purchase decisions in business markets tend to be more formalized than the consumer markets. This demonstrates which characteristic difference between consumer and business markets?

   a) Market structure and demand
   b) Nature of the buying unit
   c) Types of decisions and decision process
   d) All of the above.

   Answer: (c)   Difficulty: 2 Page: 181

10. When consumer demand increases slightly, but leads to a large increase in business market demand, we can say that the business market is experiencing:

    a) geographic demand.
    b) elastic demand.
    c) inelastic demand.
    d) fluctuating demand.

    Answer: (c)   Difficulty: 2 Page: 180

11. A drop in the price of steel will not cause automakers to buy more steel unless it results in lower car prices which will increase consumer demand for cars. Thus, in the short run, automakers' demand for steel is:

    a) elastic.
    b) inelastic.
    c) fluctuating.
    d) static.

    Answer: (b)   Difficulty: 2 Page: 180

12. Compared with consumer purchases, business purchases usually involves more buyers and a more professional purchasing effort. This is typical of which characteristic differences between business and consumer markets?

    a) Market structure and demand
    b) Nature of the buying unit
    c) Types of decisions
    d) Types of decision processes

    Answer: (b)   Difficulty: 2 Page: 180

13. Compared with consumer buyers, in the business buyers and sellers are often much more dependent on each other. This is typical of which characteristic differences between business and consumer markets?

    a) Market structure and demand
    b) Nature of the buying unit
    c) Types of decisions
    d) Types of decision processes

    Answer: (d)   Difficulty: 2 Page: 181

14. Within the organization, all the people involved in the buying decision are part of the:

    a) purchasing department.
    b) acquisition department.
    c) distribution center.
    d) buying center.

    Answer: (d)   Difficulty: 1 Page: 183

15. In a _____, the buyer reorders something without any modifications.

    a) straight rebuy
    b) modified rebuy
    c) new-task buy
    d) habitual rebuy

    Answer: (a)   Difficulty: 1 Page: 185

16. In a _____, the buyer wants to modify product specifications, prices, terms, or suppliers.

    a) straight rebuy
    b) modified rebuy
    c) new-task buy
    d) indirect rebuy

    Answer: (b)   Difficulty: 1 Page: 185

17. When the firm buys a product or service for the first time, it is facing a:

    a) straight rebuy situation.
    b) modified rebuy situation.
    c) new task situation.
    d) systems buying situation.

    Answer: (c)   Difficulty: 1 Page: 185

18. Buying a packaged solution to a problem without all the separate decisions involved is called:

    a) pre-packaged buying.
    b) systems buying.
    c) new task buying.
    d) direct competitive buying.

    Answer: (b) Difficulty: 1 Page: 183

19. Based on prior buying satisfaction, the buying situation where the buyer simply chooses from the various suppliers on its list is called:

    a) modified rebuy
    b) straight rebuy
    c) new task
    d) modified task

    Answer: (b)   Difficulty: 2 Page: 185

20. In the _____, the buyer must decide on product specifications, suppliers, price limits, payment terms, order quantities, delivery times, and service terms.

    a) modified rebuy situation
    b) straight rebuy situation
    c) new task situation
    d) systems buying situation

    Answer: (c)   Difficulty: 2 Page: 185

21. Omega Sales Corporation is seeking a supplier to produce automobile batteries to specifications which will allow Omega to profitably sell the batteries in its Omega-Mart Discount Stores. Omega's efforts to locate suitable suppliers would be best described as a:

    a) straight rebuy.
    b) report task.
    c) reciprocity agreement.
    d) new task.

    Answer: (d)   Difficulty: 3 Page: 185

22. Which of the following purchasing situations offers the greatest opportunity and challenge to the marketer?

    a) straight rebuy
    b) modified rebuy
    c) new task
    d) indirect rebuy

    Answer: (c)   Difficulty: 2 Page: 185

23. Orangeco is a firm seeking to buy a "whole solution" to its problem rather than making a series of separate decisions. It is using a _____ approach.

    a) systems buying
    b) modified rebuy
    c) straight rebuy
    d) new task

    Answer: (a)   Difficulty: 1 Page: 185

24. The Simms Corporation has enjoyed great success as a result of its strategy of selling a group of interlocking products supported by an integrated mix of services designed to meet the buyer's need for a smooth-running operation. The firm is employing:

    a) systems selling.
    b) reciprocity selling.
    c) oligoplistic selling.
    d) negative-option selling.

    Answer: (a)   Difficulty: 3 Page: 186

25. The decision-making unit of a buying organization is called:

    a) the marketing department.
    b) the acquisition department.
    c) the distribution center.
    d) the buying center.

    Answer: (d) Difficulty: 1 Page: 186

26. Which, if any, of the following is/are major influences on business buyers?

    a) Environmental factors
    b) Organizational factors
    c) Interpersonal factors
    d) All of the above are influences.

    Answer: (d)   Difficulty: 1 Page: 188

27. Factors such as the shortages of key materials and cost of money are part of which type of influence on business buyers?

    a) Environmental factors
    b) Organizational factors
    c) Interpersonal factors
    d) Individual factors

    Answer: (d)   Difficulty: 1 Page: 188

28. Which of the following is an increasingly important environmental factor influencing business buyers?

    a) the level of primary demand
    b) the cost of money
    c) shortages in key materials
    d) the economic outlook

    Answer: (c)   Difficulty: 2 Page: 188

29. Questions facing the business marketer such as who is involved in the buying decision, how many are involved, and what are their evaluative criteria, are all part of which group of factor influencing business buyers?

    a) Environmental factors
    b) Organizational factors
    c) Interpersonal factors
    d) Individual factors

    Answer: (b)   Difficulty: 1 Page: 189

30. Since participants influence the buying decision process and control rewards and punishments, are well liked, have special expertise, or have a special relationship with other important participants are all part of which factor that influences business buyers?

    a) Environmental factors
    b) Organizational factors
    c) Interpersonal factors
    d) Individual factors

    Answer: (c)   Difficulty: 1 Page: 189

31. The stage in the business buying process where someone in the company recognizes that a need can be met by acquiring product or service, is called:

    a) general need description.
    b) product specification.
    c) supplier search.
    d) problem recognition.

    Answer: (d)   Difficulty: 2   Page: 192

32. The stage in the business buying process where a team of buyers will rank the importance of product reliability, durability, price, and other product attributes desired in that item.

    a) general need description.
    b) product specification.
    c) supplier search.
    d) problem recognition.

    Answer: (a)   Difficulty: 2   Page: 192

33. _____ is an approach to cost reduction in which components are studied carefully to determine if they can be redesigned, standardized, or made by less costly methods of production.

    a) Supplier search
    b) Problem recognition
    c) Product specification
    d) Value analysis

    Answer: (d)   Difficulty: 2   Page: 192

34. The stage of the business buying process in which the buying organization decides on and specifies the best technical product characteristics for a need item is called:

    a) general need description.
    b) product specification.
    c) supplier search.
    d) problem recognition.

    Answer: (b)   Difficulty: 2   Page: 192

35. The stage of the business buying process in which the buyer tries to find the best vendors is called:

    a) general need description.
    b) product specification.
    c) supplier search.
    d) problem recognition.

    Answer: (c)   Difficulty: 2   Page: 192

36. The stage of the business buying process in which the buyer invites qualified suppliers to submit proposals is called:

    a) general need description.
    b) product specification.
    c) supplier search.
    d) proposal solicitation.

    Answer: (d)   Difficulty: 2 Page: 194

37. During this stage of the business buying process, buyers may attempt to negotiate with preferred suppliers for better prices and terms.

    a) general need description.
    b) product specification.
    c) supplier search.
    d) supplier selection.

    Answer: (d)   Difficulty: 2 Page: 194

38. Blanket contracts are typically part of which of the following stages in the business buying decision process?

    a) order routine specification.
    b) product specification.
    c) supplier search.
    d) problem recognition.

    Answer: (a)   Difficulty: 2 Page: 194

39. The stage of the business buying process where the buyer may continue, modify, or cancel the arrangement with a supplier is called:

    a) general need description.
    b) product specification.
    c) supplier search.
    d) performance review.

    Answer: (d)   Difficulty: 2 Page: 194

40. Which of the following buying process stages can always be expected to be completed for new task, modified rebuy, and straight rebuy?

    a) problem recognition and supplier search
    b) product specification and performance review
    c) general need description and supplier selection
    d) problem recognition and order routine specification

    Answer: (b)   Difficulty: 3 Page: 193

41. The _____ consists of schools, hospitals, nursing homes, prisons, and other institutions that provide goods and services to people in their care.

    a) Government markets
    b) Business markets
    c) Consumer markets
    d) Institutional markets

    Answer: (d)   Difficulty: 2   Page: 195

42. Low budgets and captive patrons are often characteristics of:

    a) government markets
    b) institutional markets
    c) business markets
    d) consumer markets

    Answer: (b)   Difficulty: 2   Page: 195

43. _____ purchase or rent goods and services for carrying out the main functions of government.

    a) Government markets
    b) Institutional markets
    c) Business markets
    d) Consumer markets

    Answer: (a)   Difficulty: 2   Page: 195

44. This particular market is carefully watched by outside publics.

    a) Government markets
    b) Institutional markets
    c) Business markets
    d) Consumer markets

    Answer: (a)   Difficulty: 2   Page: 196

TRUE/FALSE

45. The business market consists of all the organizations that buy goods and services to use in the production of other products and services that are sold, rented, or supplied to others.

    Answer: True   Difficulty: 2   Page: 179

46. The business market includes retailing and wholesaling firms that acquire goods for the purpose of reselling or renting them to others at a profit.

    Answer: True   Difficulty: 2   Page: 179

47. Companies that sell to other business organizations must do their best to understand consumer markets and consumer buyer behavior.

    Answer: False   Difficulty: 2   Page: 179

48. Business markets tend to have fewer buyers than consumer markets.

    Answer: True   Difficulty: 1 Page: 179

49. Business markets are geographically concentrated.

    Answer: True   Difficulty: 1 Page: 179

50. Business markets have less inelastic demand than consumer markets.

    Answer: False   Difficulty: 1 Page: 180

51. Business markets have far fewer but far larger buyers than consumer markets.

    Answer: True   Difficulty: 1 Page: 179

52. In large business markets, few buyers account for most of the purchasing.

    Answer: True   Difficulty: 1 Page: 179

53. As a result of inelastic demand in business markets, the demand for business goods and services fluctuates less--and less quickly--than the demand for consumer goods and services.

    Answer: False   Difficulty: 2 Page: 180

54. Business demand is a derived demand.

    Answer: True   Difficulty: 2 Page: 180

55. Business buyers usually face a more formalized process, however, the buying decisions are less complex than consumer buyers.

    Answer: False   Difficulty: 2 Page: 180

56. Business markets have less fluctuating demand than consumer markets.

    Answer: False   Difficulty: 2 Page: 180

57. The more complex the business buying purchase, the less likely that several people will participate in the decision-making process.

    Answer: False   Difficulty: 2 Page: 180

58. Compared with consumer purchases, a business purchase usually involves more buyers and a more professional purchasing effort.

    Answer: True   Difficulty: 2 Page: 180

59. Within the organization, buying activity consists of two major parts: the buying center, and the buying decision process.

    Answer: True   Difficulty: 2 Page: 183

60. In the model of business buyer behavior, the four Ps of marketing are part of the environment.

    Answer: True   Difficulty: 2 Page: 182

61. According to the model of business buyer behavior, the buying center is made up of all the people involved in the buying decision.

    Answer: True   Difficulty: 2 Page: 183

62. A firm's buying center is typically located in, and limited to, its purchasing department.

    Answer: False   Difficulty: 2 Page: 183

63. In a straight rebuy, the buyer reorders something without any modifications.

    Answer: True   Difficulty: 2 Page: 185

64. In a modified rebuy, the buyer wants to modify product specifications, prices, terms or suppliers.

    Answer: True   Difficulty: 2 Page: 185

65. The buyer makes the fewest decisions in the modified rebuy and the most in the new-task situation.

    Answer: False   Difficulty: 2 Page: 185

66. A company facing a product or service for the first time faces a new task situation.

    Answer: True   Difficulty: 2 Page: 185

67. In a modified rebuy, automatic reordering will save reordering time.

    Answer: False   Difficulty: 2 Page: 185

68. The modified rebuy situation is the marketer's greatest opportunity and challenge.

    Answer: False   Difficulty: 1 Page: 185

69. Many business buyers prefer to buy packaged solutions to problems from as many sellers as possible.

    Answer: False   Difficulty: 2 Page: 185

70. Asking bids from suppliers to supply both components and assemble the package is called system buying.

    Answer: True   Difficulty: 2 Page: 185

71. Systems buying allows a purchaser to buy a whole solution to his or her problem while avoiding the necessity of making a series of separate decisions over time.

    Answer: True   Difficulty: 2   Page: 185

72. All the individuals and units that participate in the business buying-decision process is called the buying center.

    Answer: True   Difficulty: 2   Page: 185

73. The buying center is a fixed and formally identified unit within the buying organization.

    Answer: False   Difficulty: 2   Page: 186

74. An increasingly important organizational factor is shortages in key materials.

    Answer: False   Difficulty: 2   Page: 188

75. Business buyers respond primarily to competitive development in the environment.

    Answer: False   Difficulty: 2   Page: 188

76. An increasingly important environmental factor for business buyers is shortages in key materials.

    Answer: True   Difficulty: 2   Page: 188

77. When business buyers ask such questions as: "How many people are involved in the buying decision?" and "Who are they?," they are addressing interpersonal factors that will influence their decisions.

    Answer: False   Difficulty: 2   Page: 189

78. Regardless of the buying situation, problem recognition is always the first stage of the business buying process.

    Answer: True   Difficulty: 2   Page: 192

79. When the buyer ranks the importance of reliability, durability, and price preferred for a given product, the buyer is in the product specification stage of the business buying process.

    Answer: False   Difficulty: 2   Page: 192

80. Value analysis is an approach to cost reduction in which components are studied carefully to determine if they can be redesigned, standardized or made by less costly methods of production.

    Answer: True   Difficulty: 2   Page: 192

81. The newer the buying task, and the more complex and costly the item, the greater the amount of time the buyer will spend searching for suppliers.

    Answer: True   Difficulty: 2 Page: 192

82. In the supplier selection stage of the business buying process, the buyer invites qualified suppliers to submit proposals.

    Answer: False   Difficulty: 2 Page: 194

83. During the supplier selection, the buying center often will draw up a list of the desired supplier attributes and their relative importance.

    Answer: True   Difficulty: 2 Page: 194

84. Price is usually the determining factor in the selection of suppliers.

    Answer: False   Difficulty: 2 Page: 194

85. Many buyers prefer single sources of supplies in order to obtain the best prices.

    Answer: False   Difficulty: 2 Page: 194

86. The Soft Sofabed Corporation has outlined a marketing strategy which calls for developing long-term relationships with its customers. The firm is likely to prefer blanket contracts to achieve this goal.

    Answer: True   Difficulty: 2 Page: 194

87. Blanket contracts tend to "tie" suppliers more tightly to the buyer and make it difficult for new suppliers to compete.

    Answer: True   Difficulty: 2 Page: 194

88. During the performance review stage in the business buying process, the buyer may choose to continue, modify, or cancel its arrangements with a supplier.

    Answer: True   Difficulty: 2 Page: 194

89. The performance review stage of the business buying model is quite different from the postpurchase evaluation stage of the consumer buying model.

    Answer: False   Difficulty: 2 Page: 194

90. Product specification and performance review are the only stages of the business buying process that buyers face in new task, modified rebuy and straight rebuy.

    Answer: True   Difficulty: 2 Page: 193

91. Many institutional markets are characterized by low budgets and captive patrons.

    Answer: True   Difficulty: 2 Page: 195

92. When trying to meet the needs of institutional buyers, most marketers do not need to set a separate division.

    Answer: False   Difficulty: 2   Page: 195

93. Government organizations tend to favor domestic suppliers over foreign suppliers.

    Answer: True   Difficulty: 2   Page: 196

94. Noneconomic criteria sometimes play a role in government buying decisions.

    Answer: True   Difficulty: 2   Page: 197

ESSAY

95. Explain how business markets differ from consumer markets.

    Answer:
    Main differences include market structure and demand, nature of the buying unit, and types of decisions and decision processes. Business markets are geographically concentrated and have derived, inelastic, and fluctuating demand. Buying is more professional and involves more people. Decisions are more complex, more formalized, and the buyer and seller are more dependent upon one another.

    Difficulty: 3   Page: 180

96. Identify and discuss the three major types of buying situations.

    Answer:
    Straight rebuy is a reorder without any modifications. A modified rebuy involves some changes in product specifications, prices, terms or suppliers. New task buying occurs when a company buys a product or service for the first time. In such cases greater risk or cost will lead to a larger number of decision participants and a greater information search effort.

    Difficulty: 3   Page: 185

97. Briefly discuss the market structure and demand characteristics of business markets. What are their marketing implications?

    Answer:
    The business market is composed of a comparatively small number of very large buyers. Each buyer is sufficiently important to justify intensive marketing efforts which are typically built around personal selling. The geographic concentration of this market makes the use of personal selling feasible and encourages the location of inventory storage facilities near customers. The factor of derived demand forces organizational marketers to follow trends in the final consumer market and encourages the use of advertising directed to the final consumer. The inelasticity that characterizes demand in this market results from its derived nature. As a result, price may be less important in the supplier's marketing mix than delivery capacity. The derived nature of demand in this market also creates greater demand fluctuations

    Difficulty: 3   Page: 179

98. Identify the two major parts of the buying activity as it occurs within an organization. Briefly describe the composition of the buying center and identify the types of influences which affect its operation.

Answer:
The buying activity consists of the buying center and the buying decision process. The buying center is composed of all those individuals involved in the buying decision. The buying center and the buying process are influenced by internal organizational, interpersonal, and individual factors as well as by external environmental factors.

Difficulty: 1 Page: 161

99. What are the environmental factors that influence industrial buying behavior? Give an example of their impact on purchase decisions.

Answer:
The major environmental influences on industrial buying behavior include the current and expected economic environment, shortages in key materials, technological, political and competitive developments as well as culture and customs. As uncertainty in the economic environment increases, industrial buyers cut back on new investments and attempt to reduce their inventories.

Difficulty: 3 Page: 168

100. List and define the stages in the business buying decision process.

Answer:
1) Problem recognition, the first step in the buying process, occurs when someone in the organization recognizes a problem or need that can be met by acquiring a specific good or service. 2) General need description describes the general characteristics and quality of the needed item. 3) Product specification, technical specifications are developed--often with the aid of value analysis. 4) Supplier search, locate the best vendors. 5) Proposal solicitation, Qualified suppliers submit presentations designed to convince the buyer to select their products or services. 6) Supplier selection, the buyer considers the technical competence of various suppliers. 7) Order-routine specification, the buyer writes the final order. 8) Performance review, the buyer rates its satisfaction with suppliers.

Difficulty: 3 Page: 192-195

Chapter 7

1. To a marketer, a/an _____ is the set of all actual and potential buyers of a product or service.

   a) segment
   b) target
   c) market
   d) industry

   Answer: (c)   Difficulty: 1 Page: 203

2. When Coca-Cola produced only one drink for the whole market, it was practicing which marketing strategy:

   a) mass marketing
   b) product-variety marketing
   c) target marketing
   d) demand marketing

   Answer: (a)   Difficulty: 1 Page: 203

3. Wal-Mart is adopting a strategy that aims for the lowest costs and prices and creates the largest potential market. This strategy would include:

   a) product variety marketing.
   b) target marketing.
   c) chain marketing.
   d) mass marketing.

   Answer: (d)   Difficulty: 2 Page: 203

4. Based on the argument that consumers have different tastes that change over time and that they seek variety and change, sellers should adopt which of the following strategies:

   a) product variety marketing.
   b) target marketing.
   c) chain marketing.
   d) mass marketing.

   Answer: (a)   Difficulty: 2 Page: 203

5. In _____ marketing, the seller identifies market segments, selects one or more of those segments, and develops products and marketing mixes tailored to each.

   a) product variety marketing.
   b) target marketing.
   c) chain marketing.
   d) mass marketing.

   Answer: (b)   Difficulty: 2 Page: 203

6. Which of the following is not a reason why companies are moving toward target marketing?

   a) Target marketing can better help sellers find their marketing opportunities.
   b) Sellers can develop the right product for each target market and adjust their prices, distribution channels, and advertising to reach the target market efficiently.
   c) Sellers can focus on the buyers who have the greater purchase interest.
   d) Sellers can focus their marketing efforts on the shotgun approach.

   Answer: (d)   Difficulty: 3 Page: 204

7. With the increasing fragmentation of the American mass markets into hundreds of smaller markets with different needs and lifestyles, marketing has taken on a new form called:

   a) segmentation marketing.
   b) micromarketing.
   c) macromarketing.
   d) market mixing.

   Answer: (b)   Difficulty: 2 Page: 204

8. Dividing a market into distinct groups of buyers with different needs, characteristics, or behavior who might require separate products or marketing mixes is called:

   a) market targeting.
   b) market segmentation.
   c) market positioning.
   d) market mixing.

   Answer: (b)   Difficulty: 1 Page: 204

9. The Coca-Cola Company is attempting to identify consumer groups that might require different products or marketing mixes. Coca-Cola is applying the concept of:

   a) market targeting.
   b) market positioning.
   c) market probing.
   d) market segmentation.

   Answer: (d)   Difficulty: 3 Page: 204

10. The process of evaluating each market segment's attractiveness and selecting one or more segments to enter is called:

    a) market targeting.
    b) market segmentation.
    c) market positioning.
    d) market mixing.

    Answer: (a)   Difficulty: 1 Page: 204

11. The Bluesky Corporation is engaged in determining which of several possible market segments to enter; the firm is involved in:

    a) mass marketing.
    b) market segmentation.
    c) market positioning.
    d) market targeting.

    Answer: (d)   Difficulty: 3 Page: 204

12. Setting the competitive positioning for the product and creating a detailed marketing mix is called:

    a) mass marketing.
    b) market segmentation.
    c) market positioning.
    d) market targeting.

    Answer: (c)   Difficulty: 3 Page: 204

13. The Beta Corporation is preparing the strategy it will use in marketing its product against the competition it will face in its selected market segments. The firm is engaged in:

    a) target marketing.
    b) market segmentation.
    c) market positioning.
    d) market promotion.

    Answer: (c)   Difficulty: 3 Page: 204

14. Which, if any, of the following is not a major market segmentation variable?

    a) Geographic segmentation
    b) Demographic segmentation
    c) Psychographic segmentation
    d) All of the above are major segmentation variables.

    Answer: (d)   Difficulty: 1 Page: 205

15. Dividing a market into different units based upon such criteria as nations, regions, states, counties, cities, or neighborhoods is called:

    a) geographic segmentation.
    b) demographic segmentation.
    c) psychographic segmentation.
    d) behavioral segmentation.

    Answer: (a)   Difficulty: 1 Page: 205

16. The trend toward regionalizing marketing programs by localizing their products, advertising, promotion, and sales efforts to fit the needs of individual regions is an example of:

    a) geographic segmentation.
    b) demographic segmentation.
    c) psychographic segmentation.
    d) behavioral segmentation.

    Answer: (a)   Difficulty: 1 Page: 205

17. When Campbell Soup sells Cajun gumbo soup in Louisiana and Mississippi, and makes its nacho cheese soup spicier in Texas and California, this is an example of:

    a) geographic segmentation.
    b) demographic segmentation.
    c) psychographic segmentation.
    d) behavioral segmentation.

    Answer: (a)   Difficulty: 1 Page: 205

18. Dividing the market into groups based upon such variables as age, gender, income and occupation is called:

    a) geographic segmentation.
    b) demographic segmentation.
    c) psychographic segmentation.
    d) behavioral segmentation.

    Answer: (b)   Difficulty: 1 Page: 209

19. When Toyota markets automobiles to women who "aren't only working hard, but playing hard," this is an example of:

    a) gender segmentation.
    b) age and life-cycle segmentation.
    c) income segmentation.
    d) psychographic segmentation.

    Answer: (a)   Difficulty: 1 Page: 210

20. When American Express markets gold cards, corporate cards and platinum cards aimed at different customer groups, this is an example of:

    a) gender segmentation.
    b) age and life-cycle segmentation.
    c) income segmentation.
    d) psychographic segmentation.

    Answer: (c)   Difficulty: 1 Page: 211

21. All of the following are common demographic segmentation variables except:

    a) lifestyle segmentation.
    b) family life-cycle segmentation.
    c) occupation segmentation.
    d) income segmentation.

    Answer: (a)   Difficulty: 2 Page: 209

22. Dividing buyers into different groups based on social class, lifestyle, or personality characteristics is called:

    a) geographic segmentation.
    b) demographic segmentation.
    c) psychographic segmentation.
    d) behavioral segmentation.

    Answer: (c)   Difficulty: 1 Page: 211

23. According to your text, successful market segmentation strategies based on _____, have been used for products such as cosmetics, cigarettes, insurance, and liquor.

    a) personality
    b) lifestyle
    c) occasions
    d) benefit

    Answer: (a)   Difficulty: 3 Page: 210

24. Pork producers are positioning pork as a "healthy" alternative to beef. The industry is attempting to take advantage of recent changes in the American:

    a) lifestyle.
    b) life cycle.
    c) personality.
    d) social class.

    Answer: (a)   Difficulty: 3 Page: 211

25. Dividing buyers into groups based upon their knowledge, attitudes, uses, or responses to a product is called:

    a) geographic segmentation.
    b) demographic segmentation.
    c) psychographic segmentation.
    d) behavioral segmentation.

    Answer: (d)   Difficulty: 1 Page: 212

26. Kodak has developed special versions of its single-use camera for just about any picture-taking occasion, is an example of which type of segmentation?

    a) Benefit
    b) Occasions
    c) Psychographic
    d) Personality

    Answer: (b)   Difficulty: 2 Page: 213

27. Dividing a market into groups according to the different advantages that consumers seek from the product is called:

    a) psychographic segmentation
    b) lifestyle segmentation
    c) benefit segmentation
    d) life-cycle segmentation

    Answer: (c)   Difficulty: 2 Page: 214

28. Segmentation based upon groups of nonusers, ex-users, potential users, first-time users, and regular users of a product is called segmentation based on:

    a) occasions.
    b) user status.
    c) usage rate.
    d) loyalty status.

    Answer: (b)   Difficulty: 2 Page: 214

29. Segmenting markets who have similar needs and buying behavior even though they are located in different countries is called:

    a) intramarket segmentation.
    b) intermarket segmentation.
    c) geographic segmentation.
    d) psychographic segmentation.

    Answer: (b)   Difficulty: 2 Page: 218

30. Which of the following is among the characteristics of effective market segments?

    a) measurability.
    b) accessibility.
    c) substantiality.
    d) All of the above.

    Answer: (d)   Difficulty: 1 Page: 219

31. The size, purchasing power, and profiles of a market segment are all part of which of the following characteristics?

    a) measurability.
    b) accessibility.
    c) substantiality.
    d) actionability.

    Answer: (a)   Difficulty: 1   Page: 219

32. The ability to effectively reach and serve a given market segment defines the characteristic of:

    a) measurability.
    b) accessibility.
    c) substantiality.
    d) actionability.

    Answer: (b)   Difficulty: 1   Page: 219

33. Whether or not the market segment is large or profitable enough to serve is part of the characteristics of:

    a) measurability.
    b) accessibility.
    c) substantiality.
    d) actionability.

    Answer: (c)   Difficulty: 1   Page: 219

34. Designing effective programs for attracting and serving market segments is part of the characteristic of:

    a) measurability.
    b) accessibility.
    c) substantiality.
    d) actionability.

    Answer: (d)   Difficulty: 1   Page: 220

35. In market targeting, a firm evaluates all of the following factors except:

    a) segment size and growth.
    b) segment structural attractiveness.
    c) company objectives and resources.
    d) All of the above are factors to consider.

    Answer: (d)   Difficulty: 2   Page: 220

36. In market targeting, collecting and analyzing data on current segment sales, growth rates, and expected profitability is part of:

    a) segment size and growth.
    b) segment structural attractiveness.
    c) company objectives and resources.
    d) All of the above.

    Answer: (a)   Difficulty: 2 Page: 220

37. In market targeting, the existence of many actual or potential substitute products that may limit prices and the profits that can be earned is part of:

    a) segment size and growth.
    b) segment structural attractiveness.
    c) company objectives and resources.
    d) All of the above are factors to consider.

    Answer: (b)   Difficulty: 2 Page: 220

38. A market-coverage strategy in which a firm decides to ignore market segment differences and go after the whole market with one offer is called:

    a) undifferentiated marketing.
    b) differentiated marketing.
    c) concentrated marketing.
    d) superior marketing.

    Answer: (a)   Difficulty: 2 Page: 222

39. When a firm maintains a narrow product line in order to keep down product, inventory, and transportation costs to the absolute minimum, they are likely to practice:

    a) undifferentiated marketing.
    b) differentiated marketing.
    c) concentrated marketing.
    d) superior marketing.

    Answer: (b)   Difficulty: 2 Page: 224

40. When a firm decides to target several market segments and design separate offers for each, this is called:

    a) undifferentiated marketing.
    b) differentiated marketing.
    c) concentrated marketing.
    d) superior marketing.

    Answer: (b)   Difficulty: 2 Page: 224

41. The Simms Corporation desires to generate the greatest possible total sales volume. The firm is most likely to use:

    a) undifferentiated marketing.
    b) differentiated marketing.
    c) concentrated marketing.
    d) superior marketing.

    Answer: (b)   Difficulty: 2 Page: 224

42. The practice of a firm going after a large share of one of a few submarkets is called:

    a) undifferentiated marketing.
    b) differentiated marketing.
    c) concentrated marketing.
    d) superior marketing.

    Answer: (c)   Difficulty: 2 Page: 224

43. _____ provides an excellent way for small new businesses to get a foothold in the climb against larger, more resourceful competitors.

    a) Undifferentiated marketing.
    b) Differentiated marketing.
    c) Concentrated marketing.
    d) Superior marketing.

    Answer: (c)   Difficulty: 2 Page: 225

44. Which of the following marketing approaches typically carries the greatest risk?

    a) Undifferentiated marketing.
    b) Differentiated marketing.
    c) Concentrated marketing.
    d) Superior marketing.

    Answer: (c)   Difficulty: 2 Page: 225

45. Which, if any, of the following is not a factor to consider when choosing a market-coverage strategy?

    a) Company resources
    b) Product and market variability
    c) Product's stage in the life cycle
    d) All of the above are factors to consider.

    Answer: (d)   Difficulty: 2 Page: 225

46. The way a product is defined by consumers on important attributes is called:

    a) position.
    b) segment.
    c) target.
    d) strategy.

    Answer: (a)   Difficulty: 1 Page: 225

47. The BMW Corporation has launched a series of ads in which it highlights the differences between its product and competitors' products. BMW is attempting to _____ its product.

    a) position.
    b) segment.
    c) target.
    d) strategy.

    Answer: (a)   Difficulty: 1   Page: 226

48. Citibank VISA uses ads to compare itself directly with American Express. Citibank is:

    a) using an illegal advertising technique.
    b) positioning its product away from competitors.
    c) positioning its product against its competitors.
    d) positioning its product as similar to its competition.

    Answer: (c)   Difficulty: 3   Page: 228

49. When choosing and implementing a positioning strategy, firms should:

    a) Identify possible competitive advantages
    b) Select the right competitive advantages
    c) Communicate and deliver the chosen position
    d) All of the above.

    Answer: (d)   Difficulty: 2   Page: 232

50. The strategy of choosing one attribute to excel at to create competitive advantage is known as (a):

    a) unique selling proposition.
    b) underpositioning.
    c) overpositioning.
    d) confused positioning.

    Answer: (a)   Difficulty: 2   Page: 233

TRUE/FALSE

51. Theoretically, mass marketing should lead to the lowest costs and prices and create the largest potential market.

    Answer: True   Difficulty: 2   Page: 203

52. Currently, there is a trend away from target and toward product-variety marketing.

    Answer: False   Difficulty: 2   Page: 203

53. By segmenting the market, a firm can avoid the need for developing a variety of products and/or marketing mixes.

    Answer: False   Difficulty: 2   Page: 204

54. Micromarketing is a form of target marketing in which companies tailor their marketing programs to the needs and wants of narrowly defined segments.

    Answer: True   Difficulty: 2 Page: 204

55. Market segmentation is dividing a market into distinct groups of buyers with different needs, characteristics, or behavior wo might require separate products or marketing mixes.

    Answer: True   Difficulty: 2 Page: 204

56. Market targeting evaluates each market segment's attractiveness and selects one or more of the market segments to enter.

    Answer: True   Difficulty: 2 Page: 204

57. Market positioning is the setting of the competitive position for the product and creating a detailed marketing mix.

    Answer: True   Difficulty: 2 Page: 204

58. Most marketers agree that there is typically a single way to segment a market.

    Answer: False   Difficulty: 1 Page: 205

59. Dividing a market into different geographical units such as nations, states, regions, countries, cities, or neighborhoods is called psychographic segmentation.

    Answer: False   Difficulty: 2 Page: 205

60. Geographic segmentation is not feasible for products that are used in all parts of the country.

    Answer: False   Difficulty: 2 Page: 205

61. Dividing the market into groups based on demographic variables such as age, gender, life-cycle stage and income is called demographic segmentation.

    Answer: True   Difficulty: 2 Page: 209

62. Consumer needs and wants rarely change with age.

    Answer: False   Difficulty: 1 Page: 209

63. Dividing a market into different age and life-cycle groups is called age and life-cycle segmentation.

    Answer: True   Difficulty: 1 Page: 209

64. Age is often a good predictor of a person's life cycle, health, work or family status, needs, and buying power.

    Answer: False   Difficulty: 2 Page: 210

65. Age is often a poor predictor of a person's life cycle, health, needs and buying power.

    Answer: True   Difficulty: 2 Page: 210

66. Life-cycle segmentation has long been used in clothing, cosmetics, and magazines.

    Answer: False   Difficulty: 1 Page: 210

67. Dividing a market into different groups based on sex is called gender segmentation.

    Answer: True   Difficulty: 1 Page: 210

68. Most marketers refuse to use gender as a segmentation variable for fear of an adverse public reaction.

    Answer: False   Difficulty: 2 Page: 210

69. Automobiles, boats, clothing, cosmetics, financial services, and travel have used income segmentation exclusively.

    Answer: False   Difficulty: 1 Page: 211

70. Income segmentation is effective only for companies targeting affluent customers.

    Answer: False   Difficulty: 2 Page: 211

71. Psychographic segmentation divides buyers into groups based on social class, lifestyle, or personality characteristics.

    Answer: True   Difficulty: 1 Page: 211

72. People in the same demographic group can have very different psychographic makeups.

    Answer: True   Difficulty: 1 Page: 211

73. Demographic factors are the most popular bases for segmenting consumer groups.

    Answer: True   Difficulty: 1 Page: 211

74. Marketers often use personality variables to segment markets, giving products personalities that correspond to consumer personalities.

    Answer: True   Difficulty: 2 Page: 212

75. Behavioral segmentation divides buyers into groups based on their knowledge, attitudes, uses, or responses to a product.

    Answer: True   Difficulty: 1 Page: 212

76. Many marketers believe that life-cycle variables are the best starting point for building market segments.

    Answer: False   Difficulty: 1 Page: 212

77. Occasion segmentation can help firms build up product usage.

    Answer: True   Difficulty: 1 Page: 213

78. Linking product purchases to events such as Mother's Day is consistent with occasion segmentation.

    Answer: True   Difficulty: 1 Page: 213

79. A powerful form of segmentation is to group buyers according to the different product attributes that they seek.

    Answer: False   Difficulty: 2 Page: 213

80. Market share leaders focus on attracting potential users, whereas smaller firms focus on attracting users away from the market leader.

    Answer: True   Difficulty: 2 Page: 214

81. Segmenting the market into groups such as nonusers, potential users, and regular users are examples of segmentation by usage rate.

    Answer: False   Difficulty: 2 Page: 214

82. Market segmentation by light, heavy, and medium users groups is an example of segmentation by user status.

    Answer: False   Difficulty: 2 Page: 214

83. Demographic segmentation is used in consumer market segmentation but not in business market segmentation.

    Answer: False   Difficulty: 2 Page: 216

84. Forming segments of consumers who have similar needs and buying behavior even though they are located in different countries is called international segmentation.

    Answer: False   Difficulty: 2 Page: 218

85. The best way to segment international markets is to be based on geographic, economic, political, cultural, and other factors.

    Answer: False   Difficulty: 2 Page: 218

86. The size, purchasing power, and profiles of the segments are all aspects of effective segmentation relating to measurability.

    Answer: True   Difficulty: 1 Page: 219

87. A market must be effectively reached and served to be considered accessible.

    Answer: True   Difficulty: 1 Page: 219

88. Substantiality means that the market segments are large or profitable enough to serve.

    Answer: True   Difficulty: 1 Page: 219

89. The ability to design effective programs for attracting and serving a market segment refers to its actionability.

    Answer: True   Difficulty: 1 Page: 220

90. Even though buyers have unique needs and wants, each buyer usually will fit into an undifferentiated market segment.

    Answer: False   Difficulty: 1 Page: 221

91. Targeting several market segments and designing separate offers for each is using a differentiated marketing strategy.

    Answer: True   Difficulty: 1 Page: 224

92. Differentiated marketing strategy typically creates more total sales than does undifferentiated marketing strategy.

    Answer: True   Difficulty: 2 Page: 224

93. Concentrated marketing allows a firm to develop a strong position in the segment it serves, but may also increase the risk faced by the seller.

    Answer: True   Difficulty: 2 Page: 224

94. A product's position is the way that the product is defined by the company relative to its competition on relevant attributes.

    Answer: False   Difficulty: 2 Page: 225

ESSAY

95. Define market segmentation, market targeting, and market positioning.

    Answer:
    Market segmentation is dividing a market into distinct groups of buyers with different needs, characteristics, or behaviors who might require separate products or marketing mixes. Market targeting is involving each segment's attractiveness and deciding which segments to enter. Market positioning is the setting of the competitive position and creating a detailed marketing mix.

    Difficulty: 3 Page: 204

96. Identify and discuss the steps in market segmentation, targeting, and positioning.

    Answer:
    (1) Identify bases for segmenting the market. (2) Develop profiles of resulting segments. (3) Develop measures of segment attractiveness. (4) Select the target segment(s). (5) Develop positioning for each target segment. (6) Develop marketing mix for each target segment.

    Difficulty: 3 Page: 204

97. List and discuss the major bases for segmenting consumer and business markets.

   Answer:
   The major basis for segmenting consumer markets are geographic, demographic, psychographic and behavioral variables. The major basis for segmenting business markets are demographics, operating characteristics, purchasing approaches, situational factors, and personal characteristics.

   Difficulty: 3   Page: 205

98. Identify and discuss the basic requirements for effective segmentation.

   Answer:
   Measurability: the size, purchasing power, and profiles of the segments. Accessibility: the market segments can be effectively reached and served. Substantiality: the market segments are large or profitable enough to serve. Actionability: effective programs can be designed for attracting and serving the segments.

   Difficulty: 3   Page: 219

99. After evaluating different segments, the company must decide which and how many segments to serve. Discuss the different market-coverage strategies that a firm can adopt.

   Answer:
   (1) Undifferentiated marketing: a market-coverage strategy in which a firm decides to ignore market segment differences and go after the whole market with one offer. (2) Differentiated marketing: a market-coverage strategy in which a firm decides to target several market segments and designs separate offers for each. (3) Concentrated marketing: a market coverage strategy in which a firm goes after a large share of one or a few submarkets.

   Difficulty: 3   Page: 222-224

100. Explain how companies can position their products for maximum competitive advantage in the marketplace.

   Answer:
   First, the company identifies its competitive advantage. A company or market offer can be differentiated along the lines of product services, personnel or image. After the company has identified its potential competitive advantages, it must choose the ones upon which it will build its positioning strategy. And finally, it must take strong steps to deliver and communicate the desired position to target customers.

   Difficulty: 3   Page: 229

Chapter 8

1. Anything that can be offered to a market for attention, acquisition, use, or consumption and that might satisfy a want or need is called a(n):

   a) attribute.
   b) idea.
   c) product.
   d) service.

   Answer: (c)   Difficulty: 1 Page: 241

2. The most basic level of a product is called the:

   a) core product.
   b) actual product.
   c) basic product.
   d) fundamental product.

   Answer: (a) Difficulty: 1 Page: 241

3. The problem-solving benefits that consumers seek when they buy a product or service is called the:

   a) actual product.
   b) augmented product.
   c) core product.
   d) tangible product.

   Answer: (c) Difficulty: 1 Page: 241

4. Quality level, features, design, brand name, and packaging are all part of the:

   a) actual product.
   b) augmented product.
   c) core product.
   d) tangible product.

   Answer: (a) Difficulty: 1 Page: 242

5. The additional consumer services and benefits built around the actual product is called the:

   a) actual product.
   b) augmented product.
   c) core product.
   d) tangible product.

   Answer: (b)   Difficulty: 1 Page: 242

6. _____ are those bought by final consumers for personal consumption.

   a) Consumer products
   b) Services
   c) Shopping goods
   d) Convenience goods

   Answer: (a)   Difficulty: 1 Page: 243

7. Products that the consumer purchases frequently, immediately, and with a minimum of comparison and buying effort are called:

   a) convenience products.
   b) shopping products.
   c) specialty products.
   d) consumer products.

   Answer: (a)   Difficulty: 1 Page: 244

8. Products that the consumer purchases less frequently and usually compares on suitability, quality, price and style are called:

   a) convenience products.
   b) shopping products.
   c) specialty products.
   d) consumer products.

   Answer: (b)   Difficulty: 1 Page: 244

9. Consumers spend much time and effort in gathering information and making comparisons when buying:

   a) convenience products.
   b) shopping products.
   c) specialty products.
   d) unsought products.

   Answer: (b)   Difficulty: 2 Page: 244

10. Products with unique characteristics or brand identification for which a significant group of buyers is willing to make a special purchase effort are called:

    a) convenience products.
    b) shopping products.
    c) specialty products.
    d) consumer products.

    Answer: (c)   Difficulty: 1 Page: 244

11. Products that the consumer does not know about or does not normally think about buying are called:

    a) convenience products.
    b) shopping products.
    c) specialty products.
    d) unsought products.

    Answer: (d)   Difficulty: 1   Page: 244

12. Products purchased by individuals and organizations for further processing or for use in conducting a business are called:

    a) consumer products.
    b) convenience products.
    c) business products.
    d) industrial products.

    Answer: (d)   Difficulty: 1   Page: 244

13. Ford Motor Company purchases thousands of tires for use in producing its automobiles. The tires that Ford buys would be best classified as:

    a) raw materials
    b) component materials
    c) component parts.
    d) supplies.

    Answer: (c)   Difficulty: 3   Page: 244

14. Industrial products that aid in the buyer's production or operations are called:

    a) materials and parts.
    b) capital items.
    c) supplies.
    d) services.

    Answer: (b)   Difficulty: 2   Page: 244

15. Industrial goods that usually are purchased with a minimum of effort or comparison are called:

    a) materials and parts.
    b) capital items.
    c) supplies.
    d) services.

    Answer: (c)   Difficulty: 2   Page: 245

16. Decisions about product quality, features, design relate to which of the following?

    a) Product attributes
    b) Branding
    c) Packaging
    d) Labeling

    Answer: (a)   Difficulty: 1 Page: 246

17. The ability of a product to perform its functions in terms of durability, reliability, precision, ease of operation and repair, and other valued attributes is called its:

    a) core product.
    b) actual product.
    c) augmented product.
    d) product quality.

    Answer: (d)   Difficulty: 2 Page: 246

18. An effort to constantly improve product and process quality in every phase of the operation is called:

    a) Total Quality Management (TQM)
    b) Return on Quality (ROQ)
    c) Customer-defined quality (CDQ)
    d) Total customer satisfaction (TQS)

    Answer: (a)   Difficulty: 2 Page: 246

19. A name, term, sign, symbol, or design, or a combination of these that identifies the maker or seller of a product is called a:

    a) brand.
    b) product feature.
    c) package.
    d) trademark.

    Answer: (a)   Difficulty: 1 Page: 249

20. All of the following are advantages that branding offers the seller except:

    a) Branding makes it easier for the seller to process orders.
    b) Branding makes it easier for the seller to track down problems
    c) Branding provides legal protection.
    d) All of the above are advantages.

    Answer: (d)   Difficulty: 3 Page: 250

21. The value of a brand, based on the extent to which it has high brand loyalty, name awareness, perceived quality, strong brand associations, and other assets such as patents, trademarks, and channel relationships is called:

    a) brand endurance.
    b) brand equity.
    c) brand loyalty.
    d) brand consistency

    Answer: (b)   Difficulty: 2 Page: 250

22. All of the following are advantages that high brand equity provides a company except:

    a) Powerful brands have a high level of consumer brand awareness and loyalty.
    b) Companies have more leverage in bargaining with resellers.
    c) Companies are less likely to launch brand extensions.
    d) Powerful brands offer the company defense against fierce price competition.

    Answer: c   Difficulty: 2 Page: 250

23. Which of the following is not a desirable quality for a brand name?

    a) It should suggest something about the product's benefits and qualities.
    b) It should be easy to pronounce, recognize, and remember.
    c) The name should translate easily into foreign languages.
    d) All of the above are desirable qualities for a brand name.

    Answer: (d)   Difficulty: 2 Page: 252

24. A brand created and owned by the producer of a product or service is called:

    a) private brand.
    b) manufacturer's brand.
    c) store brand.
    d) licensed brand.

    Answer: (b)   Difficulty: 1 Page: 252

25. The term retailer brand, distributor brand, or store brand all refer to:

    a) the manufacturer's brand.
    b) the private brand.
    c) the licensed brand.
    d) the independent brand.

    Answer: (a)   Difficulty: 1 Page: 252

26. If Bubble-Right makes all the world's bubble gum but sells it through middlemen who market under individual store brand, Bubble-Right is utilizing which type of brand-sponsorship?

    a) Manufacturer's brand
    b) National brand
    c) Private brand
    d) Licensed brand

    Answer: c   Difficulty: 3   Page: 253

27. Payments demanded by retailers from producers before they will accept new product for their store shelves is called:

    a) slotting fees
    b) manufacturer's fees
    c) shelving fees
    d) stocking fees

    Answer: (a)   Difficulty: 1   Page: 253

28. Decisions about line extensions fall under which category of major brand decisions?

    a) Brand sponsorship
    b) Brand strategy
    c) Brand repositioning
    d) Co-branding

    Answer: (b)   Difficulty: 1   Page: 255

29. When a company introduces additional items in a given product category under the same brand name, it is following which brand strategy?

    a) Line extensions.
    b) Brand extensions
    c) Multibrands
    d) New brands

    Answer: (a)   Difficulty: 1   Page: 255

30. When a company uses a successful brand name to launch a new or modified product in a new category, it is following which brand strategy?

    a) Line extensions.
    b) Brand extensions
    c) Multibrands
    d) New brands

    Answer: (b)   Difficulty: 1   Page: 256

31. The practice of Honda to use its company name to cover such different products as its automobiles, motorcycles, lawn mowers, and snowmobiles, it is following which brand strategy?

    a) Line extensions.
    b) Brand extensions
    c) Multibrands
    d) New brands

    Answer: (b)   Difficulty: 1   Page: 256

32. A strategy under which a seller develops two or more brands in the same product category is called:

    a) line extensions.
    b) brand extensions
    c) multibrands
    d) new brands

    Answer: (c)   Difficulty: 1   Page: 257

33. When a company enters a new product category for which its current brand names are not appropriate, it will likely follow which of the following brand strategies?

    a) New brands
    b) Brand extensions
    c) Line extensions
    d) Product extensions

    Answer: (a)   Difficulty: 2   Page: 258

34. The activities of designing and producing the container or wrapper for a product are referred to as:

    a) promoting.
    b) producing.
    c) packaging.
    d) placing.

    Answer: (c)   Difficulty: 1   Page: 258

35. The _____ states what the package should be or do for the product.

    a) marketing concept
    b) brand strategy
    c) branding concept
    d) packaging concept

    Answer: (d)   Difficulty: 2   Page: 259

36. At the very least, a label should:

    a) promote the product.
    b) grade the product.
    c) provide information about the product.
    d) identify the product.

    Answer: (d)   Difficulty: 2 Page: 259

37. Effective labeling can perform which of the following functions?

    a) Identify the product or brand.
    b) Grade the product.
    c) Promote the product through attractive graphics.
    d) All of the above.

    Answer: (d)   Difficulty: 2 Page: 259

38. Services that augment actual products are called:

    a) core product services.
    b) marketing-support services.
    c) branding-support services.
    d) product-support services.

    Answer: (d)   Difficulty: 1 Page: 260

39. A group of products that are closely related because they function in a similar manner is called:

    a) marketing line
    b) product line
    c) brand strategy
    d) similar product strategy

    Answer: (b)   Difficulty: 1 Page: 263

40. Product line _____ occurs when a company lengthens its product line beyond its current range.

    a) amalgamation
    b) concentration
    c) stretching
    d) specialization

    Answer: (c)   Difficulty: 2 Page: 263

41. The Maytag Company has been long noted for its line of high-quality, high-priced major appliances. The firm is preparing to offer a new line of medium-priced appliances this fall. This decision would be an example of product line:

a) amalgamation
b) concentration
c) stretching
d) specialization

Answer: (c)   Difficulty: 2 Page: 263

42. Companies which add "low-end" products to their existing line of "high-end" products may describe their move as a(n):

a) line filling decision
b) downward stretch.
c) two-way stretch
d) upward stretch

Answer: (b)   Difficulty: 2 Page: 263

43. A company may initiate a downward stretch of its product line for all of the following reasons except:

a) to establish a quality image.
b) to attract new customers.
c) to "plug" a market hole.
d) to respond to competitive attacks.

Answer: (a)   Difficulty: 2 Page: 263

44. A company may add more items within the present range of the line for all the following reasons except:

a) reaching for extra profits.
b) try to satisfy dealers.
c) to establish a "value" image.
d) plug holes to keep out competitors.

Answer: (c)   Difficulty: 2 Page: 265

45. The total number of items that the company carries is called its:

a) depth.
b) length.
c) width.
d) consistency.

Answer: (b)   Difficulty: 1 Page: 265

46. The number of versions offered of each product in the line is called its:

    a) depth.
    b) length.
    c) width.
    d) consistency.

    Answer: (a)   Difficulty: 1 Page: 265

47. How closely related the various product lines are in end use, production requirements, distribution channels, or in other ways is called:

    a) depth.
    b) length.
    c) width.
    d) consistency.

    Answer: (d)   Difficulty: 1 Page: 266

48. Any activity or benefit that one party can offer to another party that is essentially intangible and does not result in the ownership of anything is referred to as a(n):

    a) manufacturing.
    b) marketing.
    c) product.
    d) service.

    Answer: (d)   Difficulty: 1 Page: 267

49. The characteristic of a service in that it cannot be seen, tasted, felt, heard, or smelled before it is purchased is called:

    a) inseparability.
    b) intangibility.
    c) perishability.
    d) variability.

    Answer: (b)   Difficulty: 1 Page: 267

50. The fact that services are produced and consumed at the same time refers to which service characteristic?

    a) Inseparability.
    b) Intangibility.
    c) Perishability.
    d) Variability.

    Answer: (a)   Difficulty: 1 Page: 268

51. The nature of provider-client interaction is part of which characteristic of services?

    a) Inseparability.
    b) Intangibility.
    c) Perishability.
    d) Variability.

    Answer: (d)   Difficulty: 1 Page: 268

52. The fact that a service cannot be stored for later sale or use refers to which characteristic of a service?

    a) Inseparability.
    b) Intangibility.
    c) Perishability.
    d) Variability.

    Answer: (c)   Difficulty: 1 Page: 268

53. Providing employee incentives for quality service and checking customer satisfaction through suggestion boxes and complaint departments in an effort to standardize customer experiences are all steps that address which aspect of services?

    a) Inseparability.
    b) Intangibility.
    c) Perishability.
    d) Variability.

    Answer: (d)   Difficulty: 1 Page: 268

54. The fact that a business traveler may have one very positive check-in experience at a hotel and then a very negative check-in experience with a different employee on a subsequent visit is evidence of service:

    a) inseparability.
    b) intangibility.
    c) perishability.
    d) variability.

    Answer: (c)   Difficulty: 1 Page: 268

55. The fact that hotels and resorts charge lower prices in the off-season to attract more guests is an example of which characteristic of services?

    a) Inseparability.
    b) Intangibility.
    c) Perishability.
    d) Variability.

    Answer: (a)   Difficulty: 1 Page: 268

56. Marketing of a service firm that recognizes that perceived service depends heavily on the quality of buyer-seller interaction is called:

    a) external marketing.
    b) internal marketing.
    c) interactive marketing.
    d) service marketing.

    Answer: (c)   Difficulty: 1   Page: 272

57. The activities undertaken to create, maintain, or change the attitudes and behavior of target customers toward a firm, group or company are called:

    a) place marketing.
    b) person marketing.
    c) organization marketing.
    d) idea marketing.

    Answer: (c)   Difficulty: 1   Page: 275

58. When politicians market themselves to get votes for their programs, they are engaging in:

    a) place marketing.
    b) person marketing.
    c) organization marketing.
    d) idea marketing.

    Answer: (b)   Difficulty: 1   Page: 275

59. _____ involves activities undertaken to create, maintain, or change attitudes or behavior toward particular places.

    a) Place marketing.
    b) Person marketing.
    c) Organization marketing.
    d) Idea marketing.

    Answer: (a)   Difficulty: 1   Page: 275

60. The design, implementation, and control of programs seeking to increase the acceptability of a social idea, cause, or practice among a target group is called:

    a) target marketing.
    b) cause marketing.
    c) social marketing.
    d) program marketing.

    Answer: (c) Difficulty: 1   Page: 277

TRUE/FALSE

61. A product is anything that can be offered to a market for attention, acquisition, use, or consumption and that might satisfy a want or need.

    Answer: True   Difficulty: 1   Page: 241

62. Products, when broadly defined, includes physical objects, services, person's place, organization, ideas, or mixes of these entities.

    Answer: True   Difficulty: 1   Page: 241

63. The problem-solving benefits that the consumer seeks when they purchase a product or service is called the actual product.

    Answer: False   Difficulty: 1   Page: 241

64. The actual product can have as many as five characteristics including quality level, features, design, brand name, and packaging.

    Answer: True   Difficulty: 1   Page: 242

65. The additional consumer services and benefits that support the actual and core product make up the augmented product.

    Answer: True   Difficulty: 1   Page: 242

66. Consumer products are those bought by final consumers for personal consumption.

    Answer: True   Difficulty: 1   Page: 243

67. Convenience products are consumer and industrial goods that are purchased frequently, immediately, and with a minimum of comparison and buying effort.

    Answer: False   Difficulty: 1   Page: 244

68. Shopping products are less frequently purchased consumer products that customers compare carefully on suitability, quality, price and style.

    Answer: True   Difficulty: 1   Page: 244

69. When buying specialty products, consumers spend much time and effort in gathering information and making comparisons.

    Answer: False   Difficulty: 1   Page: 244

70. Shopping products are consumer products and services that the customer usually buys frequently, immediately; and with a minimum of comparison and buying effort.

    Answer: False   Difficulty: 1   Page: 244

71. Most major innovations are unsought until the consumer becomes aware of them through advertising.

    Answer: True   Difficulty: 1   Page: 244

72. Industrial products are those purchased for further processing or for use in conducting a business.

    Answer: True   Difficulty: 1   Page: 244

73. The distinction between a consumer product and an industrial product is based on the purpose for which the product is bought.

    Answer: True   Difficulty: 2 Page: 244

74. Honda supplies engines for a wide variety of lawn mower manufacturers. The engines purchased by these producers would be best classified as a component part.

    Answer: True   Difficulty: 3 Page: 244

75. Supplies and services are capital items that do not enter the finished product at all.

    Answer: False   Difficulty: 2 Page: 245

76. Capital items are industrial products that aid in the buyer's production or operations, including installations and accessory equipment.

    Answer: True   Difficulty: 2 Page: 244

77. Product quality means that a product will perform its functions.

    Answer: True   Difficulty: 1 Page: 246

78. Product quality has two dimensions: quality level and quality consistency.

    Answer: True   Difficulty: 1 Page: 246

79. Product features are a competitive tool for differentiating the company's product from competitors' products.

    Answer: True   Difficulty: 2 Page: 247

80. Product design is synonymous with product style.

    Answer: False   Difficulty: 1 Page: 247

81. It is the buyer's promise to expect that the seller will deliver consistently a specific set of features, benefits, and services to buyers.

    Answer: False   Difficulty: 2 Page: 249

82. A brand is a name, term, sign, symbol, or design that identifies the goods and services of one seller and helps differentiate them from those of the competition.

    Answer: True   Difficulty: 2 Page: 249

83. The value of a brand, based on the extent to which it has high brand loyalty, name awareness, perceived quality, strong brand associations, and other assets such as patents, trademarks and channel relationships is called brand equity.

    Answer: True   Difficulty: 2 Page: 250

84. Manufacturers brands are typically priced lower than retailer brands, thereby appealing to budget-conscious shoppers.

    Answer: False   Difficulty: 2 Page: 253

85. General Mills and Hershey Foods combined brands to create Reese's Peanut Butter Puffs cereal. This is an example of a licensed brand.

    Answer: False   Difficulty: 2 Page: 252

86. Line extensions occur when a company introduces additonal items in a given product category under the same brand name.

    Answer: True   Difficulty: 1 Page: 255

87. Offering several brands within a product category to suggest different functions or benefits is called a multibrand strategy.

    Answer: True   Difficulty: 1 Page: 257

88. A major drawback of multibranding is that each brand might obtain only a small market share, and none may be very profitable.

    Answer: True   Difficulty: 2 Page: 257

89. Product line breadth is used to describe the total number of versions offered of each product in the line.

    Answer: False   Difficulty: 1 Page: 266

90. Any activity or benefit that one part can offer to another that is essentially intangible and does not result in the ownership of anything is called a service.

    Answer: True   Difficulty: 1 Page: 267

91. Service variability means that the quality of service depends on who provides them, as well as when, where, and how they are provided.

    Answer: True   Difficulty: 1 Page: 268

92. Service perishability means that services cannot be separated from their providers, whether the providers are people or machines.

    Answer: False   Difficulty: 1 Page: 268

93. A key aspect of services is that they are easily standardized.

    Answer: False   Difficulty: 1 Page: 268

94. Internal marketing means that the service firm effectively trains and motivates its customer-contact personnel to work as a team.

    Answer: True   Difficulty: 1 Page: 272

ESSAY

95. Differentiate between the core product, the actual product, and the augmented product as these concepts apply to the automobile industry.

Answer:
The core product is the basic problem-solving services desired by the consumer. In this case, the core product is transportation. The actual product includes quality level, product features, design, brand name and packaging. In this example, the actual product would be the actual automobile. The augmented product are the additional consumer services and benefits that are built around the core and actual products. In this example, the repair services, product warranty on parts, etc., would be considered the augmented product.

Difficulty: 3 Page: 241-242

96. Explain why companies use brands. Identify desirable qualities for a brand name.

Answer:
Companies use brands as a means of differentiating their products from the competition. It is a name, term, sign, symbol, or design, or a combination of these that identifies the maker or seller of a product.
Among desirable qualities for a brand name: 1) It should suggest something about the product's benefits and qualities. 2) It should be easy to pronounce, recognize, and remember. 3) The brand name should be distinctive. 4) The name should translate into foreign languages. 5) It should be capable of registration and legal protection.

Difficulty: 3 Page: 252

97. Describe the difference between manufacturer's brand and private brand. How do manufacturers benefit from private branding?

Answer:
A manufacturer's brand is created and owned by the producer of a product while a private brand is created and owned by a reseller of a product. Manufacturers benefit from private branding because they can be very profitable. Private brands give middlemen exclusive products that cannot be bought from competitors, resulting in greater store traffic and loyalty.

Difficulty: 3 Page: 233

98. What relationship, if any, exists between product branding and product quality? Support your position.

Answer:
The relationship is complex. On the one side, branding tends to enhance PERCEIVED quality--in the absence of other information, consumers tend to use brand name and/or price as indicators of quality. Branding, then, may aid sales. Of course, quality is a subjective entity--only the consumer can determine if the quality provided by a particular brand is suitable to him or her. Branding cannot be reasonably used as an indicator of the highest possible quality, but it does generally serve as a "guarantee" of consistent quality at some level. Only the consumer can decide if that level is sufficient. The manufacturer must be prepared to maintain consistency of quality, and promote the brand aggressively, to gain the benefits of branding.

Difficulty: 3 Page: 253

99. Discuss why companies use co-branding. Identify the advantages and disadvantages of co-branding.

Answer:
Co-branding is the practice of using the established brand names of two different companies on the same product. In most co-branding situations, one company licenses another company's well-known brand to use in combination with its own. Co-branding advantages include: 1) broader consumer appeal and greater brand equity. 2) expand its existing brand into a new category that it might not have entered alone. Co-branding disadvantages include: 1) relationships are very complex. 2) partners must coordinate advertising, sales promotion , other marketing efforts. 3) trusting co-branding partner.

Difficulty: 3 Page: 255

100. Define services and describe four characteristics that affect the marketing of a service.

Answer:
A service is any activity or benefit that one party can offer to another that is essentially intangible and does not result in the ownership of anything. The four characteristics of services are intangibility, inseparability, variability, and perishability.

Difficulty: 2 Page: 267-268

Chapter 9

1. Original products, product improvements, product modifications, and new brand through its own research and development efforts are called:

   a) new product development
   b) private brand development
   c) co-brand product development
   d) brand extension

   Answer: (a)   Difficulty: 1 Page: 287

2. As the cost of developing and introducing major new products increase, many large companies obtain new products and services through:

   a) new product development
   b) acquisition
   c) brand expansion
   d) product line stretching

   Answer: (b)   Difficulty: 2 Page: 287

3. New products continue to fail at a disturbing rate. One study estimated that new consumer packaged goods fail at a rate of:

   a) 90%
   b) 65%
   c) 40%
   d) 80%

   Answer: (d)   Difficulty: 2 Page: 287

4. Reasons for new product failure include:

   a) that the market size was overestimated.
   b) that the product may have been incorrectly positioned.
   c) that a high-level executive might have pushed a favorite idea.
   d) All of the above.

   Answer: (d)   Difficulty: 2 Page: 287

5. In terms of new product development, the number one success factor is:

   a) a well-defined product concept.
   b) a unique superior product.
   c) products with a high product advantage.
   d) a systematic new-product development process.

   Answer: (b)   Difficulty: 2 Page: 287

6. The systematic search for new-product ideas is characteristic of which stage of the new product development process?

   a) Idea generation
   b) Idea Screening
   c) Concept development and testing
   d) Marketing strategy

   Answer: (a)   Difficulty: 1 Page: 288

7. Major sources of new product ideas include:

   a) internal sources.
   b) customer.
   c) competitors.
   d) All of the above.

   Answer: (d)   Difficulty: 1 Page: 288

8. Screening new product ideas in order to spot good ideas and drop poor ones as soon as possible is called:

   a) idea generation
   b) idea screening
   c) concept development and testing
   d) marketing strategy

   Answer: (b)   Difficulty: 1 Page: 292

9. The first idea-reducing stage in the new product development process is:

   a) marketing strategy.
   b) concept development and testing.
   c) idea screening.
   d) idea generation.

   Answer: (c)   Difficulty: 2 Page: 292

10. Spotting good ideas and dropping poor ones as soon as possible is the purpose of idea:

    a) generation.
    b) development.
    c) screening.
    d) testing.

    Answer: (c)   Difficulty: 1 Page: 292

11. A detailed version of the new product idea stated in meaningful consumer terms is called a:

    a) product idea.
    b) product concept.
    c) product image.
    d) product analysis.

    Answer: (b)   Difficulty: 1 Page: 292

12. The way consumers perceive an actual or potential product is called a:

    a) product idea.
    b) product concept.
    c) product image.
    d) product analysis.

    Answer: (c)   Difficulty: 1 Page: 292

13. The process of transforming a new product idea into alternative product concepts, finding out how attractive each concept is to target customers, and choosing the best one is called:

    a) concept development.
    b) concept image.
    c) concept testing.
    d) marketing strategy development.

    Answer: (a)   Difficulty: 1 Page: 292

14. Presenting new product concepts with consumers before attempting to turn them into actual new product is called:

    a) idea generation.
    b) concept development.
    c) concept testing.
    d) marketing strategy development.

    Answer: (c)   Difficulty: 2 Page: 293

15. Designing an initial marketing strategy for a new product based on the product concept is called:

    a) idea generation.
    b) concept development.
    c) concept testing.
    d) marketing strategy development.

    Answer: (d)   Difficulty: 2 Page: 294

16. Which of the following is not part of the marketing strategy statement?

    a) Business analysis.
    b) Describing the target market.
    c) Outline of product's planned price, distribution, and marketing budget.
    d) Planned long-run sales, profit goals, and marketing mix strategy.

    Answer: (a)   Difficulty: 2 Page: 296

17. The stage in the new product development process that describes the target market is called:

    a) idea generation.
    b) concept development and testing.
    c) marketing strategy development.
    d) business analysis.

    Answer: (c)   Difficulty: 2   Page: 294

18. The stage in the new product development process that outlines the product's planned price, distribution, and marketing budget for the first year is called:

    a) idea generation.
    b) concept development and testing.
    c) marketing strategy development.
    d) business analysis.

    Answer: (c)   Difficulty: 2   Page: 295

19. The stage in the new product development process that describes the planned long-run sales, profit goals, and marketing mix strategy is called:

    a) idea generation.
    b) concept development and testing.
    c) marketing strategy development.
    d) business analysis.

    Answer: (c)   Difficulty: 2   Page: 296

20. A review of the sales, costs, and profit projections for a new product to determine whether these factors satisfy the company's objectives is called:

    a) idea generation.
    b) concept development and testing.
    c) marketing strategy development.
    d) business analysis.

    Answer: (d)   Difficulty: 2   Page: 296

21. Douglas Peroff is currently involved in reviewing sales projections and cost estimates associated with several potential new products. Douglas' analysis would most accurately be described as:

    a) idea generation.
    b) concept development and testing.
    c) marketing strategy development.
    d) business analysis.

    Answer: (d)   Difficulty: 2   Page: 296

22. The R & D or engineering department develops the product concept into a physical product during which of the following stages?

    a) Business analysis.
    b) Marketing strategy development
    c) Product development
    d) Test marketing.

    Answer: (c)   Difficulty: 1 Page: 296

23. The stage in the new product development process that develops a prototype that will satisfy and excite consumers is called:

    a) idea generation.
    b) marketing strategy development.
    c) product development.
    d) test marketing.

    Answer: (c)   Difficulty: 2 Page: 297

24. The stage in the new product development where the product and marketing program are introduced into more realistic market settings is called:

    a) idea generation.
    b) marketing strategy development.
    c) product development.
    d) test marketing.

    Answer: (d)   Difficulty: 2 Page: 297

25. To test the new product under real market conditions is the basic reason for:

    a) idea generation.
    b) marketing strategy development.
    c) product development.
    d) test marketing.

    Answer: (d)   Difficulty: 2 Page: 297

26. Introducing the new product into the market takes place in which stage of the new product development process?

    a) Commercialization
    b) Test marketing
    c) Marketing strategy
    d) Product development

    Answer: (a)   Difficulty: 2 Page: 298

27. Firms which lack the necessary capital to support an immediate launch into full national distribution should generally:

    a) borrow the funds required for the national launch.
    b) develop a planned market roll out over time.
    c) delay introduction until they can afford to launch nationally.
    d) sell the marketing rights to the product to a competitor that can afford to distribute nationally.

    Answer: (b)   Difficulty: 2 Page: 298

28. An approach to developing new products in which various company departments work closely together, overlapping the steps in the product development process to save time and increase effectiveness is called:

    a) sequential product development.
    b) simultaneous product development.
    c) standard product development
    d) effective product development.

    Answer: (b)   Difficulty: 2 Page: 299

29. An approach to developing new products in which one company department works independently to complete its stage of the process before passing the new product along is called:

    a) sequential product development.
    b) simultaneous product development.
    c) standard product development
    d) effective product development.

    Answer: (a)   Difficulty: 2 Page: 299

30. IBM competes in the dynamic, highly competitive technology market. In order to get their new products to market more quickly, IBM is most likely in favor of the:

    a) progressive product development approach.
    b) sequential product development approach.
    c) simultaneous product development approach.
    d) standardized product development approach.

    Answer: (c)   Difficulty: 3 Page: 299

31. The sequential product development approach differs from the simultaneous product development approach in the:

    a) time needed to complete the process.
    b) cost of the process.
    c) average success ratio of new product introductions.
    d) managerial expertise required.

    Answer: (a)   Difficulty: 2 Page: 299

32. The course that a product's sales and profits take over the time it is in the market is called:

   a) the profit-sales life cycle.
   b) the product life cycle.
   c) the profit-growth cycle.
   d) the marketing S-shape cycle.

   Answer: (b)   Difficulty: 1 Page: 302

33. The stage in the product life cycle when profits are nonexistent due to heavy expenses is called:

   a) maturity.
   b) growth.
   c) product development
   d) introduction.

   Answer: (d)   Difficulty: 1 Page: 302

34. The stage in the product life cycle when sales growth is slow is called:

   a) maturity.
   b) growth.
   c) product development
   d) introduction.

   Answer: (d)   Difficulty: 1 Page: 302

35. A period of rapid market acceptance and increasing profits characterizes which stage in the product life cycle?

   a) maturity.
   b) growth.
   c) product development
   d) introduction.

   Answer: (b)   Difficulty: 1 Page: 302

36. The period of slowdown in sales growth because the product has achieved acceptance by most potential buyers characterizes which stage in the product life cycle?

   a) maturity.
   b) growth.
   c) product development
   d) decline.

   Answer: (a)   Difficulty: 1 Page: 302

37. Sales fall off and profits drop during which stage in the product life cycle?

    a) maturity.
    b) growth.
    c) product development
    d) decline

    Answer: (d)   Difficulty: 1 Page: 302

38. In terms of special product life cycles, a _____ is the currently accepted popular style in a given field.

    a) style
    b) fashion
    c) fad
    d) trend

    Answer: (b)   Difficulty: 1 Page: 303

39. In terms of special product life cycles, _____ enter the market quickly, are adopted with great zeal, peak early, and decline very fast.

    a) styles
    b) trends
    c) fads
    d) fashions

    Answer: (c)   Difficulty: 1 Page: 303

40. In terms of special product life cycles, a _____ would have the shortest life cycle.

    a) style
    b) fashion
    c) fad
    d) trend

    Answer: (c)   Difficulty: 1 Page: 303

41. In terms of the product life cycle, a new product is launched in which stage?

    a) Product development
    b) Introduction
    c) Growth
    d) Maturity

    Answer: (b)   Difficulty: 1 Page: 304

42. In terms of the product life cycle, profits are negative or low because of the low sales and high distribution and promotion expenses.

    a) Introduction
    b) Growth
    c) Maturity
    d) Decline

    Answer: (a)   Difficulty: 1 Page: 304

43. An increase in competition, attracted by the opportunities for profit, is typical of which stage of the product life cycle?

    a) Introduction
    b) Growth
    c) Maturity
    d) Decline

    Answer: (b)   Difficulty: 1 Page: 305

44. The stage in the product life cycle where the strategic focus is on building product conviction and purchase is:

    a) introduction
    b) growth
    c) maturity
    d) decline

    Answer: (b)   Difficulty: 1 Page: 304

45. The firm faces a trade-off between high market share and high current profit, is typical of which stage of the product life cycle?

    a) Introduction
    b) Growth
    c) Maturity
    d) Decline

    Answer: (b)   Difficulty: 1 Page: 305

46. The stage in the product life cycle that normally lasts longer than the previous stages, and it poses strong challenges to marketing management.

    a) Introduction
    b) Growth
    c) Maturity
    d) Decline

    Answer: (c)   Difficulty: 1 Page: 305

47. The stage in the product life cycle where the strategic focus is on defending market share and sustaining brand loyalty is:

    a) introduction
    b) growth
    c) maturity
    d) decline

    Answer: (c)   Difficulty: 1   Page: 305

48. The stage in the product life cycle characterized by intensive distribution and improved products at lower prices is:

    a) introduction
    b) growth
    c) maturity
    d) decline

    Answer: (c)   Difficulty: 1   Page: 305

49. Cutting prices, using aggressive sales promotions, or launching a better advertising campaign, are all typical elements of which stage used during the maturity stage of the product life cycle?

    a) Modify the market
    b) Modify the product
    c) Modify the marketing mix
    d) Modify the target market

    Answer: (c)   Difficulty: 2   Page: 305

50. During the decline stage of the product life cycle, management may decide to _____ the product, and hope that sales hold up.

    a) maintain
    b) harvest
    c) drop
    d) none of the above.

    Answer: (b)   Difficulty: 1   Page: 309

TRUE/FALSE

51. Many large companies acquire existing brands rather than create new ones.

    Answer: True   Difficulty: 1   Page: 287

52. New product products refer to product innovations that the firm develops through its own research and development efforts.

    Answer: False   Difficulty: 1   Page: 287

53. With the tremendous improvement that has taken place in marketing research techniques, the product failure rate for consumer products rarely exceeds ten percent.

   Answer: False   Difficulty: 2   Page: 287

54. New products fail because the product was incorrectly positioned in the market, priced too high, or advertised poorly.

   Answer: True   Difficulty: 2   Page: 287

55. The number one success factor for new products is a unique superior product, one with higher quality, new features and higher value in use.

   Answer: True   Difficulty: 2   Page: 287

56. Contrary to conventional wisdom, very few new product ideas come from customers.

   Answer: False   Difficulty: 2   Page: 289

57. In order to maintain its reputation for innovativeness a firm should never copy the features of competitive products.

   Answer: False   Difficulty: 2   Page: 290

58. While idea generation seeks to produce as many new product ideas as possible, the succeeding stages of the product development process is to reduce that number.

   Answer: True   Difficulty: 1   Page: 292

59. The purpose of idea screening is to spot good ideas and turn them into profitable products.

   Answer: False   Difficulty: 2   Page: 292

60. An idea for a possible product that the company can see itself offering to the market is called a product idea.

   Answer: True   Difficulty: 1   Page: 292

61. A product concept is a detailed version of the idea stated in meaningful consumer terms.

   Answer: True   Difficulty: 1   Page: 292

62. A product idea is the way that consumers perceive an actual or potential product.

   Answer: False   Difficulty: 1   Page: 292

63. Concept testing involves testing new product concepts with a group of target consumers.

   Answer: True   Difficulty: 1   Page: 293

64. Designing an initial marketing strategy for a new product based on the product concept is called the marketing strategy development.

    Answer: True   Difficulty: 1 Page: 294

65. Describing the target market; the planned product positioning; and the sales, market share and profit goals for the first few years are part of the business analysis stage of the new product development process.

    Answer: False   Difficulty: 2 Page: 294

66. The business analysis involves a review of the sales, costs, and profit projections for a new product to find out whether they satisfy the company's objectives.

    Answer: True   Difficulty: 2 Page: 296

67. Test marketing is the stage of the new product development process where the product and marketing program are tested in more realistic marketing settings.

    Answer: True   Difficulty: 2 Page: 297

68. Since test marketing gives the marketer experience with marketing the product before going to the great expense of full introduction, management must conduct test marketing on all new products.

    Answer: False   Difficulty: 2 Page: 297

69. The stage in the new product development process when the product is introduced in to market is called commercialization.

    Answer: True   Difficulty: 2 Page: 298

70. When one company department works individually to complete its stage of the process before passing it on to the next department, it is called simultaneous product development.

    Answer: False   Difficulty: 2 Page: 299

71. Simultaneous product development is an approach to developing new products in which various departments work closely together, overlapping the steps in the product development process to save time and increase effectiveness.

    Answer: True   Difficulty: 2 Page: 299

72. The course of a product's sales and profits over its lifetime is called the product life cycle.

    Answer: True   Difficulty: 1 Page: 302

73. All new products follow the S-shaped product life cycle.

    Answer: False   Difficulty: 2 Page: 302

74. In terms of the product life cycle during product development, sales are zero and the company's investment costs mount.

   Answer: True   Difficulty: 1   Page: 302

75. In terms of the product life cycle, profits are nonexistent in the introduction stage due to heavy expenses of product introduction.

   Answer: True   Difficulty: 1   Page: 302

76. In terms of the PLC, the introduction stage is a period of rapid market acceptance and increasing profits.

   Answer: False   Difficulty: 1   Page: 302

77. In terms of the PLC, the decline stage is a period when sales fall off and profits drop.

   Answer: True   Difficulty: 1   Page: 302

78. In terms of the PLC, during the maturity stage profits level off or decline because of increased marketing outlays to defend the product against competition.

   Answer: True   Difficulty: 1   Page: 302

79. A style is a basic and distinctive mode of expression.

   Answer: True   Difficulty: 1   Page: 302

80. A fashion is a currently accepted or popular style.

   Answer: True   Difficulty: 1   Page: 302

81. Fashions do not survive for long because they normally do not satisfy a strong need or satisfy it well.

   Answer: False   Difficulty: 1   Page: 303

82. Fads last only a short time and tend to attract only a limited following.

   Answer: True   Difficulty: 1   Page: 303

83. A fad is a fashion with a very short product life cycle.

   Answer: True   Difficulty: 1   Page: 303

84. A specific brand's life cycle can change quickly because of changing competitive attacks and responses.

   Answer: True   Difficulty: 2   Page: 303

85. Marketing strategy is both a cause and result of the product life cycle.

   Answer: True   Difficulty: 1   Page: 303

86. During the growth stage of the PLC, the firm typically improves product quality and adds new product features and models.

    Answer: True   Difficulty: 2   Page: 304

87. During the mature stage of the PLC, the firm faces a trade-off between high market share and high current profit.

    Answer: False   Difficulty: 2   Page: 305

88. During the growth stage of the PLC, product managers should do more than simply continue with or defend their products, a good offense is the best defense.

    Answer: True   Difficulty: 2   Page: 305

89. During the decline stage of the PLC, product managers should consider modifying the market, modifying the product or modifying the marketing mix.

    Answer: False   Difficulty: 2   Page: 305

90. Generally speaking, most marketing management decisions deal with products in the maturity stage of the PLC.

    Answer: True   Difficulty: 2   Page: 305

91. The maturity stage of the PLC, normally lasts longer and poses strong challenges to marketing management.

    Answer: True   Difficulty: 2   Page: 305

92. During the decline stage of the PLC, marketing managers should turn their efforts to defending their product's position.

    Answer: False   Difficulty: 2   Page: 309

93. When a product reaches the decline phase of its life cycle, it should be automatically harvested.

    Answer: False   Difficulty: 2   Page: 309

94. Harvesting a declining product refers to gradually reducing marketing support in order to increase short-run profits.

    Answer: True   Difficulty: 2   Page: 309

ESSAY

95. List and define the steps in new product development.

    Answer:
    Steps include idea generation, idea screening, concept development and testing, marketing strategy development, business analysis, product development, test marketing, and commercialization. At each level, the marketing manager must evaluate whether the company should continue with the development of the new product.

    Difficulty: 2   Page: 287-298

96. Explain how companies find and develop new product ideas.

Answer:
Major new sources of new product ideas include internal sources, customers, competitors, distributors and suppliers, and the general public or societal trends.
Difficulty: 2   Page: 288-292

97. Differentiate between sequential product development and simultaneous product development. Describe the advantages and disadvantages of these development approaches.

Answer:
Under the sequential product development approach, one company department works individually to complete its stage of the process before passing the new product along to the next department and stage; while under the simultaneous product development approach, various company departments work closely together, overlapping the steps in the product-development process to save time and increase effectiveness.
Difficulty: 3   Page: 299

98. Identify and describe the distinct stages of the product life cycle. Include a diagram in your response.

Answer:
The stages in the product life cycle include product development, introduction, growth, maturity, and decline.
Difficulty: 2   Page: 302

99. Explain how marketing strategy changes during a product's life cycle.

Answer:
During introduction, strategy focuses on awareness and acceptance of basic product. Growth attracts competitors and more product features. Maturity strategy focuses on modifying the product, market, or mix. Decline forces choices on maintaining, harvesting or dropping the product.

100. Should a firm automatically drop a product that appears to be in its decline stage? Justify your position.

Answer:
No, the drop decision should not be automatic. The firm probably has a lot invested in the production of the product--it should not be dropped unless no other alternative exists. Management may decide to maintain its brand without change in hopes that competitors will leave the industry. Management may decide to harvest the product, which means reducing various costs and hope that sales will hold up. Finally, management may decide to drop the product from the line.
Difficulty: 2   Page: 309

Chapter 10

1. Simply defined, _____ is the amount of money charged for a product or service.

   a) product.
   b) place.
   c) price.
   d) promotion.

   Answer: (c)   Difficulty: 1 Page: 316

2. The sum of the values consumers exchange for the benefits of having or using the product or service defines its:

   a) cost.
   b) price.
   c) satisfaction.
   d) worth.

   Answer: (b)   Difficulty: 1 Page: 316

3. The only element of the marketing mix that produces revenue is called:

   a) place.
   b) price.
   c) product.
   d) promotion.

   Answer: (b)   Difficulty: 1 Page: 316

4. The following are common mistakes regarding pricing except:

   a) pricing is too cost oriented.
   b) prices are too demand oriented.
   c) prices are not revised often enough.
   d) prices are not varied enough.

   Answer: (b)   Difficulty: 2 Page: 316

5. All of the following statements about pricing are true except:

   a) pricing must reflect market changes.
   b) pricing must consider the rest of the marketing mix.
   c) pricing must be primarily cost oriented.
   d) pricing must be appropriate for different product items and market segments.

   Answer: (c)   Difficulty: 2 Page: 316

6. Pricing decisions that include the company's marketing objectives, marketing-mix strategy, costs, and organization are called:

a) controllable factors
b) external factors
c) internal factors
d) marketing factors

Answer: (c)   Difficulty: 1 Page: 316

7. Companies set _____ as their major pricing objective if they are troubled by too much capacity, heavy competition, or changing consumer wants.

a) survival
b) current profit maximization
c) product-quality leadership
d) market-share leadership

Answer: (a)   Difficulty: 1 Page: 317

8. Pricing to cover variable costs and some fixed costs is typical of which of the following pricing objectives?

a) Survival
b) Current profit maximization
c) Product-quality leadership
d) Market-share leadership

Answer: (a)   Difficulty: 1 Page: 317

9. Choosing a price that will produce the maximum current profit, cash flow, or return on investment reflects which of the following pricing objectives?

a) Survival
b) Current profit maximization
c) Product-quality leadership
d) Market-share leadership

Answer: (b)   Difficulty: 1 Page: 317

10. Companies that set price to obtain current financial results rather than long-run performance are using which of the following pricing objectives?

a) Survival
b) Current profit maximization
c) Product-quality leadership
d) Market-share leadership

Answer: (b)   Difficulty: 1 Page: 317

11. Companies which strive for _____ believe that the company which dominates the market will enjoy the lowest costs and highest long-run profit.

    a) survival
    b) market-share leadership
    c) product quality leadership
    d) current profit maximization

    Answer: (b)   Difficulty: 2   Page: 317

12. Companies that price products as low as possible typically pursue which of the following pricing objectives?

    a) Survival
    b) Current profit maximization
    c) Product-quality leadership
    d) Market-share leadership

    Answer: (d)   Difficulty: 1   Page: 317

13. Companies that charge a high price to cover higher performance quality and the high cost of R&D typically pursue which of the following pricing objectives?

    a) Survival
    b) Current profit maximization
    c) Product-quality leadership
    d) Market-share leadership

    Answer: (c)   Difficulty: 1   Page: 317

14. When a company sets a price for a new product on the basis of what it thinks the product should cost, then develops estimates on what each component should cost to meet proposed price with an acceptable profit margin, the company is practicing:

    a) predatory pricing.
    b) target costing.
    c) strategic costing.
    d) product line pricing.

    Answer: (b)   Difficulty: 2   Page: 318

15. Some Japanese firms have adopted a strategy where they determine a price at which the product is most likely to appeal to buyers. That price then determines features and production costs. This strategy is called:

    a) current profit maximization.
    b) target pricing.
    c) target costing.
    d) market share leadership.

    Answer: (c)   Difficulty: 2   Page: 318

16. The "floor" for the price that a company can ask for its product is set by:

    a) revenues.
    b) resources.
    c) production capacity.
    d) costs.

    Answer: (d)   Difficulty: 2 Page: 319

17. Costs that do not vary with production or sales levels are called:

    a) variable costs.
    b) long-term costs.
    c) fixed costs.
    d) nonnegotiable costs.

    Answer: (c)   Difficulty: 1 Page: 319

18. Labor costs, lumber and hardware are examples of what type of costs for a construction company?

    a) variable costs
    b) direct costs
    c) fixed costs
    d) total costs

    Answer: (a)   Difficulty: 2 Page: 319

19. In small companies, prices are typically set by the:

    a) marketing department
    b) sales department.
    c) divisional or product-line managers.
    d) top management.

    Answer: (d)   Difficulty: 2 Page: 319

20. The type of market that consists of many buyers and sellers trading in a uniform commodity such as wheat, copper is called:

    a) pure competition.
    b) monopolistic competition.
    c) oligopolistic competition.
    d) pure monopoly.

    Answer: (a)   Difficulty: 1 Page: 322

21. The type of market structure in which no single buyer or seller has much effect on the going market price is called:

    a) pure competition.
    b) monopolistic competition.
    c) oligopolistic competition.
    d) pure monopoly.

    Answer: (a)   Difficulty: 1 Page: 322

22. The type of market that consists of many buyers and sellers who trade over a range of prices rather than a single market price is called:

    a) pure competition.
    b) monopolistic competition.
    c) oligopolistic competition.
    d) pure monopoly.

    Answer: (b)   Difficulty: 1   Page: 322

23. The type of market in which sellers try to develop differentiated offers for different customer segments is called:

    a) pure competition.
    b) monopolistic competition.
    c) oligopolistic competition.
    d) pure monopoly.

    Answer: (b)   Difficulty: 1   Page: 322

24. The type of market that consists of a few sellers who are highly sensitive to each other's pricing and marketing strategies is called:

    a) pure competition.
    b) monopolistic competition.
    c) oligopolistic competition.
    d) pure monopoly.

    Answer: (c)   Difficulty: 1   Page: 322

25. The type of market in which the product can be uniform or nonuniform, but in which sellers are alert to competitors' strategies and moves, is called:

    a) pure competition.
    b) monopolistic competition.
    c) oligopolistic competition.
    d) pure monopoly.

    Answer: (c)   Difficulty: 1   Page: 322

26. The type of market that consists of one seller is called:

    a) pure competition.
    b) monopolistic competition.
    c) oligopolistic competition.
    d) pure monopoly.

    Answer: (d)   Difficulty: 1   Page: 322

27. When the consumer perceives that the price of a product is greater than the product's value, they will:

    a) purchase the product for "snob" appeal.
    b) not purchase the product.
    c) purchase the product even though the seller loses profit opportunities
    d) all of the above.

    Answer: (b)   Difficulty: 2 Page: 323

28. The relation between the price charged and the resulting demand level is shown in the:

    a) learning curve.
    b) experience curve.
    c) demand curve.
    d) cost curve.

    Answer: (c)   Difficulty: 1 Page: 323

29. In the case of prestige goods, the slope of the demand curve can be:

    a) flat.
    b) S-shaped.
    c) downward.
    d) upward.

    Answer: (d)   Difficulty: 2 Page: 324

30. Buyers are less price sensitive when the product they are buying is:

    a) the product is unique, or high in quality, prestige or exclusiveness.
    b) total expenditures for a product is low relative to their income.
    c) substitute products are difficult to find.
    d) All of the above.

    Answer: (d)   Difficulty: 3 Page: 324

31. If demand changes greatly with a small change in price, we can say that demand is:

    a) elastic.
    b) constant.
    c) inelastic.
    d) weak.

    Answer: (a)   Difficulty: 1 Page: 324

32. Adding a standard markup to the cost of the product refers to:

    a) cost-based pricing.
    b) break-even analysis.
    c) target profit pricing.
    d) going-rate pricing.

    Answer: (a)   Difficulty: 1 Page: 326

33. Markup pricing remains popular for many reasons. Which of the following are not reasons why sellers use markup pricing?

    a) Because it simplifies the pricing process.
    b) Because it reduces price competition when all firms in the industry use it.
    c) Because many people feel that it is fairer to both buyers and sellers.
    d) Because it is based ultimately on demand for the product.

    Answer: (d)   Difficulty: 3 Page: 328

34. When the firm tries to determine the price at which it will break even or make the target profit that it is seeking, it is using which form of pricing?

    a) Cost-based pricing.
    b) Break-even analysis.
    c) Target profit pricing.
    d) Going-rate pricing.

    Answer: (b)   Difficulty: 1 Page: 328

35. The pricing method that sets price based on the buyers' perceptions of value rather than on the seller's cost is called:

    a) cost plus pricing.
    b) value based pricing.
    c) target profit pricing.
    d) sealed-bid pricing

    Answer: (b)   Difficulty: 1 Page: 329

36. The pricing method that bases its price on how it thinks that competitors will price rather than on its own costs or on the demand is called:

    a) sealed-bid pricing
    b) going-rate pricing
    c) competition-based pricing
    d) perceived-value pricing

    Answer: (c)   Difficulty: 2 Page: 331

37. When demand elasticity is hard to measure, firms tend to price according to the "collective wisdom" of the industry. The pricing method most likely to be used is called:

    a) sealed-bid pricing
    b) going-rate pricing
    c) competition-based pricing
    d) perceived-value pricing

    Answer: (b)   Difficulty: 2 Page: 331

38. According to the price/quality strategy matrix, when a company overprices the product in relation to its quality it is considered which type of strategy?

    a) Premium strategy
    b) Good-value strategy
    c) Overcharging strategy
    d) Economy strategy

    Answer: (c)   Difficulty: 2 Page: 334

39. According to the price/quality strategy matrix, when a company produces a lower-quality product and charges a low price, it is considered which type of strategy?

    a) Premium strategy
    b) Good-value strategy
    c) Overcharging strategy
    d) Economy strategy

    Answer: (d)   Difficulty: 2 Page: 334

40. According to the price/quality strategy matrix, when a company produces a high-quality product and charges the highest price possible, it is considered which type of strategy?

    a) Premium strategy
    b) Good-value strategy
    c) Overcharging strategy
    d) Economy strategy

    Answer: (a)   Difficulty: 2 Page: 334

41. The process of setting prices for new products where the company initially sets a high price, then lowering the price subsequently so as to gain best profit from each market segment with the next price, is called:

    a) market-layer pricing.
    b) market-penetration pricing.
    c) market-skimming pricing.
    d) market-saturation pricing.

    Answer: (c)   Difficulty: 2 Page: 334

42. Which of the following conditions does not support market skimming pricing?

    a) a high-quality product is sold.
    b) the product has a prestige image.
    c) more efficient competitors can enter the market easily.
    d) small volumes can be economically produced.

    Answer: (c)   Difficulty: 2 Page: 335

43. The process of setting prices for new products where the company sets a low price in order to attract a large number of buyers quickly and win a large market share, is called:

    a) market-competitive pricing.
    b) market-penetration pricing.
    c) market-skimming pricing.
    d) market-saturation pricing.

    Answer: (b)   Difficulty: 2   Page: 335

44. Which of the following is not a condition favorable to a market-penetration pricing strategy?

    a) When the market is highly price sensitive.
    b) When production and distribution costs fall as sales volume increases.
    c) When low prices keep out competition.
    d) When the prospect of gaining a large market share is small.

    Answer: (d)   Difficulty: 2   Page: 336

45. Firms that produce a group of related products should price in a manner calculated to:

    a) maximize profits for each individual product.
    b) maximize profits on the total product mix.
    c) minimize production costs.
    d) minimize competitive reaction.

    Answer: (b)   Difficulty: 2   Page: 337

46. The price steps between products in a product line should take into account all of the following except:

    a) cost differences between products.
    b) customer evaluations of different features.
    c) resale price maintenance.
    d) competitors' prices.

    Answer: (c)   Difficulty: 2   Page: 337

47. Companies that make products that must be used in conjunction with a main product are practicing:

    a) optional-product pricing.
    b) captive-product pricing.
    c) by-product pricing.
    d) product-bundle pricing.

    Answer: (c)   Difficulty: 1   Page: 337

48. Selling season tickets for less than the cost of the tickets for each game if purchased separately is a form of:

    a) optional-product pricing.
    b) captive-product pricing.
    c) by-product pricing.
    d) product-bundle pricing.

    Answer: (d)   Difficulty: 1 Page: 338

49. A price reduction to buyers who pay their bills promptly is called a:

    a) cash discount.
    b) quantity discount.
    c) functional discount.
    d) seasonal discount.

    Answer: (a)   Difficulty: 1 Page: 339

50. When companies adjust their prices to allow for differences in customers, products, and locations, it is practicing

    a) psychological pricing.
    b) geographical pricing.
    c) segmented pricing.
    d) discriminatory pricing.

    Answer: (c) Difficulty: 1 Page: 339

TRUE/FALSE

51. Price is the amount of money charged for a product or service.

    Answer: True   Difficulty: 1 Page: 316

52. Price is the only element in the marketing mix that produces revenue.

    Answer: True   Difficulty: 2 Page: 316

53. Price is one of the most flexible elements of the marketing mix.

    Answer: True   Difficulty: 2 Page: 316

54. Generally speaking, most sellers set one price for all buyers.

    Answer: True   Difficulty: 1 Page: 316

55. Since pricing is of primary importance to the firm, it must be considered in isolation from the other elements of the marketing mix.

    Answer: False   Difficulty: 2 Page: 316

56. Internal factors affecting pricing decisions include the company's marketing objectives, marketing-mix strategy, costs, and organization.

    Answer: True   Difficulty: 1   Page: 316

57. External factors affecting pricing decisions include the nature of the market and demand, competition, and other environmental elements.

    Answer: True   Difficulty: 1   Page: 320

58. Companies facing too much capacity or heavy competition should adopt a survival objective in setting prices.

    Answer: True   Difficulty: 1   Page: 317

59. Companies that want short-term financial results rather than long-run performance may set current profit maximization as their marketing objective.

    Answer: True   Difficulty: 1   Page: 317

60. Companies with the largest market share and enjoy the lowest costs and highest long-run profit adopt a product-quality leadership as their marketing objective.

    Answer: False   Difficulty: 1   Page: 317

61. Companies seeking to dominate a market often choose market-share leadership marketing objective in setting price.

    Answer: True   Difficulty: 1   Page: 317

62. Charging a high price to cover the cost of offering superior quality and a high R&D budget is typical of a product quality leadership marketing objective.

    Answer: True   Difficulty: 1   Page: 317

63. Setting a product's price by starting with cost and working back is called target costing.

    Answer: True   Difficulty: 1   Page: 318

64. Companies often market their marketing-mix decision first and then make their pricing decisions.

    Answer: False   Difficulty: 1   Page: 318

65. Costs set the floor for the price that the company can charge for its product.

    Answer: True   Difficulty: 1   Page: 319

66. When a firm ceases to produce a product, the variable costs associated with that product's production cease to exist.

    Answer: True   Difficulty: 2   Page: 319

67. Generally speaking, management should charge a price that will at least cover its total production costs at a given level of production.

    Answer: True   Difficulty: 2 Page: 319

68. In small companies, prices are often set by top management rather than by the marketing or sales department.

    Answer: True   Difficulty: 2 Page: 319

69. Pure competition consists of a market with many buyers and sellers trading in a uniform commodity.

    Answer: True   Difficulty: 2 Page: 322

70. Under pure competition; marketing research, product development, pricing, advertising and sales promotion play an important role.

    Answer: False   Difficulty: 3 Page: 322

71. In monopolistic competition, buyers and sellers trade over a range of prices.

    Answer: True   Difficulty: 2 Page: 322

72. A company operating in a monopolistic competition type of market is less affected by competitors' marketing strategies than in oligopolistic markets.

    Answer: True   Difficulty: 2 Page: 322

73. Monopolistic competition is characterized by the enforcement of a single market price established by the only seller in the market.

    Answer: False   Difficulty: 2 Page: 322

74. A characteristic of oligopolistic competition is that it is very easy for new competitors to enter the market.

    Answer: False   Difficulty: 2 Page: 322

75. The price is "right" if the consumers perceive the satisfactions or benefits received as equal to or greater than the price they must pay.

    Answer: True   Difficulty: 2 Page: 323

76. Price elasticity refers to how responsive demand will be to a change in price.

    Answer: True   Difficulty: 2 Page: 324

77. The Major Corporation found that a decrease in the price of its product produces more total revenue. The demand for Major's product is elastic.

    Answer: True   Difficulty: 3 Page: 324

78. The simplest pricing method is cost-plus pricing.

    Answer: True   Difficulty: 1 Page: 326

79. An appliance manufacturer who desires to earn a 25 percent markup on cost for a toaster which has a unit cost of $20 would use a markup price of $25.

    Answer: True   Difficulty: 3 Page: 326

80. Markup pricing remains popular since sellers are more certain about costs than about demand.

    Answer: True   Difficulty: 2 Page: 328

81. Target profit pricing is a variation of breakeven pricing.

    Answer: True   Difficulty: 1 Page: 328

82. On a breakeven chart, the firm will break even at a volume of sales at which total revenues exactly equals total costs.

    Answer: True   Difficulty: 2 Page: 328

83. The major advantage of the breakeven analysis and target profit pricing is that it takes into account the price-demand relationship.

    Answer: False Difficulty: 2 Page: 329

84. Value-based pricing uses buyers' perceptions of value, not the seller's cost, as the key to pricing.

    Answer: True   Difficulty: 2 Page: 329

85. When a firm bases its price on how it thinks competitors will price rather than on its own costs or on demand, it is practicing going-rate pricing.

    Answer: False Difficulty: 2 Page: 331

86. Market-skimming pricing means setting a high initial price and taking revenues layer by layer from each price-sensitive segment of the market.

    Answer: True   Difficulty: 1 Page: 334

87. Market-skimming pricing takes advantage of the fact that some customers are willing to pay more to be the first to own a new, or unique product.

    Answer: True   Difficulty: 2 Page: 334

88. Market-penetration pricing involves setting a low initial price to capture a large market share quickly.

    Answer: True   Difficulty: 1 Page: 335

89. Market-penetration pricing is used to generate profits quickly.

    Answer: False   Difficulty: 2   Page: 336

90. The judicious use of price points allows consumers to easily form quality images appropriate to the various items which compose a product line.

    Answer: True   Difficulty: 2   Page: 337

91. The use of captive product pricing allows a seller to keep the price of the basic product low while making a nice profit on extras the consumer would like to add to that product.

    Answer: False   Difficulty: 2   Page: 337

92. Quantity discounts are typically offered only to large customers and may even exceed the seller's cost savings associated with the sale of the large amount.

    Answer: False   Difficulty: 2   Page: 339

93. A seller must offer the same cash discount to all similar buyers who meet the terms of the offer in order to avoid charges of price discrimination.

    Answer: True   Difficulty: 2   Page: 339

94. The Alpha Corporation typically seeks to have its products displayed beside more expensive brands. The firm is probably hoping to influence the consumer's reference price.

    Answer: True   Difficulty: 3   Page: 340

ESSAY

95. Identify and explain how marketing objectives affect pricing decisions.

    Answer:
    Marketing objectives are among the internal factors that affect pricing. The clearer a firm is about its objectives, the easier it is to set price. Common objectives include survival that sets a low price; current profit maximization: setting price to maximize profits; market-share leadership: setting prices as low as possible since these companies have the lowest costs; product-quality leadership: charging a high price to cover higher performance quality and the high cost of R&D.

    Difficulty: 2   Page: 317

96. Identify the different types of markets and explain how the different types of markets affect pricing decisions.

Answer:
Pure competition, the market consists of many buyers and sellers trading in a uniform commodity. No single buyer or seller has much effect on the going market price. Monopolistic competition, the market consists of many buyers and sellers who trade over a range of prices rather than a single market price. Sellers try to differentiate offers for different customer segments. Oligopolistic competition, the market consists of a few sellers who are highly sensitive to each other's pricing and marketing strategies. Pure monopoly, the market consists of one seller. Pricing is handled differently in each case.

Difficulty: 2   Page: 322

97. Compare the three general pricing approaches.

Answer:
Cost-plus pricing adds a standard markup to the cost of the product. Breakeven analysis and target profit pricing are common cost-oriented methods. Value-based pricing uses buyers' perceptions of value, not the seller's cost as the key to pricing. Competition-based pricing uses prices that competitors charge for similar products. Going-rate pricing and sealed-bid pricing are two popular competition-based pricing approaches.

Difficulty: 2   Page: 326-331

98. Identify and describe the major strategies for pricing imitative new products.

Answer:
Premium strategy: producing a high quality product and charging the highest price. Economy pricing strategy: producing a lower-quality product but charging a low price. Good-value strategy: producing a high quality product but charging a low price. Overcharging strategy: the company overprices the product in relation to its quality.

Difficulty: 2   Page: 334

99. Describe the major strategies for pricing innovative products.

Answer:
Market skimming: setting a high price for a new product to skim maximum revenues layer by layer from the segments that are willing to pay the high price; the company makes fewer, but more profitable, sales. Market penetration: setting a low price for a new product in order to attract a large number of buyers and a large market share.

Difficulty: 2   Page: 334-336

100. Discuss the major reasons why companies decide to change prices.

Answer:
Companies may change prices if faced with excess capacity to stimulate demand. Other price changes may come from loss of market share, a strategy of low cost leadership, or competitive moves. Increases may result from inflation or over demand. All price changes should be weighed carefully and evaluated in terms of customer and competitive reactions.

Difficulty: 2 Page: 344-346

Chapter 11

1. A set of interdependent organizations involved in the process of making a product or service available for use or consumption by the consumer or business user is called:

   a) a retailer.
   b) a wholesaler.
   c) a distribution channel.
   d) a selling channel.

   Answer: (c)   Difficulty: 1 Page: 358

2. Which of the following are reasons why producers use marketing intermediaries?

   a) Because they offer greater efficiency in making goods available to target markets.
   b) Because of their contacts and experience with customers
   c) Because of their specialization in delivering goods as needed.
   d) All of the above.

   Answer: (d)   Difficulty: 2 Page: 358

3. From the economic system's point of view, which of the following is not a role of marketing intermediaries:

   a) transform assortments made by producers into assortments wanted by consumers.
   b) reduce the amount of work done by both producers and consumers.
   c) match supply and demand
   d) transform consumer needs and wants into product desires.

   Answer: (d)   Difficulty: 2 Page: 358

4. Gathering and distributing marketing research and intelligence information about the marketing environment is part of which of the following marketing channel functions?

   a) Information
   b) Promotion
   c) Contact
   d) Negotiation

   Answer: (a)   Difficulty: 2 Page: 359

5. Developing and spreading persuasive communications about an offer is part of which of the following marketing channel functions?

   a) Information
   b) Promotion
   c) Contact
   d) Negotiation

   Answer: (b)   Difficulty: 2 Page: 359

6. Finding and communicating with prospective buyers is part of which of the following marketing channel functions?

   a) Information
   b) Promotion
   c) Contact
   d) Negotiation

   Answer: (c)   Difficulty: 2 Page: 359

7. Shaping and fitting the offer to the buyer's needs, including such activities as manufacturing, grading, assembling, and packaging is part of which of the following marketing channel functions?

   a) Information
   b) Promotion
   c) Contact
   d) Negotiation

   Answer: (c)   Difficulty: 2 Page: 359

8. Reaching an agreement on price and other terms of the offer so that ownership or possession can be transformed is part of which of the following marketing channel functions?

   a) Information
   b) Promotion
   c) Contact
   d) Negotiation

   Answer: (d)   Difficulty: 2 Page: 359

9. Acquiring and using funds to cover the costs of the channel work are characteristics of which of the following key functions?

   a) Physical distribution
   b) Contact
   c) Negotiation
   d) Financing

   Answer: (d)   Difficulty: 2 Page: 359

10. Regarding the key functions of marketing channels, all of the following statements are true except:

    a) all functions use up scarce resources.
    b) all functions need to be performed for all products.
    c) the functions can be performed better through specialization.
    d) the functions can be shifted among channel members.

    Answer: (b)   Difficulty: 2 Page: 359

11. A(n) _____ has no intermediary levels between the producer and the consumer.

    a) direct-marketing channel
    b) primary-marketing channel
    c) indirect-marketing channel
    d) manufacturer-marketing channel

    Answer: (a)   Difficulty: 1 Page: 360

12. In consumer markets with one intermediary level, the intermediary is typically called:

    a) wholesaler
    b) retailer
    c) jobber
    d) vendor

    Answer: (b)   Difficulty: 1 Page: 360

13. Disagreements among channel members regarding roles and goals generate:

    a) healthy competition which improves channel efficiency.
    b) channel conflict.
    c) an increase in channel length.
    d) improved communication.

    Answer: (b)   Difficulty: 2 Page: 362

14. Conflict between channel members at the same level of the channel is called:

    a) vertical competition.
    b) middleman conflict.
    c) horizontal conflict.
    d) functional conflict.

    Answer: (c)   Difficulty: 1 Page: 362

15. The Polo Company sells to both full-price retailers and discounters. The full price dealers have complained about this arrangement. The resulting friction would be best described as:

    a) middleman conflict.
    b) horizontal conflict.
    c) channel conflict.
    d) vertical conflict.

    Answer: (b)   Difficulty: 3 Page: 362

16. Conflict between the different levels of the same channel are referred to as:

    a) level-based conflict.
    b) channel conflict.
    c) horizontal conflict.
    d) vertical conflict.

    Answer: (d)   Difficulty: 1 Page: 362

17. When a company like Coca-Cola has disagreements with some of its bottlers over business practices, it is a form of:

    a) horizontal conflict.
    b) vertical conflict.
    c) channel conflict.
    d) conventional conflict

    Answer: (b)   Difficulty: 3 Page: 362

18. When one or more independent producers, wholesalers, and retailers operate as a separate business in the channel of distribution, it comprises which type of distribution channel?

    a) Vertical distribution channel
    b) Conventional distribution channel
    c) Horizontal distribution channel.
    d) Independent distribution channel

    Answer: (b)   Difficulty: 2 Page: 363

19. A distribution channel structure in which producers, wholesalers, and retailers act as a unified system is called:

    a) corporate marketing system.
    b) horizontal marketing system.
    c) vertical marketing system.
    d) direct marketing system.

    Answer: (c)   Difficulty: 2 Page: 364

20. A vertical marketing system (VMS) that combines successive stages of production and distribution under single ownership is called:

    a) corporate VMS.
    b) contractual VMS.
    c) administered VMS.
    d) conventional VMS.

    Answer: (a)   Difficulty: 2 Page: 366

21. A vertical marketing system (VMS) in which independent firms at different levels of production and distribution join together through contracts to obtain more economies or sales impact than they could achieve alone is called a:

    a) corporate VMS.
    b) contractual VMS.
    c) administered VMS.
    d) conventional VMS.

    Answer: (b)   Difficulty: 2 Page: 367

22. A vertical marketing system (VMS) in which wholesalers organize voluntary chains of independent retailers to help them compete with large chain organizations is called a:

    a) corporate VMS.
    b) wholesaler-sponsored voluntary chains.
    c) retailer cooperatives.
    d) franchise organizations.

    Answer: (b)   Difficulty: 2 Page: 367

23. A vertical marketing system (VMS) in which retailers organize a new, jointly owned business to carry on wholesaling and possibly production is called a:

    a) corporate VMS.
    b) wholesaler-sponsored voluntary chains.
    c) retailer cooperatives.
    d) franchise organizations.

    Answer: (c)   Difficulty: 2 Page: 367

24. A vertical marketing system (VMS) in which a channel member links several stages in the production-distribution process is called a:

    a) corporate VMS.
    b) wholesaler-sponsored voluntary chains.
    c) retailer cooperatives.
    d) franchise organizations.

    Answer: (d)   Difficulty: 2 Page: 367

25. The fastest growing retailing form in recent years is which type of vertical marketing system?

    a) Franchise organizations.
    b) Wholesaler-sponsored voluntary chains.
    c) Retailer cooperative.
    d) Manufacturer-owned chains

    Answer: (a)   Difficulty: 2 Page: 367

26. The type of franchise organizations used by the automobile industry is called a:

    a) manufacturer-sponsored retailer franchise system.
    b) manufacturer-sponsored wholesaler franchise system.
    c) service-firm-sponsored retailer franchise system.
    d) service-firm sponsored direct channel franchise system.

    Answer: (a)   Difficulty: 2 Page: 368

27. The type of franchise system that licenses wholesalers to buy products from the manufacturer, process them, and sell them as finished products, as in the soft-drink industry is called a:

    a) manufacturer-sponsored retailer franchise system.
    b) manufacturer-sponsored wholesaler franchise system.
    c) service-firm-sponsored retailer franchise system.
    d) service-firm sponsored direct channel franchise system.

    Answer: (b)   Difficulty: 2 Page: 368

28. The type of franchise system in which a service firm licenses a system of retailers to bring its service to consumers, as in the fast-food service business is called a:

    a) manufacturer-sponsored retailer franchise system.
    b) manufacturer-sponsored wholesaler franchise system.
    c) service-firm-sponsored retailer franchise system.
    d) service-firm sponsored direct channel franchise system.

    Answer: (c)   Difficulty: 2 Page: 368

29. Which type of vertical marketing system (VMS) coordinates successive stages of production and distribution through the size and power of one of the parties?

    a) Corporate VMS.
    b) Contractual VMS.
    c) Administered VMS.
    d) Conventional VMS.

    Answer: (c)   Difficulty: 2 Page: 368

30. When two or more companies at one level joint together to follow a new marketing opportunity, it is called a(n):

    a) vertical marketing system.
    b) horizonal marketing system.
    c) administered marketing system.
    d) hybrid marketing system.

    Answer: (b)   Difficulty: 2 Page: 368

31. When IBM and Apple Computer announced a joint operation to develop a new computer operating system, it was an example of a(n)

    a) vertical marketing system.
    b) horizonal marketing system.
    c) administered marketing system.
    d) hybrid marketing system.

    Answer: (b)   Difficulty: 2 Page: 368

32. Multichannel distribution systems in which a single firm sets up two or more marketing channels to reach one or more customer segments are often called:

    a) vertical marketing systems.
    b) horizonal marketing systems.
    c) administered marketing systems.
    d) hybrid marketing systems.

    Answer: (d)   Difficulty: 2 Page: 368

33. Designing the distribution channel starts with which of the following?

    a) Analyzing consumer service needs.
    b) Identifying the major channel alternatives.
    c) Setting the channel objectives and constraints.
    d) Evaluating the major alternatives.

    Answer: (a)   Difficulty: 2 Page: 372

34. Which of the following is not an area of consideration when setting the channel objectives and constraints?

    a) product characteristics.
    b) company characteristics.
    c) competitors' channels
    d) consumer characteristics

    Answer: (d)   Difficulty: 2 Page: 373

35. A distribution strategy in which the producer tries to stock their products in as many outlets as possible is called:

    a) intensive distribution.
    b) exclusive distribution.
    c) selective distribution.
    d) mass distribution.

    Answer: (a)   Difficulty: 2 Page: 375

36. The form of distribution where the producer gives only a limited number of dealers the sole right to market its products in their territories is called:

    a) intensive distribution.
    b) exclusive distribution.
    c) selective distribution.
    d) limited distribution.

    Answer: (b)   Difficulty: 2 Page: 375

37. The Rolls Royce Company, a manufacturer of expensive, prestigious automobiles, insists on maintaining control of the way in which its products are presented in its showrooms. The firm can best maintain this control through the use of:

    a) intensive distribution.
    b) exclusive distribution.
    c) selective distribution.
    d) limited distribution.

    Answer: (b)   Difficulty: 2 Page: 375

38. The type of distribution strategy whereby the producer uses more than one, but fewer than all of the intermediaries who are willing to carry the company's products is called:

    a) intensive distribution.
    b) exclusive distribution.
    c) selective distribution.
    d) alternative distribution

    Answer: (c)   Difficulty: 2 Page: 375

39. They type of distribution strategy that most television, furniture and small appliance brands use is called:

    a) intensive distribution.
    b) exclusive distribution.
    c) selective distribution.
    d) alternative distribution

    Answer: (c)   Difficulty: 2 Page: 375

40. In designing international distribution channels, marketers must take into consideration which of the following?

    a) Each country has its own unique distribution system that has evolved over time and changes slowly.
    b) Each country's distribution channel is complex and hard to penetrate.
    c) Distribution channels in developing countries may be scattered and inefficient.
    d) All of the above.

    Answer: (d)   Difficulty: 2 Page: 378

41. The tasks involved in planning, implementing, and controlling the physical flow of materials, final goods, and related information from points of origin to points of consumption to meet customer requirements at profit is called:

    a) marketing logistics.
    b) product logistics.
    c) physical distribution.
    d) performance logistics.

    Answer: (a)   Difficulty: 2 Page: 382

42. Which of the following statements regarding physical distribution objectives is true?

   a) Most companies seek maximum customer service.
   b) Most companies seek the least possible distribution costs.
   c) No physical distribution system can both maximize customer service and minimize distribution costs.
   d) Most companies let the physical distribution manager have total control over managing physical distribution costs.

   Answer: (c)   Difficulty: 3 Page: 384

43. Companies are placing greater emphasis on logistics for all of the following reasons except:

   a) distribution is an important customer service element.
   b) logistics is a major cost element for most companies.
   c) product variety has created a need for improved logistics management.
   d) All of the above are reasons for marketing logistics.

   Answer: (d)   Difficulty: 2 Page: 382

44. All of the following are major logistics functions except:

   a) order processing.
   b) warehousing.
   c) transportation.
   d) customer service.

   Answer: (d)   Difficulty: 2 Page: 384

45. A large, highly automated warehouse designed to receive goods from various plants and suppliers, take orders, fill them efficiently, and deliver goods to customers as quickly as possible is called a:

   a) warehouse center.
   b) distribution center.
   c) logistic center.
   d) service center.

   Answer: (b)   Difficulty: 2 Page: 385

46. The Just-In-Time logistics systems is a management tool that is part of which logistics function?

   a) Order processing.
   b) Warehousing.
   c) Inventory management.
   d) Transportation.

   Answer: (c)   Difficulty: 2 Page: 386

47. _____ are the most cost-effective modes for shipping large amounts of bulk products.

    a) Railroads
    b) Ships
    c) Trucks
    d) Air carriers

    Answer: (a)   Difficulty: 1   Page: 386

48. Although accounting for less than one percent of the nation's transported goods, the ideal transportation mode when speed is needed or distant markets have to reached is:

    a) Railroads
    b) Ships
    c) Trucks
    d) Air carriers

    Answer: (d)   Difficulty: 1   Page: 388

49. Putting goods in boxes or trailers that are easy to transfer between two transportation modes is called:

    a) packaging.
    b) piggyback.
    c) containerization.
    d) rail boxes.

    Answer: (c)   Difficulty: 1   Page: 389

50. The logistics concept that emphasizes teamwork, both inside the company and among all the marketing channel organizations, to maximize the performance of the entire distribution system is called:

    a) channel partnership.
    b) integrated logistics management.
    c) cross-functional teamwork.
    d) quick-response system.

    Answer: (b)   Difficulty: 2   Page: 389

TRUE/FALSE

51. A company's marketing channel decisions directly affect every other marketing decision.

    Answer: True   Difficulty: 2   Page: 358

52. A distribution channel is a set of interdependent organizations involved in the process of making a product or service available for use or consumption by the consumer or business user.

    Answer: True   Difficulty: 2   Page: 358

53. Businesses use intermediaries because they provide greater efficiency in making goods available to target markets.

    Answer: True   Difficulty: 2   Page: 358

54. Intermediaries play an important role in matching supply and demand.

    Answer: True   Difficulty: 2   Page: 358

55. The promotion function in a distribution system involves finding and communicating with prospective buyers.

    Answer: False   Difficulty: 2   Page: 359

56. The promotion function in a distribution system involves developing and spreading persuasive communications about an offer.

    Answer: True   Difficulty: 2   Page: 359

57. The negotiation function in a distribution system involves reaching an agreement on price and other terms of the offer so that ownership or possession can be transferred.

    Answer: True   Difficulty: 2   Page: 359

58. The length of a channel is determined by the number of intermediary levels it contains.

    Answer: True   Difficulty: 2   Page: 360

59. A direct-marketing channel has no intermediary levels.

    Answer: True   Difficulty: 2   Page: 360

60. From the producer's point of view, a smaller number of levels means greater control and less channel complexity.

    Answer: False   Difficulty: 2   Page: 361

61. Channel members share a common interest in selling the product and therefore, there is rarely conflict between members.

    Answer: False   Difficulty: 2   Page: 362

62. Horizontal conflict refers to conflicts between different levels of the same channel.

    Answer: False   Difficulty: 2   Page: 362

63. Because the success of individual channel members depends on overall channel success, all channel firms should work together smoothly.

    Answer: True   Difficulty: 2   Page: 362

64. Conflict in the channel is never healthy competition and can ultimately damage the channel.

    Answer: False   Difficulty: 2   Page: 363

65. A conventional distribution channel consists of one or more independent producers, wholesalers, and retailers with a separate business seeking to maximize its own profits.

    Answer: True   Difficulty: 2   Page: 364

66. A vertical marketing system consists of producers, wholesalers, and retailers acting as a unified system under contractual arrangements or through the ownership or domination of one of the members.

    Answer: True   Difficulty: 1   Page: 364

67. Vertical marketing systems evolved to control channel behavior and manage channel conflict.

    Answer: True   Difficulty: 2   Page: 365

68. A vertical marketing system (VMS) that combines successive stages of production and distribution under single ownership is called a corporate VMS.

    Answer: True   Difficulty: 2   Page: 366

69. Giant Food Stores operates an ice-making facility, a soft-drink bottling operation, an ice-cream-making plant, and a bakery that supplies Giant stores with everything from bagels to birthday cakes. Giant distributes its products through a corporate VMS.

    Answer: True   Difficulty: 3   Page: 366

70. A contractual VMS consists of independent firms at different levels of production and distribution who join together to obtain more economies or sales impact than each could achieve alone is called a contractual VMS.

    Answer: True   Difficulty: 2   Page: 367

71. Wholesaler-sponsored voluntary chains are a form of administered VMS.

    Answer: False   Difficulty: 2   Page: 367

72. In retailer cooperatives profits are passed back to members in proportion to their purchases.

    Answer: True   Difficulty: 1   Page: 367

73. Franchising is the fastest-growing retailing form in the United States.

    Answer: True   Difficulty: 1   Page: 367

74. Retailer cooperatives are a form of franchise organizations.

    Answer: False   Difficulty: 1   Page: 367

75. Automobile dealers represent the most common form of manufacturer-sponsored wholesaler franchise systems.

    Answer: False   Difficulty: 2   Page: 368

76. An administered VMS coordinates successive stages of production and distribution through the size and power of one of the channel members.

    Answer: True   Difficulty: 1   Page: 368

77. The Beta Corporation uses its position as the acknowledged leader in its industry to dominate its marketing channels. Beta probably distributes through an administered VMS.

    Answer: True   Difficulty: 3   Page: 368

78. When two or more companies at one level join together to follow a new marketing opportunity it is called a hybrid marketing system.

    Answer: False   Difficulty: 1   Page: 368

79. The horizontal marketing system is a channel arrangement in which two or more companies at one level join together to follow a new marketing opportunity.

    Answer: True   Difficulty: 2   Page: 368

80. Multichannel distribution systems in which a single firm sets up two or more marketing channels to reach one or more customer segments is often called hybrid marketing channels.

    Answer: True   Difficulty: 2   Page: 369

81. The major disadvantage of hybrid channel systems is that they generate conflict as more channels compete for customers and sales.

    Answer: True   Difficulty: 2   Page: 370

82. The best marketing channel design from a marketing standpoint is the lowest cost one.

    Answer: False   Difficulty: 2   Page: 370

83. Analyzing consumer service needs requires first setting the channel objectives and constraints.

    Answer: False   Difficulty: 2   Page: 372

84. Providing higher levels of service results in lower costs for the channel, however, prices for consumers tend to be higher.

    Answer: False   Difficulty: 2   Page: 373

85. Stocking the product in as many outlets as possible is called intensive distribution.

    Answer: True   Difficulty: 1 Page: 375

86. Producers of convenience products and common raw materials typically seek selective distribution.

    Answer: False   Difficulty: 2 Page: 375

87. Selective distribution lies between intensive and exclusive distribution in terms of the number of intermediaries used.

    Answer: True   Difficulty: 2 Page: 375

88. The Ruby Jewel Company offers a line of prestige jewelry. The firm is most likely to utilize intensive distribution.

    Answer: False   Difficulty: 3 Page: 375

89. Under exclusive distribution, a limited number of dealers are chosen to represent the manufacturer in each of the territories it serves.

    Answer: True   Difficulty: 1 Page: 375

90. The Japanese distribution system utilizes fewer intermediaries than the American distribution system.

    Answer: False   Difficulty: 2 Page: 377

91. A distribution center is a large, highly automated warehouse designed to receive goods from various plants and suppliers, take orders, fill them efficiently, and deliver goods to customers as quickly as possible.

    Answer: True   Difficulty: 2 Page: 385

92. During the past decade, many companies have greatly reduced their inventory costs through just-in-time logistics systems.

    Answer: True   Difficulty: 2 Page: 386

93. A properly designed physical distribution system can achieve the dual goals of maximizing customer service and minimizing distribution costs.

    Answer: False   Difficulty: 2 Page: 384

94. Although the cost of air transportation is high, savings resulting from smaller inventories and reduced warehousing needs may make its use economically attractive.

    Answer: True   Difficulty: 2 Page: 388

ESSAY

95. Explain why companies use distribution channels. What are the functions these channels perform?

Answer:
Producers use marketing intermediaries because they give greater efficiency in making goods available to target markets. Through their contacts, experience, specialization, and scale of operation, intermediaries offer the firm more than it can achieve on its own. Distribution channels move goods from producers to consumers. Members of the marketing channel perform many functions including information, promotion, contact, matching, negotiation as well as physical distribution, financing and risk taking.

Difficulty: 3   Page: 358-359

96. Briefly explain the concept of vertical marketing systems. Identify the three major types of VMSs.

Answer:
A vertical marketing system consists of producers, wholesalers, and retailers acting as a unified system. There are three major types of VMSs. In a corporate VMS, coordination and conflict management are attained through common ownership at different levels of the channel. In a contractual VMS, they are attained through contractual agreements among channel members. In an administered VMS, leadership is assumed by one or a few dominant channel members.

Difficulty: 2   Page: 363-368

97. Briefly explain the concept of horizontal marketing systems. How can this approach benefit its participants?

Answer:
In a horizontal marketing system, two or more firms work with each other on a temporary or permanent basis to take advantage of an opportunity neither could pursue alone. By working together, companies can combine their capital, production capabilities, or marketing resources to accomplish more than any one could working alone. In some cases, the firms may form a new company.

Difficulty: 2   Page: 368

98. Briefly explain the concept of hybrid marketing systems. What are the advantages and disadvantages of this marketing system?

Answer:
Hybrid marketing channels are defined as multichannel distribution systems in which a single firm sets up two or more marketing channels to reach one or more customer segments. There are several advantages of hybrid marketing channels. With each new channel, the company expands its sales and market coverage and gains opportunities to tailor its products and services to the specific needs of diverse customer segments. However, some channel systems are harder to control, and they generate conflict as more channels compete for customers and sales.

Difficulty: 2   Page: 369-370

99. Define and discuss the nature of physical distribution and marketing logistics.

    Answer:
    Physical distribution or marketing logistics includes planning, implementing, and controlling the physical flow of materials, final goods, and related information from points of origin to points of consumption to meet customer requirements at a profit. Companies are placing greater emphasis on logistics for several reasons. First, effective logistics is becoming a key to winning and keeping customers. Second, logistics is a major cost element for most companies. Third, the explosion in product variety has created a need for improved logistics management.

    Difficulty: 2 Page: 382

100. The Garden Company is evaluating different modes of transporting its products. Please discuss the pros and cons of the various choices.

    Answer:
    Railroads are one of the most cost-effective modes for shipping large amounts of bulk products over long distances. Trucks are highly flexible in their routing and time schedules. In many cases, their rates are competitive with railway rates, and trucks can usually offer faster, more flexible service. The cost of water transportation is low but it is the slowest mode and sometimes affected by the weather. Air is best when speed is needed.

    Difficulty: 3 Page: 386-388

Chapter 12

1. All the activities involved in the selling of goods or services directly to final consumers for their personal, nonbusiness use is called:

   a) wholesalers.
   b) retailers.
   c) consumer marketing.
   d) nonbusiness marketing.

   Answer: (b)   Difficulty: 2 Page: 397

2. Describing retailers by the breadth and depth of their product assortment is classification by:

   a) amount of service.
   b) product line.
   c) relative prices.
   d) control of outlets.

   Answer: (b)   Difficulty: 1 Page: 397

3. When describing a retail store as self-service, limited-service, or full-service, it is classification by:

   a) amount of service.
   b) product line.
   c) relative prices.
   d) control of outlets.

   Answer: (a)   Difficulty: 1 Page: 397

4. The type of retail stores that carry a narrow product lines with deep assortments within those lines is called:

   a) convenience stores.
   b) department stores.
   c) specialty stores.
   d) supermarkets.

   Answer: (c)   Difficulty: 1 Page: 398

5. A retail organization that carries a wide variety of product lines, each managed by specialist buyers or merchandisers is called:

   a) convenience stores.
   b) department stores.
   c) specialty stores.
   d) supermarkets.

   Answer: (b)   Difficulty: 1 Page: 399

6. Retailers that are large, low-cost, low-margin, high-volume, self-service and that carry a wide variety of food, laundry and household products are called:

   a) convenience stores.
   b) department stores.
   c) specialty stores.
   d) supermarkets.

   Answer: (d)   Difficulty: 1 Page: 400

7. Small stores that carry a limited line of high-turnover, easily available goods are called:

   a) convenience stores.
   b) department stores.
   c) superstores.
   d) supermarkets.

   Answer: (a)   Difficulty: 1 Page: 400

8. Retail stores that are almost twice the size of a regular supermarket that carries a large assortment of routinely purchased food and nonfood items are called:

   a) convenience stores.
   b) department stores.
   c) superstores.
   d) supermarkets.

   Answer: (c)   Difficulty: 1 Page: 401

9. Huge superstores that carry only limited product variety are called:

   a) convenience stores.
   b) superstores.
   c) hypermarkets.
   d) supermarkets.

   Answer: (c)   Difficulty: 1 Page: 401

10. The largest retail stores, perhaps as large as six football fields, that combine food, discount, and warehouse retailing are called:

    a) supermarkets.
    b) superstores.
    c) category killers.
    d) hypermarkets.

    Answer: (d)   Difficulty: 2 Page: 401

11. The type of retailer that sells standard merchandise at lower prices by accepting lower margins and selling at higher volume is called:

    a) discount stores.
    b) supermarkets.
    c) hypermarkets.
    d) warehouse clubs.

    Answer: (a)   Difficulty: 2   Page: 401

12. The type of retailer that buys at less than regular wholesale prices and charge consumers less than traditional retail prices is called:

    a) discount stores.
    b) off-price retailers.
    c) warehouse clubs.
    d) catalog showrooms.

    Answer: (d)   Difficulty: 2   Page: 402

13. The type of off-price retailer that is owned and operated by manufacturers and that normally carry the manufacturer's surplus, discounted, or irregular goods is called:

    a) independent off-price retailers.
    b) factory outlets.
    c) warehouse clubs.
    d) catalog showrooms.

    Answer: (b)   Difficulty: 2   Page: 402

14. The type of off-price retailer that sells a limited selection of brand-name grocery items, appliances, clothing, and a hodgepodge of other goods at deep discounts is called:

    a) independent off-price retailers.
    b) factory outlets.
    c) warehouse clubs.
    d) catalog showrooms.

    Answer: (c)   Difficulty: 2   Page: 403

15. A retail location comprised of manufacturer's outlets, off-price independent retailers, and department store clearance outlets is called:

    a) factory outlet malls.
    b) value-retail centers.
    c) catalog showroom shopping centers.
    d) independent off-price centers.

    Answer: (b)   Difficulty: 2   Page: 402

16. A _____ sells a wide selection of high-markup, fast-moving, brand-name goods at discount prices.

    a) independent off-price retailer
    b) factory outlet
    c) warehouse club
    d) catalog showroom

    Answer: (d)   Difficulty: 2 Page: 403

17. Two or more outlets that are commonly owned and controlled and that have central buying and merchandising, and sell similar lines of merchandise are called:

    a) corporate chains.
    b) voluntary chains.
    c) retailer cooperative.
    d) consumer conglomerates.

    Answer: (a)   Difficulty: 2 Page: 403

18. Groups of independent retailers who set up a central buying organization and conduct joint promotions are called:

    a) voluntary chain.
    b) retailer cooperative.
    c) franchise organization.
    d) merchandising conglomerates.

    Answer: (b)   Difficulty: 2 Page: 404

19. The type of retail organization that is a free-form corporation that combines several diversified retailing lines and forms under central ownership is called a:

    a) voluntary chain.
    b) retailer cooperative.
    c) franchise organization.
    d) merchandising conglomerates.

    Answer: (d)   Difficulty: 2 Page: 404

20. Corporate chains provide which of the following advantages over independent retailers?

    a) They buy in large quantities at lower prices.
    b) They hire corporate-level specialists to make decisions regarding pricing and sales.
    c) They spread their advertising costs over many stores.
    d) All of the above.

    Answer: (d)   Difficulty: 2 Page: 404

21. The form of retailing that uses various advertising media to interact directly with consumers, is called:

    a) direct marketing.
    b) direct selling.
    c) automatic vending.
    d) merchandising conglomerates.

    Answer: (a)   Difficulty: 2 Page: 405

22. Which of the following trends have fueled the growth of direct marketing?

    a) The increasing "demassification" of consumer markets.
    b) The increasing number of women entering the work force.
    c) The inconvenience associated with in-store shopping.
    d) All of the above.

    Answer: (d)   Difficulty: 2 Page: 405

23. Among the advantages direct marketing provides to consumers is:

    a) the ability to compare products and prices from their homes.
    b) convenient, hassle-free, and fun shopping.
    c) ordering and receiving products without having to leave their homes.
    d) All of the above.

    Answer: (d)   Difficulty: 2 Page: 407

24. Among the advantages direct marketing provides sellers is:

    a) selectivity in targeting consumers.
    b) higher readership and response rates.
    c) messages can be personalized and customized.
    d) All of the above.

    Answer: (d)   Difficulty: 2 Page: 407

25. Historically, roving peddlers are an early form of:

    a) direct marketing.
    b) automatic vending.
    c) door-to-door retailing.
    d) sales management.

    Answer: (c)   Difficulty: 2 Page: 409

26. Selling door to door, office to office, or at home-sales parties is called:

    a) direct marketing.
    b) automatic vending.
    c) door-to-door retailing.
    d) sales management.

    Answer: (c)   Difficulty: 2 Page: 409

27. In 217 B.C. Egyptians could buy sacrificial water from which method of direct marketing?

    a) Catalog marketing
    b) Automatic vending
    c) Door-to-door retailing
    d) Sales management

    Answer: (b)   Difficulty: 2 Page: 409

28. Which of the following is not an advantage of automatic vending?

    a) Vending machines are found everywhere.
    b) Vending machines offer consumers greater convenience.
    c) Vending machines offer fewer damaged goods.
    d) Vending machines prices are typically lower.

    Answer: (d)   Difficulty: 2 Page: 410

29. The first major marketing decision facing retailers is:

    a) product assortment decisions.
    b) pricing decisions.
    c) promotion decisions.
    d) target market decisions.

    Answer: (d)   Difficulty: 2 Page: 411

30. When a retailer asks "should the store focus on upscale, midscale, or downscale shoppers" it is rethinking which marketing strategy?

    a) product assortment decisions.
    b) pricing decisions.
    c) promotion decisions.
    d) target market decisions.

    Answer: (d)   Difficulty: 2 Page: 411

31. Determining the quality of goods to carry is part of which retailer marketing decision?

    a) product assortment decisions.
    b) pricing decisions.
    c) promotion decisions.
    d) target market decisions.

    Answer: (a)   Difficulty: 2 Page: 414

32. The decision to turn retail stores into theaters that transport customers into unusual, exciting environments is part of which retailer marketing decision?

    a) product assortment decisions.
    b) pricing decisions.
    c) promotion decisions.
    d) target market decisions.

    Answer: (a)   Difficulty: 2 Page: 411

33. A retailer's _____ is a crucial factor and must be decided in relation to its target market, its product and service assortment, and its competition.

    a) promotion decision
    b) placing decision
    c) pricing decision
    d) positioning decision

    Answer: (c)   Difficulty: 2   Page: 415

34. The choice of high markups and high volume is part of which of the following retailer marketing decisions?

    a) Promotion decision
    b) Placing decision
    c) Pricing decision
    d) Positioning decision

    Answer: (c)   Difficulty: 2   Page: 415

35. The use of some combination of advertising, personal selling, sales promotion, and public relations to reach target consumers is part of which of the following retailer marketing decisions?

    a) Promotion decision
    b) Placing decision
    c) Pricing decision
    d) Positioning decision

    Answer: (a)   Difficulty: 2   Page: 415

36. A group of retail businesses planned, developed, owned, and managed as a unit is called a:

    a) franchise.
    b) shopping center.
    c) voluntary chain.
    d) merchandising conglomerate.

    Answer: (b)   Difficulty: 1   Page: 416

37. The main form of retail store clusters that were popular in the 1950s was the:

    a) central business district.
    b) regional shopping center.
    c) free-standing store.
    d) drive-in retailer.

    Answer: (a)   Difficulty: 2   Page: 416

38. The largest and most dramatic shopping center that typically contains from 40 to 200 stores is called:

    a) community shopping centers.
    b) neighborhood shopping centers.
    c) strip malls.
    d) regional shopping centers.

    Answer: (d)   Difficulty: 2 Page: 416

39. A concept of retailing states that new types of retailers usually begin as low-margin, low-price, low-status operations but later evolve into higher-priced, higher-service operations, eventually becoming like the conventional retailers that they replaced is called the:

    a) retail life cycle.
    b) wheel of retailing.
    c) accordion theory of retailing.
    d) retail evolutionary theory.

    Answer: (b)   Difficulty: 2 Page: 418

40. The activities involved in selling goods and services to those buying for resale or business use is called:

    a) retailing.
    b) wholesaling.
    c) marketing.
    d) jobbers.

    Answer: (b)   Difficulty: 1 Page: 419

41. When wholesalers help retailers train their salesclerks, improve store layouts and displays, and set up accounting and inventory control systems, they are performing which of the following channel functions?

    a) Bulk-breaking.
    b) Warehousing.
    c) Financing.
    d) Management services and advice.

    Answer: (d)   Difficulty: 2 Page: 419

42. When wholesalers hold inventories, thereby reducing the inventory costs and risks of suppliers and customers, they are performing which of the following channel functions?

    a) Bulk-breaking.
    b) Warehousing.
    c) Financing.
    d) Management services and advice.

    Answer: (b)   Difficulty: 2 Page: 419

43. The largest single group of wholesalers accounting for roughly 50 percent of all wholesaling is called:

    a) warehouse clubs
    b) brokers and agents.
    c) merchant wholesalers.
    d) manufacturers' sales branches and offices.

    Answer: (c)   Difficulty: 1   Page: 419

44. The form of limited service wholesaler that performs a selling and delivery function is called a:

    a) cash-and-carry wholesaler.
    b) truck wholesaler.
    c) drop shipper.
    d) rack jobber.

    Answer: (b)   Difficulty: 2   Page: 420

45. The type of wholesaler who represents buyers or sellers on a relatively permanent basis, performs only a few functions, and does not take title to goods is called:

    a) merchant wholesalers.
    b) industrial distributors.
    c) brokers and agents.
    d) manufacturers' sales branches and offices

    Answer: (d)   Difficulty: 2   Page: 422

46. In order to survive, wholesalers must:

    a) purchase their own production facilities.
    b) develop an overall promotion strategy.
    c) resist the temptation to expand geographically.
    d) serve only the largest retail chains.

    Answer: (b)   Difficulty: 1   Page: 423

47. Which of the following is a predicted trend for the wholesaling industry?

    a) Consolidation will significantly reduce the number of wholesaling firms.
    b) Wholesaling firms will grow larger.
    c) Geographic expansion will require wholesalers to compete over wider and more diverse areas.
    d) All of the above.

    Answer: (d)   Difficulty: 2   Page: 425

48. All of the following wholesaling trends are expected to continue in the future except:

    a) Increase use of computerized and automated systems.
    b) The distinction between large and small wholesalers continues to blur.
    c) Increase in energy costs will mean that future sales will come from domestic markets.
    d) Increase the services they provide retailers.

    Answer: (c)   Difficulty: 3 Page: 425

TRUE/FALSE

49. All the activities involved in selling goods or services directly to final consumers for their personal, nonbusiness use is called retailing.

    Answer: True   Difficulty: 1 Page: 397

50. Today, limited-service is the basis of all discount operations and typically is used by sellers of convenience goods and nationally branded, fast-moving shopping goods.

    Answer: False   Difficulty: 2 Page: 397

51. In full-service retailers, salespeople assist customers in every phase of the shopping process.

    Answer: True   Difficulty: 1 Page: 397

52. Today, limited-service retailers provide more liberal return policies, various credit plans, free delivery, and home servicing.

    Answer: False   Difficulty: 1 Page: 397

53. A specialty store carries a narrow product line with deep assortments within those lines.

    Answer: True   Difficulty: 1 Page: 398

54. A department store carries a wide variety of product lines typically clothing, home furnishings, and household goods.

    Answer: True   Difficulty: 1 Page: 399

55. Supermarkets are the most frequently shopped type of retail store.

    Answer: True   Difficulty: 1 Page: 400

56. Superstores are large, low-cost, low-margin, high-volume, self-service stores that carry a wide variety of food, laundry and household products.

    Answer: False   Difficulty: 1 Page: 400

57. Convenience stores are small stores that carry a limited line of high turnover convenience goods.

    Answer: True   Difficulty: 1 Page: 400

58. In the 1990s, the supermarket suffered from overcapacity as its primary market of young, blue-collar men shrunk.

    Answer: False   Difficulty: 1   Page: 400

59. "Category killers" are a kind of superstore that carries a very deep assortment of a particular line and knowledgeable staff.

    Answer: True   Difficulty: 2   Page: 401

60. Hypermarkets are huge superstores, perhaps as large as six football fields.

    Answer: True   Difficulty: 2   Page: 401

61. A discount store sells standard merchandise at lower prices by accepting lower margins and selling higher volume.

    Answer: True   Difficulty: 1   Page: 401

62. Discount stores buy at less than regular wholesale prices and charge consumers less than standard retail.

    Answer: False   Difficulty: 2   Page: 402

63. Value-retail centers have become one of the hottest growth areas of retailing.

    Answer: False   Difficulty: 2   Page: 402

64. Off-price retailers--such as factory outlet stores and outlet malls--benefited from the decision of many discount chains to "trade up."

    Answer: True   Difficulty: 2   Page: 402

65. Warehouse clubs are owned and operated by manufacturers and normally carry the manufacturer's surplus, discontinued, or irregular goods.

    Answer: False   Difficulty: 2   Page: 402

66. Independent off-price retailers are either owned and run by entrepreneurs or are divisions of larger retail corporations.

    Answer: True   Difficulty: 2   Page: 402

67. A catalog showroom sells a wide selection of low-markup, fast-moving, brand-name goods at discount prices.

    Answer: False   Difficulty: 2   Page: 403

68. Chain stores are two or more outlets that are commonly owned and controlled, employ central buying and merchandising, and sell similar lines of merchandise.

    Answer: True   Difficulty: 2   Page: 403

69. A franchise is a group of independent retailers that band together to set up a jointly owned central wholesale operation and conduct joint merchandising and promotion efforts.

    Answer: False   Difficulty: 2 Page: 404

70. Voluntary chains were developed by small, independent retailers in response to the price competition of corporate retail chains.

    Answer: False   Difficulty: 2 Page: 404

71. The main difference between franchise organizations and other contractual systems is that franchise systems are normally based on some unique product or service.

    Answer: True   Difficulty: 1 Page: 404

72. Merchandising conglomerates are corporations that combine several different retailing forms under a central ownership.

    Answer: True   Difficulty: 2 Page: 405

73. Direct marketing is a major form of nonstore retailing in the consumer market but has not grown rapidly in the business-to-business marketing area.

    Answer: False   Difficulty: 2 Page: 405

74. The information superhighway is the newest method of direct selling.

    Answer: False   Difficulty: 2 Page: 405

75. The biggest criticism of direct marketing is the lack of privacy.

    Answer: False   Difficulty: 2 Page: 408

76. Door-to-door selling started centuries ago with roving peddlers.

    Answer: True   Difficulty: 2 Page: 409

77. The advantage of door-to-door retailing is lower costs.

    Answer: False   Difficulty: 2 Page: 410

78. In 215 B.C. Egyptians could buy sacrificial water from automatic vending dispensers.

    Answer: True   Difficulty: 2 Page: 410

79. The target market decision is the first marketing decision that retailers must make.

    Answer: True   Difficulty: 2 Page: 411

80. The product assortment is one of the key tools of nonprice competition for setting one store apart from another.

    Answer: False   Difficulty: 2 Page: 414

81. Retailers are turning their stores into theaters that transport customers into unusual, exciting shopping environments.

    Answer: True   Difficulty: 2   Page: 414

82. Generally, retailers must choose between high markups and high volume in setting retail prices.

    Answer: True   Difficulty: 2   Page: 415

83. Retailers that put low prices on some items to serve as "loss leader" are following a survival pricing objective.

    Answer: False   Difficulty: 3   Page: 415

84. Central business districts were the main form of retail cluster until the 1950s.

    Answer: True   Difficulty: 2   Page: 416

85. A shopping center is a group of retail businesses that are planned, developed, owned, and managed as a unit.

    Answer: True   Difficulty: 2   Page: 416

86. A megamall is the largest and most dramatic shopping center that contains from 40 to 200 stores.

    Answer: False   Difficulty: 2   Page: 416

87. According to the wheel-of-retailing concept, the most successful stores are those that discover a successful formula and stick to it.

    Answer: False   Difficulty: 2   Page: 418

88. Wholesaling is involved in selling goods and services to businesses for resale or business use.

    Answer: True   Difficulty: 1   Page: 419

89. Merchant wholesalers are the largest single group of wholesalers, accounting for 90 percent of all wholesaling.

    Answer: False   Difficulty: 2   Page: 419

90. Brokers and agents are essentially the same as merchant wholesalers.

    Answer: False   Difficulty: 2   Page: 422

91. Unlike retailers, wholesalers do not need to define their target markets and position themselves effectively since they basically serve everyone.

    Answer: False   Difficulty: 2   Page: 422

92. Since many retailers now operate formats such as wholesale clubs and hypermarkets, the distinction between retailers and wholesalers is not clear.

Answer: True   Difficulty: 2 Page: 425

ESSAY

93. The Yamito Corporation is preparing to enter the U.S. market for the first time. The firm has developed a technologically sophisticated holographic camera capable of producing three-dimensional prints from regular 35mm film through the use of a special processing procedure. What type of stores should the firm sell through? Why?

Answer:
This unique new product should be sold through specialty or super-specialty stores. The product will require the support of highly knowledgeable dealers who can explain its operation and answer technical questions. Yamito may have to limit its distribution to those outlets which are able and willing to provide processing.

Difficulty: 3 Page: 397

94. Supermarkets are best known for their introduction of self-service retailing. What other innovations, both in supermarkets and/or other areas of marketing, followed naturally? What is likely to happen to supermarkets in the future?

Answer:
Self-service retailing placed much greater emphasis upon the design of packaging and its role in promotion and product identification. Advertising also became more significant as consumers had to learn to identify products for themselves. Self-service also placed greater emphasis upon store layout--and supermarkets became a leader in layout research and design. Scrambled merchandising was also a logical outgrowth--and will likely become more important in the future. Supermarket chains may use their experience in non-food items to evolve into combination stores and/or hypermarkets.

Difficulty: 3 Page: 400-401

95. Off-price retailers have replaced discount stores in the low price, high volume market. Describe the three main types of off-price retailing.

Answer:
The three main types of off-price retailing are factory outlets, independents and warehouse clubs. Factory outlets are owned and operated by manufacturers and sell the manufacturer's surplus, discontinued or irregular goods. Independent retailers are owned by entrepreneurs or are divisions of larger retail corporations. Warehouse clubs sell a limited selection of brand name grocery items, appliances and other goods to members who pay a fee to join.

Difficulty: 3 Page: 402-403

96. Discount chains, after serving a well-defined market for years, traded up by building larger, more expensive stores, adding better-known, more expensive brands, and offering more services. Describe and define the theory of retailing that would best explain these changes.

   Answer:
   The wheel of retailing would explain these change in discount stores. According to this concept, discount stores began as low-margin, low-price, low-status operations. The discount chains' success lead them to upgrade their facilities and offer more services. In turn, their costs increase, forcing them to increase their prices. Eventually, discount stores become like the conventional retailers they displaced.

   Difficulty: 3 Page: 418

97. What trends have fueled the growth in direct marketing in recent years?

   Answer:
   Direct marketing is well suited to the growing segmentation of markets. It allows sellers to focus efficiently on minimarkets. Also, the increasing number of women entering the workforce has decreased the time households have to shop. The development of toll-free telephone numbers and the increased use of credit cards have also helped. Growth in computer power has led to better data.

   Difficulty: 3 Page: 405

98. Under what circumstances would a firm consider using a manufacturer's agent? A selling agent? What dangers face a manufacturer who employs a selling agent?

   Answer:
   Manufacturer's agents may be used to replace, or more commonly, supplement the manufacturer's own sales force. While small manufacturers may rely on several manufacturer's agents to provide distribution, larger firms are more likely to use them to open new territories or introduce new products with which their sales force is not familiar. Risk and cost are held to a minimum by the fact that such agents are paid by commission. As sales become larger, and commission payments exceed the cost of using the firm's sales force, agents are typically replaced. The firm gets fast representation--and its sales force has time to learn the new product or market. Selling agents always replace the sales force--and may replace the marketing department--of small, financially weak firms.

   Difficulty: 3 Page: 419

Chapter 13

1. The specific blend of advertising, personal selling, sales promotion, and public relations tools that the company uses to pursue its advertising and marketing objectives is called:

   a) marketing mix.
   b) advertising mix.
   c) promotion mix.
   d) distribution mix.

   Answer: (c)   Difficulty: 1 Page: 431

2. Which tool of the promotion mix consists of any paid form of nonpersonal presentation and promotion of ideas, goods, or services by an identified sponsor?

   a) Advertising.
   b) Personal selling.
   c) Sales promotion.
   d) Public relations.

   Answer: (a)   Difficulty: 1 Page: 432

3. Which tool of the promotion mix consists of short-term incentives to encourage the purchase of sale of a product or service?

   a) Advertising.
   b) Personal selling.
   c) Sales promotion.
   d) Public relations.

   Answer: (c)   Difficulty: 1 Page: 432

4. Which tool of the promotion mix is designed to build a good "corporate image?"

   a) Advertising.
   b) Personal selling.
   c) Sales promotion.
   d) Public relations.

   Answer: (d)   Difficulty: 1 Page: 432

5. Which tool of the promotion mix includes sales presentations, trade shows, and incentive programs to build customer relationships?

   a) Advertising.
   b) Personal selling.
   c) Sales promotion.
   d) Public relations.

   Answer: (b)   Difficulty: 1 Page: 432

6. Working with a reporter to get a favorable article written about your company in the local paper is a form of:

   a) advertising.
   b) personal selling.
   c) sales promotion.
   d) public relations.

   Answer: (d)   Difficulty: 1   Page: 432

7. Showing a shopper how a new computer game works during an in-store visit is a form of:

   a) advertising.
   b) personal selling.
   c) sales promotion.
   d) public relations.

   Answer: (b)   Difficulty: 1   Page: 432

8. A political campaign message by an identified sponsor on the radio that asks that you vote in favor of a specific proposal is a form of:

   a) advertising.
   b) personal selling.
   c) sales promotion.
   d) public relations.

   Answer: (a)   Difficulty: 1   Page: 432

9. Using the newspaper to distribute coupons good for $1 off a purchase of any item bought in the store during the following weekend is an example of:

   a) advertising.
   b) personal selling.
   c) sales promotion.
   d) public relations.

   Answer: (c)   Difficulty: 1   Page: 432

10. Marketing communicators must do which of the following first?

   a) Determine the response sought.
   b) Choose a message.
   c) Choose media.
   d) Identify target audience.

   Answer: (d)   Difficulty: 1   Page: 433

11. The stages that consumers normally pass through on their way to making a purchase is called:

    a) buyer-development stages.
    b) buyer-progressive stages.
    c) buyer-marketing stages.
    d) buyer-readiness stages.

    Answer: (d)   Difficulty: 1 Page: 433

12. Achieving name recognition is often the goal of which stage of the buyer-readiness state?

    a) Awareness
    b) Knowledge
    c) Liking
    d) Purchase

    Answer: (a)   Difficulty: 1 Page: 433

13. When Infiniti created ads that focused on the car's high quality and many innovative features, it was focusing on which stage of the buyer-readiness state?

    a) Awareness
    b) Knowledge
    c) Liking
    d) Purchase

    Answer: (b)   Difficulty: 1 Page: 433

14. If a buyer has a favorable feeling toward a particular product, the buyer is in which stage of the buyer-readiness state?

    a) Preference
    b) Knowledge
    c) Liking
    d) Purchase

    Answer: (c)   Difficulty: 1 Page: 433

15. When marketers use press releases and other public relations activities to stress the innovative features and performance of a particular product, it is focusing on which stage of the buyer-readiness states?

    a) Conviction
    b) Knowledge
    c) Liking
    d) Purchase

    Answer: (a)   Difficulty: 1 Page: 433

16. In terms of the buyer-readiness states, the consumer is in which state when they are sure of which product they wish to buy?

    a) Conviction
    b) Knowledge
    c) Liking
    d) Purchase

    Answer: (a)   Difficulty: 1   Page: 433

17. In developing an effective message, marketers sometimes refer to the AIDA model, which stands for:

    a) awareness, interest, demand, action.
    b) awareness, interest, desire, action.
    c) attention, interest, desire, action.
    d) attention, interest, demand, action.

    Answer: (c)   Difficulty: 1   Page: 434

18. An advertising message should get attention, hold interest, arouse desire, and obtain action according to a model known as:

    a) AIDA model
    b) AHDA model
    b) The Promotional model
    c) The Communication model

    Answer: (a)   Difficulty: 1   Page: 434

19. In terms of message content, appeals that relate to the audience's self-interest are:

    a) rational appeals
    b) emotional appeals
    c) moral appeals
    d) legal appeals

    Answer: (a)   Difficulty: 1   Page: 434

20. In terms of message content, the type of appeals that stir up either negative or positive feelings are:

    a) rational appeals
    b) emotional appeals
    c) moral appeals
    d) legal appeals

    Answer: (a)   Difficulty: 1   Page: 434

21. March of Dimes uses the appeal: "God made you whole. Give to help those He didn't." In terms of message content, the March of Dimes was using which type of appeal?

    a) Rational appeals
    b) Emotional appeals
    c) Moral appeals
    d) Legal appeals

    Answer: (c)   Difficulty: 1 Page: 434

22. When IBM salespeople talk about quality, performance, reliability, and improved productivity of its product, the firm is using which type of message appeal?

    a) Rational appeals
    b) Emotional appeals
    c) Moral appeals
    d) Legal appeals

    Answer: (a)   Difficulty: 1 Page: 434

23. Appeals that urge people to support social causes are:

    a) rational appeals
    b) emotional appeals
    c) moral appeals
    d) legal appeals

    Answer: (c) Difficulty: 1 Page: 435

24. In putting a message together, the marketing communicator addressing what to say is working on:

    a) message content.
    b) message channel.
    c) message format.
    d) message design.

    Answer: (a)   Difficulty: 2 Page: 434

25. Planning for the element of body language in a television advertisement relates to which message-specific area of marketing communicator decisions?

    a) Message content.
    b) Message channel.
    c) Message format.
    d) Message design.

    Answer: (c)   Difficulty: 2 Page: 435

26. Two or more people communicating directly with each other are using:

    a) multimedia communication channels.
    b) personal communication channels.
    c) nonpersonal communication channels.
    d) direct communication channels.

    Answer: (b)   Difficulty: 1 Page: 436

27. An example of a personal communication channel outside the control of a company is:

    a) promotional influence.
    b) expert judgement.
    c) trickle down process.
    d) word-of-mouth influence.

    Answer: (d)   Difficulty: 2 Page: 436

28. A person whose advice or actions influence others to purchase is known as a(n):

    a) personal influence.
    b) facilitator.
    c) opinion leader.
    d) purchase leader.

    Answer: (c)   Difficulty: 1 Page: 436

29. Media that carry messages without personal contact or feedback are called:

    a) personal communication channels.
    b) nonpersonal communication channels.
    c) primary communication channels.
    d) secondary communication channels.

    Answer: (b)   Difficulty: 1 Page: 436

30. Nonpersonal communication channels that are designed environments that create or reinforce the buyer's leanings toward purchasing a product are called:

    a) media.
    b) atmospheres.
    c) events.
    d) images.

    Answer: (b)   Difficulty: 2 Page: 437

31. Nonpersonal communication channels that are stages occurrences that communicate messages to target audiences.

    a) media.
    b) atmospheres.
    c) events.
    d) images.

    Answer: (c)   Difficulty: 2 Page: 437

32. Chez Ritz Restaurant depends heavily upon lighting, decor, music, gourmet cuisine, and impeccable service to attract its patrons. According to your text regarding nonpersonal communication channels, Chez Ritz is using:

    a) media.
    b) atmospheres.
    c) events.
    d) images.

    Answer: (b)   Difficulty: 2 Page: 437

33. When the marketing communicator conducts marketing research to assess the effect of a promotion on the target audience, this falls under which decision area?

    a) Identifying the target market.
    b) Determining the response sought.
    c) Choosing a message.
    d) Collecting feedback.

    Answer: (d)   Difficulty: 2 Page: 438

34. Determining the promotion budget at the level that management thinks the company can afford is called the:

    a) affordable method.
    b) percentage-of-sales method.
    c) competitive-parity method.
    d) objective-and-task method.

    Answer: (a)   Difficulty: 1 Page: 440

35. Determining the promotion budget on the basis of financial availability is characteristic of which method?

    a) Affordable method.
    b) Percentage-of-sales method.
    c) Competitive-parity method.
    d) Objective-and-task method.

    Answer: (a)   Difficulty: 1 Page: 440

36. The method used to set the total budget for advertising that can result in overspending, but more often results in underspending is known as:

    a) affordable method.
    b) percentage-of-sales method.
    c) competitive-parity method.
    d) objective-and-task method.

    Answer: (a)   Difficulty: 1 Page: 440

37. The method used to set the total budget for advertising by taking some predetermined portion of the actual or forecasted sales is called:

    a) affordable method.
    b) percentage-of-sales method.
    c) competitive-parity method.
    d) objective-and-task method.

    Answer: (b)   Difficulty: 1 Page: 440

38. Setting the promotion budget based on industry promotion-spending estimates is called:

    a) affordable method.
    b) percentage-of-sales method.
    c) competitive-parity method.
    d) objective-and-task method.

    Answer: (c)   Difficulty: 1 Page: 440

39. The method of budgeting for advertising that views sales as the cause of promotion rather than as the result is known as:

    a) affordable method.
    b) percentage-of-sales method.
    c) competitive-parity method.
    d) objective-and-task method.

    Answer: (b)   Difficulty: 1 Page: 440

40. The most logical budget setting method is the:

    a) affordable method.
    b) percentage-of-sales method.
    c) competitive-parity method.
    d) objective-and-task method.

    Answer: (d)   Difficulty: 1 Page: 441

41. Which of the following methods of setting the promotion budget forces management to spell out its assumptions about the relationship between spending and promotion results?

    a) Affordable method.
    b) Percentage-of-sales method.
    c) Competitive-parity method.
    d) Objective-and-task method.

    Answer: (d)   Difficulty: 1 Page: 440

42. Each of the following statements about advertising are true except:

   a) Consumers view advertised products as standard and legitimate.
   b) Large-scale advertising says something positive about the seller's size, popularity, and success.
   c) Advertising is more persuasive than personal selling.
   d) Although advertising is expensive, the cost per exposure is low.

   Answer: (c)   Difficulty: 2 Page: 441

43. The most expensive promotion tool is:

   a) advertising.
   b) promotion.
   c) personal selling.
   d) public relations.

   Answer: (c)   Difficulty: 1 Page: 442

44. To stimulate a quick purchase response from consumers who are favorably disposed toward a product, it is best to use:

   a) advertising.
   b) sales promotion.
   c) personal selling.
   d) public relations.

   Answer: (b)   Difficulty: 1 Page: 443

45. The promotion tool that marketers tend to under use or use only as an afterthought is:

   a) advertising.
   b) promotion.
   c) personal selling.
   d) public relations.

   Answer: (d)   Difficulty: 1 Page: 443

46. When a producer directs its marketing activities toward channel members in order to induce them to carry the product and promote it to final consumers, they are using which type of promotion strategy?

   a) Pull strategy.
   b) Push strategy.
   c) Product-mix strategy.
   d) Marketing-mix strategy.

   Answer: (b)   Difficulty: 2 Page: 443

47. When a producer directs its marketing activities toward the final consumer to induce them to buy the product, they are using which type of promotion strategy?

    a) Pull strategy.
    b) Push strategy.
    c) Product-mix strategy.
    d) Marketing-mix strategy.

    Answer: (a)   Difficulty: 2 Page: 443

48. In the introduction stage of the product life-cycle, _____ and _____ are good for producing high awareness.

    a) advertising and sales promotion.
    b) personal selling and advertising.
    c) public relations and personal selling.
    d) advertising and public relations.

    Answer: (d)   Difficulty: 3 Page: 446

49. The infomercial is a form of which type of direct marketing communication?

    a) On-line shopping.
    b) Telemarketing.
    c) Direct mail marketing.
    d) Television marketing.

    Answer: (d)   Difficulty: 2 Page: 451

50. The concept under which a company carefully coordinates its many communications channels to deliver a clear, consistent, and compelling message about the organization and its products is called:

    a) integrated direct marketing.
    b) the marketing mix.
    c) direct marketing communication.
    d) integrated marketing communications.

    Answer: (d)   Difficulty: 2 Page: 454

TRUE/FALSE

51. The communication mix consists of the specific blend of advertising, personal selling, sales promotion, and public relations tools that the company uses to pursue its marketing objectives.

    Answer: False   Difficulty: 2 Page: 431

52. Advertising is any paid form of personal presentation and promotion of ideas, goods, or services by an identified sponsor.

    Answer: False   Difficulty: 2 Page: 432

53. Personal selling is the oral presentation in a conversation with one or more prospective purchasers for the purpose of making sales.

    Answer: True   Difficulty: 2 Page: 432

54. Public relations involves building good relations with the company's various publics by obtaining favorable publicity, building up a good "corporate image," and handling or heading off unfavorable rumors, stories, and events .

    Answer: True   Difficulty: 1 Page: 432

55. Sales promotion is the use of short-term incentives to encourage the purchase or sale of a product or service.

    Answer: True   Difficulty: 1 Page: 432

56. The Jusco Corporation is preparing to introduce a unique new product. The firm's first task will be to build awareness in its target market.

    Answer: True   Difficulty: 3 Page: 433

57. The first step in developing effective communication is determining the response sought.

    Answer: False   Difficulty: 2 Page: 433

58. In planning a promotion, a marketing communicator starts with a clear target audience in mind.

    Answer: True   Difficulty: 2 Page: 433

59. Awareness and knowledge are cognitive states of buyer readiness.

    Answer: True   Difficulty: 2 Page: 433

60. Typically, marketing communications alone can create positive feeling and purchases for products.

    Answer: False   Difficulty: 2 Page: 434

61. Good marketing communication calls for "good deeds followed by good words."

    Answer: True   Difficulty: 1 Page: 434

62. According to the AIDA model, an advertising message must first generate attention if it is to be successful.

    Answer: True   Difficulty: 2 Page: 434

63. The AIDA model refers to Awareness, Interest, Demand, and Action.

    Answer: False   Difficulty: 2 Page: 434

64. Emotional appeals relate to the audience's self-interest.

    Answer: False   Difficulty: 2   Page: 434

65. Emotional appeals attempt to stir up either negative or positive feelings that can motivate purchase.

    Answer: True   Difficulty: 2   Page: 434

66. When communicators try to get people to stop smoking, they are likely to use moral appeals.

    Answer: False   Difficulty: 2   Page: 434

67. Moral appeals are directed to the audience's sense of what is right and proper.

    Answer: True   Difficulty: 1   Page: 435

68. In personal communication channels, two or more people communicate directly with each other.

    Answer: True   Difficulty: 1   Page: 436

69. Word-of-mouth influence is especially important in the sale of products that are expensive, risky, or highly visible.

    Answer: True   Difficulty: 2   Page: 436

70. Opinion leaders are especially important in a firm's attempts to utilize word-of-mouth influence.

    Answer: True   Difficulty: 2   Page: 436

71. Nonpersonal communication affects buyers directly.

    Answer: False   Difficulty: 2   Page: 436

72. Media that carry messages without personal contact or feedback are called nonpersonal communication channels.

    Answer: True   Difficulty: 1   Page: 436

73. Opinion leaders step between the mass media and their audiences and carry messages to people who are less exposed to media.

    Answer: True   Difficulty: 2   Page: 437

74. Atmospheres are occurrences staged to communicate messages to target audiences.

    Answer: False   Difficulty: 2   Page: 437

75. Messages delivered by highly credible sources are most persuasive.

    Answer: True   Difficulty: 1   Page: 437

76. When the communicator collects market research to determine message effects on target
    audience in order to obtain feedback, it is in the final step in developing effective
    communication.

    Answer: True   Difficulty: 2   Page: 438

77. The affordable method of setting the promotion budget usually results in overspending on
    advertising.

    Answer: False   Difficulty: 2   Page: 440

78. Unless it is based on forecasted sales, the percentage-of-sales method results in
    advertising being a cause rather than a result of sales.

    Answer: False   Difficulty: 2   Page: 440

79. Setting the promotion budget as a fraction of the current or anticipated sales is called
    the percentage-of-sales method.

    Answer: True   Difficulty: 2   Page: 440

80. The competitive-parity method of budgeting wrongly views sales as the cause of promotion
    rather than as the result.

    Answer: False   Difficulty: 2   Page: 440

81. The mere fact that a firm achieves competitive-parity in its advertising budget does not
    guarantee that its promotional efforts will be as effective as those of its competitors.

    Answer: True   Difficulty: 2   Page: 440

82. The objective-and-task method is the most logical of all the budgetary methods a firm
    might use.

    Answer: True   Difficulty: 1   Page: 441

83. The objective-and-task method requires management to set its promotional budget
    according to the goals it desires to accomplish with promotion.

    Answer: True   Difficulty: 2   Page: 441

84. Advertising is the main vehicle used to build a quality, differentiated image for many
    products.

    Answer: True   Difficulty: 2   Page: 441

85. Designing the promotion mix is complicated when one promotional tool must be used to promote another.

    Answer: True   Difficulty: 2   Page: 441

86. Advertising offers several unique qualities such as coupons, contests, cents-off deals, and premiums.

    Answer: False   Difficulty: 2   Page: 442

87. Personal selling is the company's most expensive promotion tool.

    Answer: True   Difficulty: 2   Page: 442

88. Sales promotion is used to stimulate immediate purchase reactions by offering attractive incentives for quick action.

    Answer: True   Difficulty: 2   Page: 443

89. Firms that rely heavily on push strategies allocate a large percentage of their promotional budget for advertising.

    Answer: False   Difficulty: 2   Page: 443

90. While the decision to use a push versus a pull strategy is important in setting the marketing mix, the product life-cycle stage has little impact on the promotion mix.

    Answer: False   Difficulty: 2   Page: 444

91. Industrial goods tend to use a pull promotion strategy, putting most of their funds into personal selling.

    Answer: False   Difficulty: 2   Page: 444

92. Marketers today are concerned with the reckless use of a push promotion strategy, since they believe it will lead to fierce price competition.

    Answer: True   Difficulty: 2   Page: 445

93. In the decline stage, advertising and public relations are kept at a reminder level.

    Answer: True   Difficulty: 2   Page: 446

94. In the introduction stage, advertising and sales promotions are good for producing high product awareness.

    Answer: False   Difficulty: 2   Page: 446

ESSAY

95. Identify and describe the four tools of the promotion mix.

Answer:
Advertising is any paid form of nonpersonal promotion of ideas, goods, or services by an identified sponsor. Personal selling is the oral presentation for the purposes of making a sale. Sales promotion consists of short-term incentives to encourage purchase or sales of a product or service. Public relations involves building good relations with the company's various publics by obtaining favorable publicity, building up a good "corporate image."

Difficulty: 3 Page: 432

96. Identify and describe each of the buyer-readiness states.

Answer:
A target audience may be in any of six buyer-readiness states, states consumers normally pass through on their way to making a purchase which include awareness, knowledge, liking, preference, conviction, and purchase. Awareness is the state at which the target audience is first aware of the product's existence. Knowledge is their degree of understanding of the product. Liking is the degree of positive or negative affect. Preference is the level at which the product is liked better than the competition. Conviction leads to demanding the product and not accepting substitutes. Purchase is buying. Promotion should be tailored to the appropriate state.

Difficulty: 3 Page: 433

97. Identify and describe the different message appeals used in advertising.

Answer:
There are three types of appeals, rational, emotional, and moral. Rational appeals relate to the audience's self-interest. They show the product will produce the desired benefits. Emotional appeals attempt to stir up either negative or positive emotions that can motivate purchase. Moral appeals are directed to the audience's sense of what is right and proper.

Difficulty: 3 Page: 434-435

98. Identify and explain the methods used for setting the promotion budget.

Answer:
There are four methods of setting the total promotion budget: affordable, percentage-of-sales, competitive-parity, and objective-and-task. The affordable method sets the budget based upon available funds. The percentage-of-sales method bases the budget on a set fraction of current or forecasted sales. The competitive parity method matches the competition's spending. The objective-and-task method defines goals; determines the tasks necessary to reach them; estimates the cost of the tasks and sets their budget.

Difficulty: 3 Page: 440-441

99. Discuss the factors that affect the design of the promotion mix.

    Answer:
    Factors used in setting the promotion mix are the type of product and market, the use of a push versus a pull strategy, the buyer readiness state, and the product's stage in the product life cycle.

    Difficulty: 2 Page: 443-446

100. Identify and describe the forms of direct marketing communication.

    Answer:
    There are four major forms of direct marketing: direct-mail and catalog marketing, telemarketing, television marketing, and online shopping.

    Difficulty: 2 Page: 448-452

Chapter 14

1. Any paid form of nonpersonal presentation and promotion of ideas, goods, or services by an identified sponsor is called:

   a) sales promotion.
   b) publicity.
   c) advertising.
   d) public relations.

   Answer: (c)   Difficulty: 1 Page: 465

2. A specific communication task to be accomplished with a specific target audience in a specific period of time is referred to as a(n):

   a) advertising objective.
   b) advertising task.
   c) promotion target.
   d) promotion mix.

   Answer: (a)   Difficulty: 1 Page: 467

3. Telling the market about a new product is the objective of which type of advertising?

   a) Informative advertising.
   b) Persuasive advertising.
   c) Reminder advertising.
   d) Demand-driven advertising.

   Answer: (a)   Difficulty: 2 Page: 467

4. Maintaining top-of-mind product awareness is the objective of which type of advertising?

   a) Informative advertising.
   b) Persuasive advertising.
   c) Reminder advertising.
   d) Demand-driven advertising.

   Answer: (c)   Difficulty: 2 Page: 467

5. Encouraging consumers to switch to your brand is the object of which type of advertising?

   a) Informative advertising.
   b) Persuasive advertising.
   c) Reminder advertising.
   d) Comparison advertising.

   Answer: (b)   Difficulty: 2 Page: 467

6. When VISA advertised: "American Express is offering you a new credit card, but you don't have to accept it. Heck, 7 million merchants don't;" they were employing which type of advertising?

    a) Informative advertising.
    b) Persuasive advertising.
    c) Reminder advertising.
    d) Comparison advertising.

    Answer: (d)   Difficulty: 2 Page: 468

7. _____ is important for mature products, it keeps consumers thinking about the product.

    a) Informative advertising.
    b) Persuasive advertising.
    c) Reminder advertising.
    d) Comparison advertising.

    Answer: (c)   Difficulty: 2 Page: 468

8. Which type of advertising is most appropriate for introducing new product categories?

    a) Informative advertising.
    b) Persuasive advertising.
    c) Reminder advertising.
    d) Comparison advertising.

    Answer: (a)   Difficulty: 2 Page: 468

9. The type of advertising most appropriate when competition increases is:

    a) Informative advertising.
    b) Persuasive advertising.
    c) Reminder advertising.
    d) Comparison advertising.

    Answer: (b)   Difficulty: 2 Page: 468

10. In evaluating advertising appeals, pointing out benefits that make the product more desirable or interesting to consumers ensures that the message will be:

    a) meaningful.
    b) believable.
    c) distinctive
    d) competitive.

    Answer: (a)   Difficulty: 1 Page: 472

11. In evaluating advertising appeals, tell how the product is better than the competing brands aims at making the ad:

   a) meaningful.
   b) believable.
   c) distinctive
   d) competitive.

   Answer: (c)   Difficulty: 1 Page: 472

12. The most difficult criteria to achieve for effective advertising to overcome consumer doubts about the truth of claims in advertising in general requires that the advertisement is:

   a) meaningful.
   b) believable.
   c) distinctive
   d) competitive.

   Answer: (b)   Difficulty: 1 Page: 472

13. In terms of execution styles, the type of advertising would have one or more people using or discussing the product in a "normal" setting is called:

   a) Slice of life
   b) Lifestyle
   c) Fantasy
   d) Testimonial

   Answer: (a)   Difficulty: 2 Page: 473

14. In terms of execution styles, the type of advertising that would show how products fit into various recreation activities is called:

   a) Slice of life
   b) Lifestyle
   c) Fantasy
   d) Testimonial

   Answer: (b)   Difficulty: 2 Page: 473

15. In terms of execution styles, which type of advertising builds a mood or image around the product, such as beauty, love, or serenity?

   a) Slice of life
   b) Lifestyle
   c) Fantasy
   d) Mood or image

   Answer: (d)   Difficulty: 2 Page: 473

16. Creating a character to represent the product is typical of which execution style of advertising?

    a) Musical
    b) Mood or image
    c) Personality symbol
    d) Fantasy

    Answer: (a)   Difficulty: 2 Page: 473

17. Which of the following is the first step in selecting advertising media?

    a) Deciding on media timing.
    b) Selecting specific media vehicles.
    c) Choosing among major media types.
    d) Deciding on reach, frequency, and impact

    Answer: (d)   Difficulty: 2 Page: 474

18. The qualitative value of an exposure through a given medium is called:

    a) reach.
    b) frequency.
    c) media timing.
    d) media impact.

    Answer: (d)   Difficulty: 2 Page: 475

19. A measure of the percentage of people in the target market who are exposed to the ad campaign during a given period of time is referred to as:

    a) frequency.
    b) reach.
    c) saturation.
    d) impact.

    Answer: (b)   Difficulty: 2 Page: 475

20. A measure of how many times the average person in the target market is exposed to the message is called:

    a) frequency.
    b) reach.
    c) saturation.
    d) impact.

    Answer: (a)   Difficulty: 2 Page: 475

21. The advantage of flexibility, timeliness, good local market coverage, broad acceptability and high believability apply to which media type?

    a) Newspapers.
    b) Television.
    c) Radio.
    d) Magazines.

    Answer: (a)   Difficulty: 2 Page: 475

22. The advantage of combining sight and sound, motion, appeals to the senses, high attention and high reach characterize which type of media?

    a) Newspapers.
    b) Television.
    c) Radio.
    d) Magazines.

    Answer: (b)   Difficulty: 2 Page: 475

23. The advantage of audience selectivity, no ad competition and personalization apply to which type of media?

    a) Newspapers.
    b) Television.
    c) Direct mail
    d) Magazines.

    Answer: (c)   Difficulty: 2 Page: 475

24. The advantage of high geographic and demographic selectivity characterize which type of media?

    a) Newspapers.
    b) Direct Mail
    c) Radio.
    d) Magazines.

    Answer: (d)   Difficulty: 2 Page: 475

25. Short life, poor reproduction quality, and small pass-along audience, are all limitations of which media type?

    a) Newspapers.
    b) Television.
    c) Radio.
    d) Magazines.

    Answer: (a)   Difficulty: 2 Page: 475

26. High absolute costs and less audience selectivity are all limitations of which media type?

    a) Newspapers.
    b) Television.
    c) Radio.
    d) Magazines.

    Answer: (b)   Difficulty: 2 Page: 475

27. Little audience selectivity and creative limitations are all limitations of which media type?

    a) Newspapers.
    b) Outdoor.
    c) Radio.
    d) Magazines.

    Answer: (b)   Difficulty: 2 Page: 475

28. In choosing among major media types, all of the following are factors media planners must consider except:

    a) media habits of target consumers
    b) nature of the product
    c) types of messages
    d) media vehicles

    Answer: (d)   Difficulty: 3 Page: 475

29. In selecting media vehicles, the media planner must balance media cost measure against several media impact factors. Which of the following is not a media impact factor?

    a) Audience quality.
    b) Audience attention.
    c) Editorial quality.
    d) Editorial experience.

    Answer: (d)   Difficulty: 3 Page: 478

30. In terms of media timing, scheduling ads evenly within a given time period refers to:

    a) continuity.
    b) pulsing.
    c) reach.
    d) frequency.

    Answer: (a)   Difficulty: 1 Page: 478

31. In terms of media timing, scheduling ads unevenly over a given time period refers to:

    a) continuity.
    b) pulsing.
    c) reach.
    d) frequency.

    Answer: (b)   Difficulty: 1 Page: 478

32. The Hallmark Company routinely concentrates its advertising around Christmas, Valentine's Day, and Mother's Day. During the rest of the year, the firm does little, or no, advertising. The scheduling approach that Hallmark uses is referred to as:

    a) continuity.
    b) pulsing.
    c) reach.
    d) frequency.

    Answer: (a)   Difficulty: 1 Page: 478

33. Which statement best describes international advertising efforts?

    a) Most international advertisers use global campaigns- the same program in each country- to achieve economies of scale.
    b) Most international advertisers spend little time considering cultural differences other than to use the language of the host country in their ads.
    c) Global advertisers use standardization to overcome differences found in various local markets.
    d) Most international advertisers develop global strategies but adapt individual programs to the needs of the local markets.

    Answer: (d)   Difficulty: 3 Page: 480

34. Short-term incentives to encourage purchase or sales of a product or service are described as:

    a) advertising.
    b) sales promotion.
    c) public relations.
    d) sales management.

    Answer: (b)   Difficulty: 1 Page: 481

35. Most analysts believe that:

    a) sales promotions build long-term consumer loyalty.
    b) sales promotions produce only short-term sales.
    c) advertising should take a back seat to sales promotions.
    d) advertising is better than sales promotion in building brand loyalty.

    Answer: (b)   Difficulty: 2 Page: 481

36. Which of the following factors have contributed to the rapid growth of sales promotion in consumer markets?

    a) Product managers face pressure to increase current sales.
    b) The company faces more competition and competing brand are less differentiated.
    c) Advertising efficiency has declined.
    d) All of the above.

    Answer: (d)   Difficulty: 2 Page: 482

37. Which type of sales promotion tool uses samples, coupons, sweepstakes and games?

    a) Consumer promotion.
    b) Trade promotion.
    c) Sales force promotion.
    d) Product promotion.

    Answer: (a)   Difficulty: 1 Page: 483

38. Which type of sales promotion tool uses buying allowances, push money, and free goods?

    a) Consumer promotion.
    b) Trade promotion.
    c) Sales force promotion.
    d) Product promotion.

    Answer: (b)   Difficulty: 1 Page: 483

39. Which type of sales promotion tool uses bonuses, contests, and rallies?

    a) Consumer promotion.
    b) Trade promotion.
    c) Sales force promotion.
    d) Product promotion.

    Answer: (c)   Difficulty: 1 Page: 483

40. Which consumer promotion tool offers a trial amount of a product?

    a) Samples.
    b) Coupons.
    c) Point-of-purchase promotion
    d) Patronage rewards.

    Answer: (a)   Difficulty: 1 Page: 483

41. Which consumer promotion tool consists of certificates that give buyers a saving when they purchase a specified product?

    a) Rebate.
    b) Coupons.
    c) Premium.
    d) Patronage rewards.

    Answer: (b)   Difficulty: 1 Page: 484

42. To stimulate sales of a mature brand or promote early trial of a new brand, a firm could effectively use:

a) Samples.
b) Coupons.
c) Point-of-purchase promotion
d) Patronage rewards.

Answer: (b)   Difficulty: 1 Page: 483

43. A price reduction that occurs after the purchase rather than at the retail outlet is called a:

a) Samples.
b) Coupons.
c) Rebate
d) Patronage rewards.

Answer: (c)   Difficulty: 1 Page: 485

44. The type of trade promotion tool in which the manufacturer takes a fixed amount off the list price on each case purchased during a stated period of time is called a(n):

a) Discount
b) Allowance
c) Push money
d) Premium.

Answer: (a)   Difficulty: 2 Page: 487

45. The type of trade promotion tool in which manufacturers agree to reduce the price on each case purchased in return for the retailer's agreement to feature the manufacturer's products in some way is called a (n):

a) Discount
b) Allowance
c) Push money
d) Premium.

Answer: (b)   Difficulty: 2 Page: 487

46. Public relations departments' function that creates and places newsworthy information in the news media to attract attention to a person, product, or service is called:

a) Press relations.
b) Product publicity.
c) Public affairs.
d) Lobbying.

Answer: (a)   Difficulty: 2 Page: 490

47. Public relations departments' function that builds and maintains relations with legislators and government officials to influence legislation and regulation is called:

    a) Press relations.
    b) Product publicity.
    c) Public affairs.
    d) Lobbying.

    Answer: (d)   Difficulty: 2   Page: 491

48. Contributing money and time to such causes as the Special Olympics and campaigns to fight illiteracy are examples of which public relations tool?

    a) Speeches.
    b) Special events.
    c) Public service activities.
    d) Corporate identity materials.

    Answer: (c)   Difficulty: 2   Page: 493

49. The easiest measure of publicity effectiveness is:

    a) readership statistics generated.
    b) impact on sales and profit.
    c) the number of exposures in the media.
    d) change in product awareness, knowledge, and attitude.

    Answer: (c)   Difficulty: 2   Page: 494

50. The Tylenol Company has just completed a very extensive public relations campaign. The best measure of their public relations effort is:

    a) readership statistics generated.
    b) impact on sales and profit.
    c) the number of exposures in the media.
    d) change in product awareness, knowledge, and attitude.

    Answer: (b)   Difficulty: 2   Page: 494

TRUE/FALSE

51. Advertising is a good way to inform and persuade, whether the purpose is to sell Coca-Cola worldwide, however it is not effective to get consumers in developing countries to drink milk or use birth control.

    Answer: False   Difficulty: 2   Page: 466

52. The top 100 national advertisers account for more than one-fourth of all advertising.

    Answer: True   Difficulty: 2   Page: 466

53. An advertising objective is a specific communication task to be accomplished with a specific target audience during a specific period of time.

    Answer: True   Difficulty: 2   Page: 467

54. Informative advertising is used heavily when introducing a new product category.

    Answer: True   Difficulty: 2 Page: 468

55. Informative advertising is used heavily when building brand preference.

    Answer: False   Difficulty: 2 Page: 467

56. Persuasive advertising becomes more important as competition increases and the firm attempts to build selective demand.

    Answer: True   Difficulty: 2 Page: 468

57. Reminder advertising is not important for mature products.

    Answer: False   Difficulty: 2 Page: 468

58. In comparison advertising, a company directly or indirectly compares its brand with one or more brands.

    Answer: True   Difficulty: 1 Page: 468

59. Expensive Coca-Cola ads on television are designed to persuade consumers about Coca-Cola, not inform them.

    Answer: False   Difficulty: 2 Page: 468

60. A large advertising budget is a guarantee that the advertising campaign will be successful.

    Answer: False   Difficulty: 1 Page: 469

61. Advertising appeals should have three basic characteristics: they should be meaningful, believable and distinctive.

    Answer: True   Difficulty: 2 Page: 472

62. When choosing a message style, the REAL Corporation prefers to show its product in use by "real people in real situations." This firm is likely to use a slice-of-life approach.

    Answer: True   Difficulty: 1 Page: 473

63. When the National Dairy Board ad shows women exercising and talks about how milk adds to a healthy, active lifestyle, they were using the advertising execution style called mood or image.

    Answer: False   Difficulty: 2 Page: 473

64. The advertising execution style that creates a character to represent the product is called personality symbol.

    Answer: True   Difficulty: 1 Page: 474

65. When Maxwell House shows one of its buyers carefully selecting coffee beans, they were using the advertising execution style called technical expertise.

    Answer: True   Difficulty: 2 Page: 474

66. When Crest toothpaste used scientific evidence to convince buyers that Crest is better than other brands in fighting cavities, they were using the advertising execution style called testimonial evidence.

    Answer: False   Difficulty: 2 Page: 474

67. The first step in media selection is deciding on reach, frequency, and impact.

    Answer: True   Difficulty: 1 Page: 474

68. Reach is a measure of the percentage of people in the target market who are exposed to the ad campaign during a given period of time.

    Answer: True   Difficulty: 1 Page: 475

69. Frequency is the measure of how many times the average person in the target market is exposed to the message.

    Answer: True   Difficulty: 1 Page: 475

70. Media impact is the measure of the percentage of people in the target market who are exposed to the ad campaign.

    Answer: False   Difficulty: 2 Page: 475

71. The Ford Motor Company wants to maximize the percentage of people in the target market who were exposed to its latest advertising campaign. One approach is to emphasize the frequency in its promotional efforts.

    Answer: False   Difficulty: 3 Page: 475

72. The media habits of target consumers will affect media choice for advertising.

    Answer: True   Difficulty: 1 Page: 475

73. A media vehicle is a specific media within each general media type.

    Answer: True   Difficulty: 1 Page: 477

74. Continuity means scheduling ads evenly within a given period.

    Answer: True   Difficulty: 1 Page: 478

75. Pulsing means scheduling ads unevenly over a given time period.

    Answer: True   Difficulty: 1 Page: 478

76. An advertiser who wishes to maintain a constant pressure in the media prefers the pulsing approach to scheduling rather than continuity.

    Answer: False   Difficulty: 2   Page: 478

77. Copy testing tells whether the ad is communicating well.

    Answer: True   Difficulty: 1   Page: 478

78. It is possible to measure the sales effects of advertising by comparing past sales with past advertising expenditures.

    Answer: True   Difficulty: 2   Page: 478

79. A good rule of thumb for international advertising decisions is to "think globally but act locally."

    Answer: True   Difficulty: 1   Page: 489

80. Sales promotion consists of short-term incentives to encourage purchase or sales of a product or service.

    Answer: True   Difficulty: 2   Page: 481

81. Sales promotions produce only short-term sales.

    Answer: False   Difficulty: 1   Page: 482

82. Samples, coupons, rebates, prices-off, premiums, and contest are all examples of trade promotion tools.

    Answer: False   Difficulty: 2   Page: 483

83. Sales promotions should be consumer relationship building, rather than creating short-term sales volume.

    Answer: False   Difficulty: 2   Page: 483

84. In many consumer packaged-goods companies, sales promotion accounts for 75 percent or more of all marketing expenditures.

    Answer: True   Difficulty: 2   Page: 482

85. Increasingly, competitors are using public relations to differentiate their offers.

    Answer: False   Difficulty: 2   Page: 482

86. Rebates are like coupons except that the price reduction occurs after the purchase rather than at the retail outlet.

    Answer: True   Difficulty: 2   Page: 485

87. Price packs offer consumers savings off the regular price of a product and are more effective than coupons in stimulating short-term sales.

    Answer: True   Difficulty: 2 Page: 486

88. Premiums are goods offered either free or at low cost as an incentive to buy a product.

    Answer: True   Difficulty: 1 Page: 486

89. Most sales-promotion dollars are directed to retailers and wholesalers than to consumers.

    Answer: True   Difficulty: 2 Page: 487

90. Public relations is important in building good relations with the company's various publics, however, it plays a limited role in product promotion.

    Answer: False   Difficulty: 2 Page: 490

91. Public relations is considered a marketing stepchild because it cannot be used effectively to enhance sales and profits.

    Answer: False   Difficulty: 2 Page: 492

92. Despite its potential strengths, public relations often is described as a marketing stepchild because of its limited and scattered use.

    Answer: True   Difficulty: 2 Page: 492

93. The easiest measure of publicity effectiveness is the number of exposures in the "clippings book" that shows all the media that carried news about the product.

    Answer: True   Difficulty: 2 Page: 494

94. Sales and profit, if obtainable, is the best measure of public relations effort.

    Answer: True   Difficulty: 2 Page: 494

ESSAY

95. Describe the roles of advertising, sales promotion, and public relations in the promotion mix.

    Answer:
    Each is part of the tools for mass-promotion. Advertising builds awareness, interest, and brand loyalty. Sales promotion provides short-term incentives to buy now. Public relations is used to create a favorable image. Effective promotion strategy considers the strengths and limitations of each mass-promotion tool and assigns specific, coordinated objectives for each in support of an overall corporate objective.

    Difficulty: 2 Page: 466

96. Identify and discuss the different types of advertising used to meet advertising objectives.

Answer:
Advertising objectives can be classified by primary purpose- whether the aim is to inform, persuade, or remind. Informative advertising is used to inform consumers about a new product or feature and to build primary demand. Persuasive advertising is used to build selective demand for a brand by persuading consumers that it offers the best quality for their money. Comparison advertising compares one brand directly or indirect with one or more other brands. Reminder advertising is used to keep consumers thinking about a product.

Difficulty: 2 Page: 468

97. One of the major decisions in advertising strategy is to select advertising media. Identify and discuss the major steps in media selection.

Answer:
The major steps in media selection are 1) deciding on reach, frequency, and impact; 2) choosing among major media types; 3) selecting specific media vehicles; and 4) deciding on media timing.

Difficulty: 2 Page: 474

98. Distinguish between reach, frequency and impact. Which would be most important to firms seeking to build awareness? Why?

Answer:
Reach is a measure of the percentage of people in the target market who are exposed to the ad campaign during a given period of time. Frequency is a measure of how many times the average person in the target market is exposed to the message. Media impact is the qualitative value of a message exposed through a given medium.

Difficulty: 2 Page: 475

99. Discuss the factors that have contributed to the rapid growth of sales promotion.

Answer:
First, inside the company, product managers face greater pressures to increase their current sales, and promotion is viewed as an effective short-run sales tool. Second, externally, the company faces more competition and competing brands are less differentiated. Third, advertising efficiency has declined because of rising costs, media clutter, and legal restraints. Finally, consumers have become more deal oriented, and retailers are demanding more deals from manufacturers.

Difficulty: 2 Page: 482

100. Explain how companies use public relations to communicate with their publics.

Answer:
Public relations seeks to manage the presentation of the corporate image thorugh press relations, product publicity, corporate communications, and lobbying efforts. Major tools for reaching various publics include news, speeches, special events, written materials, audio-visual materials, corporate identity materials, and public service activities.

Difficulty: 2 Page: 492

Chapter 15

1. The analysis, planning, implementation, and control of sales-force activities is called:

   a) sales-force training.
   b) sales-force motivation.
   c) sales-force strategy.
   d) sales-force management.

   Answer: (d)   Difficulty: 1 Page: 504

2. Which of the following is a role of personal selling?

   a) Represent the company to customers.
   b) Represent customers to the company.
   c) Carry out market research and intelligence work.
   d) All of the above.

   Answer: (d)   Difficulty: 2 Page: 504

3. The type of sales-force structure where each salesperson is assigned to an exclusive geographic area and sells the company's full line of products or services to all customers in that territory is called:

   a) territorial sales-force.
   b) product sales-force.
   c) customer sales-force.
   d) complex sales-force.

   Answer: (a)   Difficulty: 2 Page: 505

4. All of the following are advantages of territorial sales-force structures except:

   a) It clearly defines the salesperson's job.
   b) It helps keep travel expenses to a minimum.
   c) It helps the salesperson get the "big picture" view of the company's operations.
   d) It increases the salesperson's desire to build local business relationships.

   Answer: (c)   Difficulty: 2 Page: 505

5. A sales-force organization under which sales-people specialize in selling only a portion of the company's products or lines is called:

   a) territorial sales-force.
   b) product sales-force.
   c) customer sales-force.
   d) complex sales-force.

   Answer: (b)   Difficulty: 2 Page: 505

6. The Giant Corporation markets numerous unrelated products--most of which are highly complex. Which sales-force organization is Giant most likely to use?

   a) territorial sales-force.
   b) product sales-force.
   c) customer sales-force.
   d) complex sales-force.

   Answer: (b)   Difficulty: 2 Page: 505

7. A sales-force organization under which sales-people specialize in selling only to certain customers or industries is called:

   a) territorial sales-force.
   b) product sales-force.
   c) customer sales-force.
   d) complex sales-force.

   Answer: (c)   Difficulty: 2 Page: 505

8. Setting up separate sales-forces for different industries, for serving current customers versus finding new ones, or for major accounts versus regular accounts is typical of which sales-force structure?

   a) Territorial sales-force.
   b) Product sales-force.
   c) Customer sales-force.
   d) Complex sales-force.

   Answer: (c)   Difficulty: 2 Page: 505

9. When different clients exhibit widely varied needs, the firm will probably utilize the sales-force structure called:

   a) Territorial sales-force.
   b) Product sales-force.
   c) Customer sales-force.
   d) Complex sales-force.

   Answer: (c)   Difficulty: 2 Page: 505

10. The greatest disadvantage of the customer sales-force structure arises when:

    a) Products are highly similar.
    b) Customers have widely varied needs.
    c) Customers buy in large quantities.
    d) Customers are geographically dispersed.

    Answer: (d)   Difficulty: 2 Page: 505

11. In determining sales-force size, when a company groups accounts into different classes and then determines how many sales-people are needed to call on them the desired number of times, it is called the:

    a) workload approach.
    b) field sales size approach.
    c) sales-force size approach.
    d) company call approach.

    Answer: (a)   Difficulty: 2 Page: 506

12. The total number of sales calls per year divided by the average number of calls each salesperson makes is used to determine the sales-force size based on:

    a) division.
    b) call-ratio.
    c) workload.
    d) call productivity.

    Answer: (c)   Difficulty: 2 Page: 506

13. The APPLE Corporation estimates that its sales-force should make 55,000 calls per year. If each salesperson makes 1,000 calls per year, according to the workload approach the company needs how many salespeople?

    a) 60
    b) 55
    c) 50
    d) 40

    Answer: (b)   Difficulty: 3 Page: 506

14. Using the telephone to sell directly to consumer is called:

    a) team selling.
    b) call selling.
    c) telemarketing.
    d) sales assistants.

    Answer: (c)   Difficulty: 1 Page: 507

15. When members from the sales, marketing, engineering, finance, technical support, and even upper management work together to service large, complex accounts, they are using:

    a) call selling.
    b) team selling.
    c) telemarketing.
    d) sales assistants.

    Answer: (b)   Difficulty: 1 Page: 507

16. The first part of a training program should concentrate on:

    a) customer's and competitors' characteristics.
    b) sales presentations.
    c) company information.
    d) field procedures and responsibilities.

    Answer: (c)   Difficulty: 2 Page: 512

17. Training programs for new salespeople have which of the following as goals?

    a) Describing the company's history and objectives.
    b) Showing how the products are produced and how they work.
    c) Becoming informed about customers' and competitors' characteristics.
    d) All of the above.

    Answer: (d)   Difficulty: 2 Page: 512

18. In terms of sales-force compensation, a salary refers to which element in the compensation mix?

    a) The fixed amount.
    b) The variable amount.
    c) The expense allowance.
    d) The fringe benefits.

    Answer: (a)   Difficulty: 1 Page: 514

19. In terms of sales-force compensation, commissions or bonuses refers to which element in the compensation mix?

    a) The fixed amount.
    b) The variable amount.
    c) The expense allowance.
    d) The fringe benefits.

    Answer: (b)   Difficulty: 1 Page: 514

20. The element of the compensation mix that repays salespeople for undertaking job-related selling efforts is called:

    a) The fixed amount.
    b) The variable amount.
    c) The expense allowance.
    d) The fringe benefits.

    Answer: (c)   Difficulty: 1 Page: 514

21. Paid vacations, sickness or accident benefits, pensions, and life insurance are all examples of which element in the compensation mix?

    a) The fixed amount.
    b) The variable amount.
    c) The expense allowance.
    d) The fringe benefits.

    Answer: (d)   Difficulty: 1 Page: 514

22. A study of sales-force compensation plans showed that the most commonly used compensation plan is:

    a) straight salary.
    b) straight commission.
    c) salary plus commission.
    d) salary plus commission plus bonus.

    Answer: (c)   Difficulty: 3 Page: 514

23. Through supervision, a company:

    a) Keeps a suspicious eye on salespeople.
    b) Commands and controls the actions of salespeople.
    c) Directs and motivates the sales force to do a better job.
    d) Seeks to weed out the weak from the strong salespeople.

    Answer: (c)   Difficulty: 3 Page: 515

24. A company directs and motivates the sales-force to do a better job through:

    a) training.
    b) supervision.
    c) counseling.
    d) compensation.

    Answer: (b)   Difficulty: 2 Page: 515

25. The standards that a salesperson must meet in sales and how those sales should be divided among the company's products are stated in:

    a) sales forecasts.
    b) performance objectives.
    c) sales goals.
    d) sales quotas.

    Answer: (d)   Difficulty: 2 Page: 517

26. Sales-force compensation is often related to how well salespeople meet their:

    a) schedules.
    b) quotas.
    c) call norms.
    d) activity plan.

    Answer: (b)   Difficulty: 2 Page: 517

27. Since sales quotas are often used to challenge the sales-force toward extra effort, sales quotas should be:

    a) set so the majority of the sales-force can achieve them easily.
    b) set according to the individual abilities of the sales-force.
    c) set higher than the sales forecast to encourage salespeople to give best effort.
    d) set so the company makes its sales forecast.

    Answer: (c)   Difficulty: 3 Page: 517

28. Direction and motivation are part of which area of sales-force management decisions?

    a) Evaluating
    b) Supervising.
    c) Training.
    d) Recruitment and selection.

    Answer: (b)   Difficulty: 2 Page: 515

29. Ensuring that salespeople learn to use time efficiently is part of which sales-force management area?

    a) Evaluating
    b) Supervising.
    c) Training.
    d) Recruitment and selection.

    Answer: (b)   Difficulty: 2 Page: 515

30. Developing customer targets and call norms falls under which area of sales-force management area?

    a) Evaluating
    b) Supervising.
    c) Training.
    d) Recruitment and selection.

    Answer: (b)   Difficulty: 2 Page: 515

31. Sales reports and work plans may be reviewed in relation to which sales-force management decision area?

    a) Evaluating
    b) Supervising.
    c) Training.
    d) Recruitment and selection.

    Answer: (a)   Difficulty: 2 Page: 518

32. Requiring salespeople to draft annual territory marketing plans falls under which sales-force management decision area?

    a) Evaluating
    b) Supervising.
    c) Training.
    d) Recruitment and selection.

    Answer: (a)   Difficulty: 2 Page: 518

33. Many companies require their salespeople to outline plans for building new accounts and increasing sales from existing accounts in a report called:

    a) annual sales report.
    b) annual work plan.
    c) annual route plan.
    d) territory marketing plan.

    Answer: (d)   Difficulty: 2 Page: 518

34. Robert Smythe has just completed a customer contact. To provide management with information on the results of that contact, and to record information that might be useful in future contacts, Bob will probably file a:

    a) quota report.
    b) call report.
    c) route report.
    d) territory report.

    Answer: (b)   Difficulty: 1 Page: 518

35. Salespeople write up their completed activities on:

    a) sales quota reports.
    b) expense reports.
    c) call reports.
    d) annual territory marketing plans.

    Answer: (c)   Difficulty: 2 Page: 518

36. The type of report salespeople file for which they are wholly or partly repaid is called the:

    a) sales report.
    b) expense report.
    c) call report.
    d) order report.

    Answer: (b)   Difficulty: 1 Page: 518

37. Sales reports, call reports, annual territory marketing plans, expense reports, and work plans may all supply the raw data from which sales management can make which type of decision?

    a) Evaluate salespeople.
    b) Recruit and select salespeople.
    c) Train salespeople.
    d) Supervise salespeople.

    Answer: (a)   Difficulty: 2   Page: 518

38. Which type of sales-force evaluation method looks at a salesperson's knowledge of the company, products, customers, competitors, territory, and tasks?

    a) Quantitative evaluation.
    b) Qualitative evaluation.
    c) Goal-based evaluation.
    d) Sales-based evaluation.

    Answer: (b)   Difficulty: 2   Page: 519

39. The step in the selling process that identifies qualified potential customers is called:

    a) prospecting
    b) preapproach.
    c) approach.
    d) closing.

    Answer: (a)   Difficulty: 1   Page: 520

40. The step in the selling process where the salesperson learns as much as possible about a prospective customer before making a sales call is called:

    a) prospecting
    b) preapproach.
    c) approach.
    d) closing.

    Answer: (b)   Difficulty: 1   Page: 520

41. Building referral sources from suppliers and dealers to identify potential customers is part of which step in the selling process?

    a) Prospecting.
    b) Preapproach.
    c) Approach.
    d) Handling objections.

    Answer: (a)   Difficulty: 1   Page: 520

42. Screening out good leads from poor ones occurs in which stage in the selling process?

    a) Prospecting.
    b) Preapproach.
    c) Approach.
    d) Handling objections.

    Answer: (a)   Difficulty: 1 Page: 520

43. Setting call objectives is done during which stage in the selling process?

    a) Prospecting.
    b) Preapproach.
    c) Approach.
    d) Handling objections.

    Answer: (b)   Difficulty: 1 Page: 520

44. Meeting and greeting the buyer is done during which stage in the selling process?

    a) Prospecting.
    b) Preapproach.
    c) Approach.
    d) Handling objections.

    Answer: (c)   Difficulty: 1 Page: 521

45. Telling the product "story" to the buyer occurs during which stage in the selling process?

    a) Prospecting.
    b) Preapproach.
    c) Approach.
    d) Presentation

    Answer: (d)   Difficulty: 1 Page: 521

46. The step in the selling process where customer problems and concerns need to be addressed is called:

    a) Prospecting.
    b) Preapproach.
    c) Approach.
    d) Handling objections.

    Answer: (d)   Difficulty: 1 Page: 522

47. The step in the selling process where the salesperson asks for the customer's order is the:

    a) Presentation.
    b) Handling objections.
    c) Closing.
    d) Follow-up.

    Answer: (c)   Difficulty: 1 Page: 522

48. The step in the selling process that is necessary if the salesperson wants to ensure customer satisfaction and repeat business is the:

    a) Presentation.
    b) Handling objections.
    c) Closing.
    d) Follow-up.

    Answer: (d)   Difficulty: 1   Page: 522

49. Relationship marketing is:

    a) An easy and natural evolution from transaction oriented marketing.
    b) Readily available to most industrial sellers seeking stable profits.
    c) More important in domestic markets than international markets.
    d) An ongoing commitment to the buyer to meet their future product and service needs.

    Answer: (d)   Difficulty: 2   Page: 522

TRUE/FALSE

50. Sales-force management is the analysis, planning, implementation, and control of sales-force activities.

    Answer: True   Difficulty: 1   Page: 504

51. By definition, the term "salesperson" is limited to individuals who make personal contacts with present or potential customers for the purpose of selling a product or service.

    Answer: False   Difficulty: 2   Page: 502

52. Salespeople should be concerned with more than just producing sales, they must consider customer satisfaction and company profit as well.

    Answer: True   Difficulty: 1   Page: 504

53. In the territorial sales-force structure, each salesperson is assigned to an exclusive territory in which to sell the company's full line of products or services.

    Answer: True   Difficulty: 1   Page: 505

54. In the territorial sales-force structure, travel expenses are typically large.

    Answer: False   Difficulty: 1   Page: 505

55. Under a product sales-force structure, the sales-force sells along product lines.

    Answer: True   Difficulty: 1   Page: 505

56. Organizing the sales-force along customer or industry lines is typical of a customer sales-force structure.

    Answer: True   Difficulty: 1   Page: 505

57. When a company sells a wide variety of products to many types of customers over a broad geographical area, it never combines sales-force structures.

    Answer: False   Difficulty: 2   Page: 506

58. The workload approach is a method of setting the sales-force size in which the company groups accounts into different classes and then determines how many salespeople are needed to call on them the desired number of times.

    Answer: True   Difficulty: 2   Page: 506

59. Inside salespeople typically conduct business from their offices via telephone or visits from prospective buyers, while outside salespeople travel to call on customers.

    Answer: True   Difficulty: 1   Page: 506

60. It is usually less expensive to recruit and train new salespeople than to pay the salaries demanded by experienced sales representatives.

    Answer: False   Difficulty: 2   Page: 508

61. Successful sales-forces begin with a carefully planned recruitment and selection program.

    Answer: True   Difficulty: 2   Page: 508

62. For many types of products and selling situations, telemarketing can be as effective as a personal call but less expensive.

    Answer: True   Difficulty: 2   Page: 507

63. The recruitment and selection of quality sales people has been greatly simplified by the development of universal traits that should be possessed by all sales people.

    Answer: False   Difficulty: 2   Page: 509

64. Women account for the majority of the sales-force in some industries, including lodging, banking and financial services, and health services.

    Answer: True   Difficulty: 2   Page: 509

65. When selecting new salespeople, many companies may spend anywhere from a few weeks or months to a year or more in training.

    Answer: True   Difficulty: 2   Page: 511

66. The first part of a training program describes the company's products, so sales trainees are shown how products are produced and how they work.

    Answer: False   Difficulty: 2   Page: 512

67. The sales-force compensation is made up of a fixed salary, expenses and fringe benefits.

    Answer: False   Difficulty: 2 Page: 514

68. Salary is the most common form of fixed amount compensation.

    Answer: True   Difficulty: 1 Page: 514

69. Commissions and bonuses are typical examples of variable amount compensation.

    Answer: True   Difficulty: 1 Page: 514

70. Expense allowances repay salespeople for job-related expenses. This allows salespeople to undertake needed and desirable selling efforts.

    Answer: True   Difficulty: 1 Page: 514

71. Expense allowances typically discourage salespeople from undertaking needed and desirable selling efforts.

    Answer: False   Difficulty: 1 Page: 514

72. The most popular sales-force compensation plan is salary plus commission.

    Answer: True   Difficulty: 2 Page: 514

73. If the marketing goal is to maximize profitability of current accounts, the compensation plan might contain a larger base salary component with additional incentives based on current account sales or customer satisfaction.

    Answer: True   Difficulty: 2 Page: 515

74. An annual call schedule shows which customers and prospects to call on in which months and which activities to carry out.

    Answer: True   Difficulty: 2 Page: 515

75. On average, actual face-to-face selling time accounts for only 30 percent of total working time.

    Answer: True   Difficulty: 2 Page: 515

76. The most important way for management to get information about its salespeople is in the annual territory marketing plan.

    Answer: False   Difficulty: 2 Page: 518

77. The creation of an annual territory marketing plan casts salespeople in the role of marketing managers and profit centers.

    Answer: True   Difficulty: 2 Page: 518

78. In organizations that hold their salespeople in high esteem, typically there is less turnover and higher performance.

   Answer: True   Difficulty: 2   Page: 517

79. Positive incentives describe the feeling that salespeople have about their opportunities, value, and reward for good performance within the company.

   Answer: False   Difficulty: 2   Page: 517

80. Generally, sales quotas are set higher than they could actually be realized in order to encourage sales managers and salespeople to give their best effort.

   Answer: False   Difficulty: 2   Page: 517

81. Most companies take a profit-oriented approach to personal selling.

   Answer: False   Difficulty: 2   Page: 519

82. Most salespeople spend much of their time getting new customers and obtaining orders from them.

   Answer: False   Difficulty: 2   Page: 520

83. Identifying and qualifying potential customers is the first step in the selling process.

   Answer: True   Difficulty: 1   Page: 520

84. During the preapproach, the salesperson identifies and qualifies potential customers.

   Answer: False   Difficulty: 1   Page: 520

85. During the preapproach step, the salesperson should know how to meet and greet the buyer and get the relationship off to a good start.

   Answer: False   Difficulty: 2   Page: 521

86. The salesperson tells the product "story" to the buyer during the presentation step of the personal selling process.

   Answer: True   Difficulty: 2   Page: 521

87. Using a need-satisfaction approach, the salesperson investigates the customer's needs by getting the customer to do most of the talking.

   Answer: True   Difficulty: 2   Page: 521

88. If the customer has an objection during the sales presentation, this clearly indicates that the salesperson needs additional training.

   Answer: False   Difficulty: 2   Page: 522

89. Some salespeople have trouble closing a sale due to a lack of confidence.

    Answer: True   Difficulty: 2 Page: 522

90. In the last step of the selling process, the salesperson asks for the customer's order.

    Answer: False   Difficulty: 2 Page: 522

91. To ensure customer satisfaction and repeat business, the salesperson should follow-up the sale.

    Answer: True   Difficulty: 1 Page: 522

92. Relationship marketing emphasizes maintaining profitable long-term relationships with customers by creating superior customer value and satisfaction.

    Answer: True   Difficulty: 2 Page: 522

ESSAY

93. Identify the six major sales-force management steps.

    Answer:
    The major steps are 1) Designing sales force strategy and structure, 2) Recruiting and selecting salespeople, 3) Training salespeople, 4) Compensating salespeople, 5) Supervising salespeople, 6) Evaluating salespeople.

    Difficulty: 2 Page: 504

94. Explain how companies recruit, select, and train salespeople.

    Answer:
    Recruitment and selection are based upon the company's perception about what type of person will be successful representing the company. Personnel looks at applications, prospects from employees, place ads, interviews college students. Training is increasingly seen as an investment and may run several months, even more than a year, with planned continuing development during the salesperson's tenure with the company.

    Difficulty: 2 Page: 508-512

95. Explain the different methods used by companies to compensate salespeople.

    Answer:
    Compensation is made up of several elements- a fixed amount, a variable amount, expenses, and fringe benefits. The straight salary approach provides the ultimate in stable and predictable income--but, compensation is not directly tied to sales effort or effectiveness. Straight commission ties compensation to sales directly--however, it may lead to over-aggressive selling and neglect of non-selling duties. In order to offer both stability and motivation, most firms employ a combination of straight salary and commission or bonus.

    Difficulty: 3 Page: 514

96. Selling is increasingly becoming a "team" effort. Why is this true? What factors determine the composition of the sales team?

Answer:
As products have become more sophisticated, and completion more intense, it has become increasingly difficult for the sales-force to handle the complete task of obtaining and maintaining customer satisfaction. In even the most routine sales transactions, the sales-force is dependent upon office staff for accurate order processing and billing, the shipping department for efficient delivery, and customer service for prompt attention to and resolution of complaints. For larger and/or more important sales, the team may include company engineers, technical specialists, and/or management personnel. The composition of the sales team is dictated by the size of the sale, the technical complexities involved, the importance of the client to the seller, and the opportunity for profitable long-term relationships.

Difficulty: 3

97. Identify and describe the steps in the selling process.

Answer:
There are seven major steps in the selling process. Prospecting and qualifying involves identifying qualified potential customers. Preapproach involves learning about the target customer. Approach meets the buyer and gets things off to a good start. Presentation tells the story to the buyer. Handling objections solves logical and psychological problems. Closing asks for the order. Follow-up ensures contact for satisfaction and repeat business.

98. Briefly contrast relationship marketing and transaction oriented marketing. Discuss the benefits associated with relationship marketing.

Answer:
The goal of transaction oriented marketing is to help salespeople close a specific sale with a customer. Relationship marketing is the process of creating, maintaining, and enhancing strong, value-laden relationships with customers and other stakeholder. Marketers who use relationship marketing call or visit clients frequently, make useful suggestions about how their clients can improve their business, they take their clients to dinner, and take an interest in the customer as a person.

Chapter 16

1. A _____ is one in which the competitive positions of firms in given local or national markets are affected by their global positions.

   a) global industry
   b) domestic industry
   c) national industry
   d) competitive industry

   Answer: (a)   Difficulty: 1   Page: 531

2. A global firm:

   a) operates in more than one country.
   b) gains research and development advantages over domestic competitors.
   c) has marketing and financial advantages over domestic competitors.
   d) All of the above.

   Answer: (d)   Difficulty: 1   Page: 531

3. A firm that by operating in more than one country gains R&D, production, marketing and financial advantages in its costs and reputation is called a(n):

   a) international firm.
   b) foreign-owned.
   c) global firm.
   d) multinational firm.

   Answer: (c)   Difficulty: 1   Page: 531

4. The first decision that a company faces in international marketing is:

   a) deciding whether to go international.
   b) deciding which markets to enter.
   c) looking at the global marketing environment.
   d) deciding how to enter the market.

   Answer: (c)   Difficulty: 2   Page: 531

5. A tax levied by a government against certain imported products is called a(n)

   a) tariff
   b) quota
   c) embargo
   d) trade bill

   Answer: (a)   Difficulty: 1   Page: 532

6. When an importing country sets limits on the amount of goods that a foreign country will accept in certain product categories. it is called a(n):

   a) tariff
   b) quota
   c) embargo
   d) trade limit

   Answer: (b)   Difficulty: 1 Page: 532

7. When an importing country totally bans some kinds of imports, it is called a(n):

   a) tariff
   b) quota
   c) embargo
   d) trade limit

   Answer: (c)   Difficulty: 1 Page: 532

8. International trade system devices that limit the amount of foreign exchange and the exchange rate against other currencies are called:

   a) protectionism.
   b) exchange controls.
   c) exchange facilitators.
   d) nontariff trade barriers.

   Answer: (b)   Difficulty: 2 Page: 532

9. Biases against U.S. company bids or restrictive product standards that discriminate against American product features are called:

   a) exchange controls.
   b) product-origin indexing.
   c) dumping.
   d) nontariff trade barriers.

   Answer: (d)   Difficulty: 2 Page: 532

10. Nonmonetary barriers to foreign products such as biases against a foreign company's bids or product standards that discriminate a foreign company's product features are called:

    a) exchange controls.
    b) product-origin indexing.
    c) dumping.
    d) nontariff trade barriers.

    Answer: (d)   Difficulty: 2 Page: 532

11. Groups of nations organized to work toward common goals in the regulation of international trade are called:

    a) multinationals.
    b) economic communities.
    c) world unions.
    d) cartel.

    Answer: (b)   Difficulty: 2   Page: 533

12. In the global marketplace, the economic environmental factor that shapes its product and service needs, income levels, and employment levels is called the:

    a) industrial structure.
    b) industrial economy.
    c) business structure.
    d) business economy.

    Answer: (a)   Difficulty: 1   Page: 536

13. Which of the following types of economies offer the least attractive opportunity for foreign trade?

    a) raw material exporting economies
    b) industrializing economies
    c) subsistence economies
    d) industrializing economies

    Answer: (c)   Difficulty: 2   Page: 536

14. The type of industrial structure where the vast majority of people engage in simple agriculture is called:

    a) raw material exporting economies
    b) industrializing economies
    c) subsistence economies
    d) industrializing economies

    Answer: (c)   Difficulty: 2   Page: 536

15. The type of industrial structure characterized by being rich in one or more natural resources but poor in other ways is called:

    a) raw material exporting economies
    b) industrializing economies
    c) subsistence economies
    d) industrializing economies

    Answer: (a)   Difficulty: 2   Page: 536

16. The type of industrial structure where manufacturing accounts for 10 to 20 percent of the country's economy is called:

    a) raw material exporting economies
    b) industrializing economies
    c) subsistence economies
    d) industrializing economies

    Answer: (b)   Difficulty: 2   Page: 536

17. The type of industrial structure that is a major exporter of manufactured goods and investment funds is called:

    a) raw material exporting economies
    b) industrializing economies
    c) subsistence economies
    d) industrializing economies

    Answer: (d)   Difficulty: 2   Page: 536

18. Which type of market structure is characterized by a new rich class and a small but growing middle class?

    a) Raw material exporting economies
    b) Industrializing economies
    c) Subsistence economies
    d) Industrializing economies

    Answer: (b)   Difficulty: 2   Page: 536

19. The two economic factors that reflect a country's attractiveness as a market are:

    a) industrial structure and income distribution.
    b) industrial structure and political structure.
    c) industrial structure and political stability.
    d) industrial structure and monetary regulations.

    Answer: (a)   Difficulty: 2   Page: 536

20. Which of the following is a factor of the political-legal environment to consider when doing business in a foreign country?

    a) Attitudes toward international buying.
    b) Government bureaucracy.
    c) Political stability
    d) All of the above.

    Answer: (d)   Difficulty: 2   Page: 537

21. When doing business in a foreign environments, all of the following are factors to consider in the political-legal environment except:

    a) attitudes toward international buying.
    b) government bureaucracy.
    c) political stability.
    d) income distribution.

    Answer: (d)   Difficulty: 2 Page: 537

22. When governments sometimes change hands violently or that a foreign government may seize international investments without warning is characteristic of which factor in the international political-legal environment?

    a) Attitudes toward international buying.
    b) Government bureaucracy.
    c) Political stability
    d) Income distribution.

    Answer: (c)   Difficulty: 2 Page: 537

23. The type of international trade where the buyer pays the seller with other items instead of cash is called:

    a) value trade.
    b) barter.
    c) countertrade.
    d) counterpurchase.

    Answer: (c)   Difficulty: 2 Page: 538

24. The type of international trade where the seller receives full payment in cash but agrees to spend some portion of the money in the other country within a stated time period is called:

    a) barter.
    b) buy-back.
    c) countertrade.
    d) counterpurchase.

    Answer: (d)   Difficulty: 2 Page: 538

25. The type of countertrade that involves the direct exchange of goods or services is called:

    a) barter.
    b) buy-back.
    c) countertrade.
    d) counterpurchase.

    Answer: (a)   Difficulty: 2 Page: 538

26. When Goodyear provided China with materials and training for a printing plant in exchange for finished labels, Goodyear is practicing which international trade transaction?

    a) barter.
    b) buy-back.
    c) countertrade.
    d) counterpurchase.

    Answer: (b)   Difficulty: 2 Page: 538

27. The international business environmental factor that considers each country's own folkways, norms, and taboos is called:

    a) economic environment.
    b) political-legal environment.
    c) cultural environment.
    d) competitive environment.

    Answer: (c)   Difficulty: 1 Page: 538

28. Which of the following is a reason for deciding to go international?

    a) Foreign markets present higher profit opportunities.
    b) Domestic market might be shrinking.
    c) Reduce its risk of dependence on any one market.
    d) All of the above.

    Answer: (d)   Difficulty: 2 Page: 539

29. In terms of indicators of market potential for international business, the size of the population and the rate of population growth refer to which of the following:

    a) demographic characteristics.
    b) economic characteristics.
    c) sociocultural factors.
    d) geographic factors.

    Answer: (a)   Difficulty: 1 Page: 541

30. In terms of indicators of market potential for international business, the physical size of a country and its climate conditions refer to which of the following?

    a) Demographic characteristics.
    b) Economic characteristics.
    c) Sociocultural factors.
    d) Geographic factors.

    Answer: (d)   Difficulty: 1 Page: 541

31. GNP per capita and income distribution correspond to which international indicator of market potential?

    a) Demographic characteristics.
    b) Economic characteristics.
    c) Sociocultural factors.
    d) Geographic factors.

    Answer: (b)   Difficulty: 1 Page: 541

32. Education levels refers to which international indicator of market potential?

    a) Demographic characteristics.
    b) Economic characteristics.
    c) Sociocultural factors.
    d) Technological factors

    Answer: (d)   Difficulty: 1 Page: 541

33. Dominant values and lifestyle patterns correspond to which international indicator of market potential?

    a) Demographic characteristics.
    b) Economic characteristics.
    c) Sociocultural factors.
    d) Technological factors

    Answer: (c)   Difficulty: 1 Page: 541

34. Industry priorities refers to which international indicator of market potential?

    a) Demographic characteristics.
    b) Economic characteristics.
    c) Sociocultural factors.
    d) National goals and plans

    Answer: (d)   Difficulty: 1 Page: 541

35. The simplest way to enter a foreign market is through:

    a) exporting
    b) joint venturing
    c) direct ownership
    d) licensing

    Answer: (a)   Difficulty: 1 Page: 541

36. Working through independent international marketing intermediaries is called:

    a) licensing.
    b) direct exporting.
    c) indirect exporting.
    d) contract manufacturing.

    Answer: (c)   Difficulty: 1 Page: 543

37. Sellers that handle their own exports are engaged in:

    a) licensing.
    b) direct exporting.
    c) indirect exporting.
    d) contract manufacturing.

    Answer: (b)   Difficulty: 1 Page: 544

38. Joining with foreign companies to produce or market products or services is called:

    a) direct exporting.
    b) joint venturing.
    c) direct investment.
    d) joint ownership.

    Answer: (b)   Difficulty: 1 Page: 544

39. When a foreign company pays a fee or royalty for the right to use a company's manufacturing process, trademark, patent, trade secret, or other item of value, it is called:

    a) direct exporting.
    b) licensing.
    c) contract manufacturing.
    d) management contracting.

    Answer: (b)   Difficulty: 2 Page: 544

40. Which of the following is a disadvantage of an international licensing agreement?

    a) It is rarely used to gain entry.
    b) It is a very risky way to enter the market.
    c) The firm has less control over the licensee than its own facilities.
    d) All of the above

    Answer: (c)   Difficulty: 1 Page: 545

41. When a company contracts with manufacturers in the foreign market to produce its product or provide its services, it is practicing which form of international business?

    a) direct exporting.
    b) licensing.
    c) contract manufacturing.
    d) management contracting.

    Answer: (c)   Difficulty: 2 Page: 545

42. When the domestic firm supplies management know-how to a foreign company that supplies the capital, it is practicing which form of international business?

    a) direct exporting.
    b) licensing.
    c) contract manufacturing.
    d) management contracting.

    Answer: (d)   Difficulty: 2 Page: 545

43. _____ is a low-risk method of getting into a foreign market, and it yields income from the beginning.

    a) Direct exporting.
    b) Licensing.
    c) Contract manufacturing.
    d) Management contracting.

    Answer: (d)   Difficulty: 2 Page: 545

44. The form of international business that consists of one company joining forces with foreign investors to create a local business in which they share ownership and control is called:

    a) direct exporting.
    b) licensing.
    c) contract manufacturing.
    d) management contracting.

    Answer: (d)   Difficulty: 2 Page: 546

45. Entering a foreign market by developing of foreign-based assembly or manufacturing facilities is called:

    a) exporting.
    b) joint venturing.
    c) joint ownership.
    d) direct investment.

    Answer: (d)   Difficulty: 2 Page: 546

46. In terms of the product/promotion strategies, marketing a product in a foreign market without any change is called:

    a) straight product extension.
    b) product adaption.
    c) product invention.
    d) communication adaption.

    Answer: (a)   Difficulty: 2 Page: 547

47. When top management tells its marketing people: "Take the product as is and find customers for it," in terms of the international product/promotion strategies they are practicing which strategy?

   a) Straight product extension.
   b) Product adaption.
   c) Product invention.
   d) Communication adaption.

   Answer: (a)   Difficulty: 2 Page: 547

48. Which international product/promotion strategy involves changing the product to meet local conditions, needs, or wants?

   a) Straight product extension.
   b) Product adaption.
   c) Product invention.
   d) Communication adaption.

   Answer: (b)   Difficulty: 2 Page: 547

49. Which international product/promotion strategy consists of creating something new for the foreign market?

   a) Straight product extension.
   b) Product adaption.
   c) Product invention.
   d) Communication adaption.

   Answer: (c)   Difficulty: 2 Page: 547

50. When a firm either charges less than its costs or less than it charges in its home market, it is said to be:

   a) dumping
   b) discounting
   c) transferring
   d) off-pricing

   Answer: (a)   Difficulty: 1 Page: 551

TRUE/FALSE

51. A global industry is one in which competitive positions of firms in given local or national markets are affected by their global positions.

   Answer: True   Difficulty: 2 Page: 531

52. The global firm sees the wold as one market.

   Answer: True   Difficulty: 2 Page: 531

53. A global firm is one that, by operating in more than one country, gains marketing, production, R&D, and financial advantages that are not available to purely domestic competitors.

    Answer: True   Difficulty: 2 Page: 531

54. Deciding whether to go international is the first major international marketing decision facing a company.

    Answer: False   Difficulty: 2 Page: 531

55. A tax levied by a government against certain imported products is called a tariff.

    Answer: True   Difficulty: 1 Page: 532

56. Tariffs are distinguished from quotas and embargoes by the fact that tariffs are used only to raise revenue while the other regulations are designed to protect domestic firms from foreign competition.

    Answer: False   Difficulty: 2 Page: 532

57. A quota sets the limit on the amount of goods that an importing country will accept in certain product categories.

    Answer: True   Difficulty: 1 Page: 532

58. Quotas are used to conserve foreign exchange and protect local industry and employment.

    Answer: True   Difficulty: 1 Page: 532

59. An embargo totally bans some kinds of imports.

    Answer: True   Difficulty: 1 Page: 532

60. An embargo is a form of quota.

    Answer: True   Difficulty: 1 Page: 532

61. Exchange controls limit the amount of foreign exchange and the exchange rate against other currencies.

    Answer: True   Difficulty: 1 Page: 532

62. Nontariff barriers to foreign products are biases against U.S. company bids or restrictive product standards that discriminate against American product features.

    Answer: True   Difficulty: 2 Page: 532

63. The General Agreement of Tariffs and Trade (GATT) is a 45-year-old treaty designed to promote world trade by reducing tariffs and other international trade barriers.

    Answer: True   Difficulty: 2 Page: 532

64. Economic communities are groups of companies within an industry that work toward common goals in the regulation of international trade.

    Answer: False   Difficulty: 2   Page: 533

65. Groups of countries that trade freely among themselves may tend to increase barriers to countries outside the zone.

    Answer: True   Difficulty: 2   Page: 535

66. A country's industrial structure shapes its product and service needs, income levels and employment levels.

    Answer: True   Difficulty: 2   Page: 536

67. Subsistence economies offer few market opportunities.

    Answer: True   Difficulty: 1   Page: 536

68. Raw-material-exporting economies are good markets for large equipment, tools and supplies, and trucks.

    Answer: True   Difficulty: 1   Page: 536

69. If there are many foreign residents and a wealthy upper class in a subsistence economy, a market for luxury goods exists.

    Answer: False   Difficulty: 2   Page: 536

70. In industrializing countries manufacturing accounts for 10 to 20 percent of the country's economy.

    Answer: True   Difficulty: 2   Page: 536

71. Industrializing economies with their varied manufacturing activities and their large middle class, make them rich markets for all sorts of goods.

    Answer: False   Difficulty: 2   Page: 536

72. Countries with subsistence economies may consist mostly of households with very low family incomes, in contrast, industrialized economies consist mostly of high income households.

    Answer: False   Difficulty: 2   Page: 536

73. Marketers cannot make a profit when the host government runs an inefficient system for helping foreign companies.

    Answer: False   Difficulty: 1   Page: 537

74. By the year 2000, countertrade may account for more than one-half of all international trade.

    Answer: True   Difficulty: 2 Page: 538

75. As countertrade involves cash transactions, it is not considered a form of countertrade.

    Answer: False   Difficulty: 2 Page: 538

76. Counterpurchase involves international sales where the seller agrees to spend a certain amount of the profits on purchase in the host country in a specified period of time.

    Answer: True   Difficulty: 2 Page: 538

77. Counterpurchase is when the seller sells a plant, equipment, or technology to another country and agrees to take payment in the resulting products.

    Answer: False   Difficulty: 2 Page: 538

78. In the global market place, business norms and behavior rarely vary from country to country.

    Answer: False   Difficulty: 2 Page: 538

79. The simplest way to enter a foreign market is through exporting.

    Answer: True   Difficulty: 1 Page: 541

80. Joint venturing involves entering foreign markets by joining with foreign companies to produce or market a product or service.

    Answer: True   Difficulty: 1 Page: 544

81. Licensing is a simple way for a manufacturer to enter international marketing.

    Answer: True   Difficulty: 1 Page: 544

82. Under contract manufacturing the domestic firm supplies the management know-how to a foreign company that supplies the capital.

    Answer: True   Difficulty: 2 Page: 545

83. Contract manufacturing is a low-risk method of getting into a foreign market, and it yields income from the beginning.

    Answer: False   Difficulty: 2 Page: 545

84. The use of standardized marketing mix will lower marketing costs--but will usually also result in lower market share and profits.

    Answer: True   Difficulty: 2 Page: 546

85. Straight product extension means marketing a product in a foreign market without any change.

    Answer: True   Difficulty: 2 Page: 547

86. Product adoption involves changing the product to meet local conditions, needs, or wants.

    Answer: True   Difficulty: 2 Page: 548

87. Product invention consists of creating something new for the foreign market.

    Answer: True   Difficulty: 2 Page: 548

88. Product invention, as its name implies, applies only to the creation of innovative, new products.

    Answer: False   Difficulty: 2 Page: 548

89. Product invention can include reintroducing another version of a product for the foreign market.

    Answer: True   Difficulty: 2 Page: 548

90. Communication adoption is a global communication strategy of fully adopting advertising messages to local markets.

    Answer: True   Difficulty: 2 Page: 540

91. Generally, companies price the same for international markets as they do for domestic ones.

    Answer: False   Difficulty: 2 Page: 548

92. Dumping occurs when a company either charges less than its costs or less than it charges in its home market.

    Answer: True   Difficulty: 2 Page: 551

93. In the whole-channel view of international marketing, the first link between the seller and the final buyer is the seller's headquarters organization.

    Answer: True   Difficulty: 2 Page: 551

94. Moving into the twenty-first century, increasingly aggressive foreign competition will force more U.S. firms to become global marketers.

    Answer: True   Difficulty: 2 Page: 553

ESSAY

95. The U.S. company looking abroad must start by understanding the international trade system. Identify and discuss the basic trade restrictions of the industrial trade system.

Answer:
International trade is regulated and restricted by various governments. A tariff is a tax levied by a foreign government against certain imported products. A quota sets limits on the amount of goods that the importing country will accept in certain product categories. An embargo, or boycott is the strongest form of quota, which totally bans some kinds of imports. Exchange controls limit the amount of foreign exchange and the exchange rate against other currencies. Nontariff barriers include bias against U.S. companies and unfair product standards that discriminate against American product features.

Difficulty: 2 Page: 532

96. Although the need for companies to go abroad is greater today than in the past, so are the risks. Outline several major problems confronting companies that go global.

Answer:
First, high debt, inflation, and unemployment in some countries have resulted in highly unstable governments and currencies. Second, governments are placing more regulations on foreign firms, such as requiring joint ownership with domestic partners. Third, foreign governments often impose high tariffs or trade barriers in order to protect their own industries. Finally, corruption is an increasing problem.

Difficulty: 3 Page: 531

97. Once a company has decided to sell in a foreign country, it must determine the best mode of entry. Describe the three key approaches to entering international markets.

Answer:
The simplest way to enter a foreign market is through exporting (indirect, direct). A second method to enter a foreign market is joint venturing- joining with foreign companies to produce or market products or services (licensing, contract manufacturing, management contracting, joint ownership). The biggest involvement in a foreign market comes through direct investment- the development of foreign-based assembly or manufacturing facilities.

Difficulty: 3 Page: 541-546

98. Identify and explain the four types of joint ventures.

Answer:
Licensing is a simple way for a manufacturer to enter international marketing. The company enters into an agreement with a licensee in the foreign market. **Contract manufacturing** is another option. The company contracts with manufacturers in the foreign market to produce its product or provide its service. Under management contracting, the domestic firm supplies management know-how to a foreign company that supplies the capital. Joint ownership ventures consist of one company joining forces with foreign investors to create a local business in which they share joint ownership and control.

Difficulty: 3 Page: 544-546

99. Explain how companies might adopt their marketing mixes for international markets.

Answer:
Marketing mix variations include standardized marketing mix and adapted marketing mix. In the case of the standardized marketing mix, the company employs the same marketing strategy for each target market. At the other extreme, the adapted marketing mix adjusts the market mix elements to each target market.

100. Identify and explain the five marketing strategies for international marketing that allows for the adoption of product and promotion to a foreign market.

Answer:
Straight product extension means marketing a product in a foreign market without any change. Product adaption involves changing the product to meet local conditions, needs, or wants. Product invention consists of creating something new for the foreign market. Communication adaption consists of fully adapting the advertising message to local markets.

Difficulty: 3   Page: 547-551

Chapter 17

1. A philosophy of customer service and mutual gain is called the:

   a) economic concept.
   b) societal marketing concept.
   c) profit maximization concept.
   d) marketing concept.

   Answer: (a)   Difficulty: 2 Page: 558

2. Consumers, consumer advocates, government agencies, and other critics have accused marketing of harming the consumers through which of the following:

   a) high prices.
   b) deceptive practices.
   c) high-pressure selling.
   d) all of the above.

   Answer: (d)   Difficulty: 1 Page: 558

3. Among the social criticisms of marketing is high prices. The longstanding charge that greedy intermediaries markup prices beyond the value of their services refers to which price-related criticism?

   a) High costs of distribution.
   b) High advertising and promotion costs.
   c) Excessive markups.
   d) Excessive salaries of retail executives.

   Answer: (a)   Difficulty: 2 Page: 559

4. Among the social criticisms of marketing is high prices. Which of the following is not a criticism regarding the high cost of distribution?

   a) Intermediaries are inefficient and poorly run.
   b) Intermediaries provide unnecessary or duplicate services.
   c) Intermediaries practice poor management and planning.
   d) All of the above are criticisms.

   Answer: (d)   Difficulty: 2 Page: 559

5. When retailers argue that intermediaries do work that would otherwise have to be done by manufacturers or consumers, they are referring to which price-related criticism?

   a) High costs of distribution.
   b) High advertising and promotion costs.
   c) Excessive markups.
   d) Excessive salaries of retail executives.

   Answer: (a)   Difficulty: 2 Page: 560

6. When retailers argue that retail competition is so intense that margins are actually quite low, they are referring to which price-related criticism?

   a) High costs of distribution.
   b) High advertising and promotion costs.
   c) Excessive markups.
   d) Excessive salaries of retail executives.

   Answer: (a)   Difficulty: 2 Page: 560

7. The criticism of marketing that packaging decisions add only psychological value to the product rather than function value relates to which social criticism of marketing?

   a) High costs of distribution.
   b) High advertising and promotion costs.
   c) Excessive markups.
   d) Excessive salaries of retail executives.

   Answer: (b)   Difficulty: 2 Page: 560

8. Pointing out that some goods are produced ahead of demand in a mass-production economy is among the responses marketers provide in answer to which of the following criticisms of marketing?

   a) High costs of distribution.
   b) High advertising and promotion costs.
   c) Excessive markups.
   d) Excessive salaries of retail executives.

   Answer: (b)   Difficulty: 2 Page: 560

9. High markups in the drug industry are PRIMARILY caused by:

   a) greed.
   b) high research and development costs.
   c) the need to pay for expensive promotion.
   d) the desire to encourage the sale of generic brands.

   Answer: (b)   Difficulty: 2 Page: 561

10. Offering a large price reduction from a phony high retail list price is a form of:

    a) deceptive pricing.
    b) deceptive promotion.
    c) deceptive packaging.
    d) planned obsolescence.

    Answer: (a)   Difficulty: 2 Page: 561

11. Pine Furniture routinely placed inflated manufacturer suggested prices on goods in order to make their own prices look lower. Pine is guilty of:

    a) deceptive pricing.
    b) deceptive promotion.
    c) deceptive packaging.
    d) planned obsolescence.

    Answer: (a)   Difficulty: 2   Page: 561

12. Overstating the product's features or performance is a form of:

    a) deceptive pricing.
    b) deceptive promotion.
    c) deceptive packaging.
    d) planned obsolescence.

    Answer: (b)   Difficulty: 2   Page: 561

13. The practice of luring the customer to the store for a bargain that is out of stock is an example of:

    a) deceptive pricing.
    b) deceptive promotion.
    c) deceptive packaging.
    d) planned obsolescence.

    Answer: (b)   Difficulty: 2   Page: 561

14. In recent years, several mail order firms have been investigated and/or charged with running rigged, or sham, contests. This practice would be BEST described as:

    a) deceptive pricing.
    b) deceptive promotion.
    c) deceptive packaging.
    d) planned obsolescence.

    Answer: (b)   Difficulty: 2   Page: 561

15. Using misleading labeling is a form of:

    a) deceptive pricing.
    b) deceptive promotion.
    c) deceptive packaging.
    d) planned obsolescence.

    Answer: (c)   Difficulty: 2   Page: 561

16. Firms that package their products while they are still warm, know that their packages will appear to be significantly less than full after the product cools. These firms often place the notice "contents sold by weight, not volume" on their packages to avoid charges of:

    a) deceptive pricing.
    b) deceptive promotion.
    c) deceptive packaging.
    d) planned obsolescence.

    Answer: (c)   Difficulty: 2 Page: 561

17. The Wheeler-Lea Act gives the FTC the power to regulate:

    a) interstate commerce.
    b) marketing ethics.
    c) unfair and deceptive acts or practices
    d) unsafe products.

    Answer: (c)   Difficulty: 2 Page: 562

18. The existence of the "three day cooling off period" that allows buyers to reconsider and cancel a contract is a form of consumer protection from:

    a) deceptive pricing.
    b) deceptive packaging.
    c) shoddy or unsafe products.
    d) high-pressure selling.

    Answer: (d)   Difficulty: 2 Page: 562

19. Marketers today understand that customer-driven quality results in customer satisfaction, which in turn creates profitable long-term customer relationships. This contradicts the social criticism leveled against marketing for:

    a) deceptive pricing.
    b) deceptive packaging.
    c) shoddy or unsafe products.
    d) high-pressure selling.

    Answer: (c)   Difficulty: 2 Page: 563

20. Designing products that would require consumers to replace them sooner than they should from a functional standpoint is typical of which criticism of marketing?

    a) Shoddy or unsafe products.
    b) High-pressure selling.
    c) Deceptive practices.
    d) Planned obsolescence.

    Answer: (d)   Difficulty: 2 Page: 563

21. The practice in the consumer electronics and computer industries to hold back attractive functional features, then introducing them later is called:

    a) Shoddy or unsafe products.
    b) High-pressure selling.
    c) Deceptive practices.
    d) Planned obsolescence.

    Answer: (d)   Difficulty: 2   Page: 563

22. The criticism of marketing that claims that the urban poor often have to shop in smaller stores that carry inferior goods and charge higher prices is called:

    a) Shoddy or unsafe products.
    b) Poor service to disadvantaged consumers.
    c) Deceptive practices.
    d) Planned obsolescence.

    Answer: (b)   Difficulty: 2   Page: 564

23. When critics charge that marketing is responsible for people judging one another by what they own rather than by who they are, they are making which complaint against marketing?

    a) Marketing emphasizes too much materialism.
    b) Marketing creates too few social goods.
    c) Marketing spreads cultural pollution.
    d) Marketing exercises too much political power.

    Answer: (a)   Difficulty: 2   Page: 566

24. When critics charge business for overselling private goods at the expense of public goods, they are making which complaint against marketing?

    a) Marketing emphasizes too much materialism.
    b) Marketing creates too few social goods.
    c) Marketing spreads cultural pollution.
    d) Marketing exercises too much political power.

    Answer: (b)   Difficulty: 2   Page: 568

25. The fact that government requires automobile manufacturers to build cars with better pollution-control systems is an example of a response to which area of criticism of marketing?

    a) Marketing emphasizes too much materialism.
    b) Marketing creates too few social goods.
    c) Marketing spreads cultural pollution.
    d) Marketing exercises too much political power.

    Answer: (b)   Difficulty: 2   Page: 568

26. The critics who charge that advertising continuously pollutes people's minds with messages of materialism, they are making which complaint against marketing?

    a) Marketing emphasizes too much materialism.
    b) Marketing creates too few social goods.
    c) Marketing spreads cultural pollution.
    d) Marketing exercises too much political power.

    Answer: (c)   Difficulty: 2 Page: 568

27. The constant bombardment of our senses by advertisements in newspapers, on radio and television, and from other sources is used to criticize marketing for:

    a) emphasizing too much materialism.
    b) creating too few social goods.
    c) spreading cultural pollution.
    d) exercising too much political power.

    Answer: (c)   Difficulty: 2 Page: 568

28. Concerns that manufacturers of harmful products such as tobacco have influence on lawmakers to the detriment of the public interest is used as evidence of which criticism of marketing?

    a) Marketing emphasizes too much materialism.
    b) Marketing creates too few social goods.
    c) Marketing spreads cultural pollution.
    d) Marketing exercises too much political power.

    Answer: (d)   Difficulty: 2 Page: 569

29. When marketing practices are criticized for reducing competition, the criticism falls under which general area of societal marketing issues?

    a) Marketing's impact on individuals.
    b) Marketing's impact on consumers.
    c) Marketing's impact on society.
    d) Marketing's impact on other businesses.

    Answer: (d)   Difficulty: 2 Page: 569

30. All of the following are benefits to society that can result from company acquisition of other companies except:

    a) the acquiring company may gain economies of scale leading to lower prices.
    b) the acquiring company may bring better management and increased efficiency.
    c) the acquisition may make the industry more competitive.
    d) the acquisition may reduce competition.

    Answer: (d)   Difficulty: 3 Page: 570

31. The two grass-root movements that have arisen to keep business in line are:

    a) ethics and morality.
    b) socialism and liberalism.
    c) unitarianism and pluralism.
    d) consumerism and environmentalism

    Answer: (d)   Difficulty: 1 Page: 570

32. The organized movement of citizens and government agencies to improve the rights and power of buyers in relation to sellers is called:

    a) Consumerism.
    b) Environmentalism
    c) Moralism
    d) Individualism.

    Answer: (a)   Difficulty: 1 Page: 570

33. Sellers have traditionally enjoyed all of the following rights except the right to:

    a) introduce any non-hazardous product.
    b) drive out less efficient competitors by any means necessary to bring about lower prices.
    c) charge any nondiscriminatory price.
    d) use any incentive schemes that are not unfair or misleading.

    Answer: (b)   Difficulty: 3 Page: 571

34. Which of the following are traditional sellers' rights?

    a) The right to charge any price.
    b) The right to spend any amount to promote the product.
    c) The right to use any buying incentive scheme.
    d) All of the above.

    Answer: (d)   Difficulty: 2 Page: 571

35. Which of the following is not among traditional buyers' rights?

    a) The right to buy a product that is offered for sale.
    b) The right to expect the product to be safe.
    c) The right to expect the product to perform as claimed.
    d) The right to be protected against questionable products and marketing practices.

    Answer: (d)   Difficulty: 2 Page: 571

36. In addition to traditional buyers' rights, consumer advocates call for all of the following consumer rights except:

    a) the right to be well-informed about important aspects of the product.
    b) the right to be protected against questionable products and marketing practices.
    c) the right to not buy a product that is offered for sale.
    d) the right to influence products and marketing in ways that will improve the "quality of life."

    Answer: (c)   Difficulty: 2 Page: 571

37. The organized movement of concerned citizens and government agencies to protect and improve the living environment of people is called:

    a) Consumerism.
    b) Environmentalism
    c) Moralism
    d) Individualism.

    Answer: (b)   Difficulty: 1 Page: 572

38. For environmentalists, the goal of the marketing system is to:

    a) maximize consumption.
    b) maximize consumer choice.
    c) maximize consumer satisfaction.
    d) maximize life quality.

    Answer: (d)   Difficulty: 1 Page: 572

39. Marketer's response to environmentalism and the "earth decade" of the 1990s by developing ecologically safer products, recyclable and biodegradable packaging, better pollution controls, and more energy-efficient operations is called:

    a) environmental marketing.
    b) green marketing.
    c) societal marketing.
    d) earth-value marketing.

    Answer: (b)   Difficulty: 2 Page: 573

40. 3M "Pollution Prevention Pays" program is an example of:

    a) environmental marketing.
    b) green marketing.
    c) societal marketing.
    d) earth-value marketing.

    Answer: (b)   Difficulty: 2 Page: 573

41. The philosophy that holds that a company's marketing should support the best long-run performance of the marketing system is called:

    a) value marketing.
    b) environmental marketing.
    c) societal marketing.
    d) enlightened marketing.

    Answer: (d)   Difficulty: 2 Page: 577

42. When a company views and organizes its marketing activities from the consumer's point of view, this enlightened marketing principle is called:

    a) Consumer-oriented marketing.
    b) Innovative marketing.
    c) Value marketing.
    d) Societal marketing.

    Answer: (a)   Difficulty: 1 Page: 577

43. The principle of enlightened marketing that requires the company to seek real product and marketing improvements continuously is called:

    a) Consumer-oriented marketing.
    b) Innovative marketing.
    c) Value marketing.
    d) Societal marketing.

    Answer: (b)   Difficulty: 1 Page: 577

44. Which of the following principles of enlightened marketing calls for continually improving the value consumers receive from the firm's marketing offer?

    a) Consumer-oriented marketing.
    b) Innovative marketing.
    c) Value marketing.
    d) Societal marketing.

    Answer: (c)   Difficulty: 1 Page: 577

45. Which of the following principles of enlightened marketing holds that a company should define in broad social terms rather than narrow product terms?

    a) Consumer-oriented marketing.
    b) Innovative marketing.
    c) Sense-of-mission marketing
    d) Societal marketing.

    Answer: (c)   Difficulty: 1 Page: 578

46. When Johnson & Johnson reshapes the basic task of selling consumer products in the larger mission of serving the interests of consumers, employees, suppliers, and others in the world community, they are following which principle of enlightened marketing?

    a) Sense-of-mission marketing.
    b) Innovative marketing.
    c) Value marketing.
    d) Societal marketing.

    Answer: (a)   Difficulty: 1 Page: 578

47. When companies make marketing decisions by considering consumers' wants and the long-run interests of the company, consumer, and the general population, they are practicing which principle of enlightened marketing?

    a) Consumer-oriented marketing.
    b) Value marketing.
    c) Sense-of-mission marketing.
    d) Societal marketing.

    Answer: (d)   Difficulty: 1 Page: 578

48. From the societal marketing perspective, products that provide immediate satisfaction and high long-run benefits are called:

    a) deficient products.
    b) pleasing products.
    c) salutary products.
    d) desirable products.

    Answer: (d)   Difficulty: 1 Page: 579

49. From the societal marketing perspective, products that have low appeal but may benefit consumers in the long run are called:

    a) deficient products.
    b) pleasing products.
    c) salutary products.
    d) desirable products.

    Answer: (c)   Difficulty: 1 Page: 579

50. From a societal marketing perspective, products that give high immediate satisfaction, but may hurt consumers in the long run are called:

    a) deficient products.
    b) pleasing products.
    c) salutary products.
    d) desirable products.

    Answer: (b)   Difficulty: 1 Page: 579

51. From a societal marketing perspective, products that have neither immediate appeal nor long-run benefits are called:

    a) deficient products.
    b) pleasing products.
    c) salutary products.
    d) desirable products.

    Answer: (a)   Difficulty: 1   Page: 579

TRUE/FALSE

52. Many critics claim that the American marketing system causes prices to be higher than they would be under more "sensible" systems.

    Answer: True   Difficulty: 2   Page: 559

53. The longstanding charge that greedy intermediaries mark up prices beyond the value of their services is a complaint related to criticism of marketing for the high cost of distribution.

    Answer: True   Difficulty: 1   Page: 559

54. Retailers respond to criticism of high costs of distribution by pointing if some Resellers try to charge too much relative to the value they add, other Resellers will step in with lower prices.

    Answer: True   Difficulty: 1   Page: 560

55. The high cost of advertising and promotion is among the criticisms of marketing's impact on society as a whole.

    Answer: False   Difficulty: 1   Page: 560

56. Marketers respond to charges of high advertising and promotion costs by pointing out that packaging and promotion add only psychological value to the product.

    Answer: False   Difficulty: 2   Page: 560

57. Most consumer abuses are intentional according to the Better Business Bureau.

    Answer: False   Difficulty: 2   Page: 560

58. Pharmaceutical excessive markups must cover the costs of purchasing, promoting, and distributing existing medicines, plus the high research and development costs of finding new medicines.

    Answer: True   Difficulty: 2   Page: 560

59. Deceptive pricing includes practices such as offering a large price reduction from a phony high retail list price.

    Answer: True   Difficulty: 2   Page: 560

60. Falsely advertising "factory" or "wholesale" prices or a large price reduction from a phony high list price are forms of deceptive promotion.

    Answer: False   Difficulty: 2   Page: 560

61. Deceptive packaging includes practices such as overstating the product's features or performance.

    Answer: False   Difficulty: 2   Page: 560

62. Deceptive promotion includes using misleading labeling.

    Answer: False   Difficulty: 2   Page: 560

63. The Wheeler-Lea Act gave the FDA the power to regulate "unfair or deceptive acts or practices."

    Answer: False   Difficulty: 2   Page: 561

64. Since passage of the Wheeler-Lea Act making deceptive practices in marketing illegal, deceptive marketing practices have all but disappeared.

    Answer: False   Difficulty: 2   Page: 562

65. Salespeople are encouraged to use high-pressure selling since the "three-day cooling-off period" allows consumers the right to cancel a contract after rethinking it.

    Answer: False   Difficulty: 1   Page: 562

66. Marketers argue that most companies avoid deceptive practices because such practices harm their business in the long run.

    Answer: True   Difficulty: 2   Page: 521

67. Designing products to wear out and need replacement before they should is called planned obsolescence.

    Answer: True   Difficulty: 1   Page: 563

68. It is common practice that all producers in the electronics industry follow a program of planned obsolescence in order to encourage more and earlier buying.

    Answer: False   Difficulty: 2   Page: 563

69. Accusations that the marketing system provides poor service to disadvantaged consumers are among the criticisms of marketing's impact on society as a whole.

    Answer: False   Difficulty: 2   Page: 566

70. The high failure rate of new products proves that the marketing system cannot control demand simply through advertising.

    Answer: False   Difficulty: 2   Page: 566

71. When businesses are accused of overselling private goods at the expense of public goods, it is a criticism of marketing's impact on society as a whole.

Answer: True   Difficulty: 1 Page: 568

72. Commercials interrupt serious programs; pages of ads obscure printed matter; and billboards mar beautiful scenery are examples of complaints of cultural pollution caused by marketing.

Answer: True   Difficulty: 1 Page: 568

73. When marketing practices bar new companies from entering an industry, it is a criticism of marketing's impact on society as a whole.

Answer: False   Difficulty: 1 Page: 569

74. Consumerism is an organized movement of citizens and government agencies to improve the rights and power of buyers in relation to sellers.

Answer: True   Difficulty: 1 Page: 571

75. Traditional sellers' rights include the right to introduce any legal product desired, even if it is hazardous to personal health or safety.

Answer: False   Difficulty: 2 Page: 571

76. Traditional buyers' rights include the right to use any buying incentive schemes, provided they are not unfair or misleading.

Answer: False   Difficulty: 2 Page: 571

77. Traditional buyers' rights include the right to be well-informed about important aspects of the product.

Answer: False   Difficulty: 2 Page: 571

78. The traditional buyers' rights include the right to expect the product to perform as claimed.

Answer: True   Difficulty: 2 Page: 571

79. Consumers not only have the right but also the responsibility to protect themselves instead of expecting the function to be performed by sellers.

Answer: True   Difficulty: 2 Page: 571

80. Environmentalism is an organized movement of concerned citizens and government agencies to protect and improve people's living environment.

Answer: True   Difficulty: 2 Page: 572

81. According to environmentalists, the marketing system's goal should not be to maximize consumption, consumer choice, or life quality, but rather to maximize consumer satisfaction.

    Answer: False   Difficulty: 2   Page: 572

82. Developing ecologically safer products, recyclable and biodegradable packaging, better pollution controls, and more energy-efficient operations is called green marketing.

    Answer: True   Difficulty: 2   Page: 573

83. The enlightened marketing concept holds that a company's marketing should support the best long-run performance of the marketing system.

    Answer: True   Difficulty: 1   Page: 577

84. Consumer-oriented marketing means that the company should view and organize its marketing activities from the consumer's point of view.

    Answer: True   Difficulty: 1   Page: 577

85. The principle of innovation marketing requires the marketer to continuously seek real product and marketing improvements.

    Answer: True   Difficulty: 2   Page: 577

86. According to the principle of value marketing, the company should put most of its resources into value-building marketing investments.

    Answer: True   Difficulty: 2   Page: 577

87. Examples of value marketing practices include one-shot sales promotions, minor packaging changes, and advertising designed to raise sales in the short run.

    Answer: False   Difficulty: 2   Page: 577

88. Sense-of-mission marketing requires the company to think in broad social terms rather than narrow product terms.

    Answer: True   Difficulty: 2   Page: 578

89. Sense-of-mission marketing means that the company should define its mission in specific product terms rather than in vague social terms.

    Answer: False   Difficulty: 2   Page: 578

90. Making marketing decisions by considering consumers' wants and interests, the company's requirements, and society's long-run interests is called societal marketing.

    Answer: True   Difficulty: 2   Page: 578

91. Desirable products offer high immediate satisfaction in spite of the fact that their long-run impacts tend to be negative.

    Answer: False   Difficulty: 2   Page: 579

92. Pleasing products are easy to sell, but may raise ethical issues with regard to their long-term impacts.

    Answer: True   Difficulty: 2   Page: 579

93. The challenge posed by salutary products is to add some pleasing qualities so that they will become more desirable in the consumers' minds.

    Answer: True   Difficulty: 2   Page: 579

94. To be effective, programs of marketing ethics must be part of the corporate culture of the company.

    Answer: True   Difficulty: 1   Page: 580

95. Ethical conduct requires marketers to go beyond merely complying with the law to consider the morality of their actions.

    Answer: True   Difficulty: 2   Page: 580

96. The problem of morality in marketing can be effectively dealt with by simply developing a comprehensive corporate code of ethics.

    Answer: False   Difficulty: 2   Page: 585

ESSAY

97. List and discuss the social criticisms of marketing's impact on individual consumers.

    Answer:
    Criticisms of marketing's impact on individual consumers include high prices, deceptive practices, high-pressure selling, shoddy or unsafe product, planned obsolescence, and poor service to disadvantaged consumers.

    Difficulty: 3   Page: 559-566

98. Planned obsolescence attempts to persuade consumers to purchase new products before existing products are worn out. Critics say such attempts are wasteful. Discuss.

    Answer:
    Planned product obsolescence, designing products to become obsolete before they should actually need to be replaced. Consumer receives psychological and/or functional satisfaction from having the latest product. Planned obsolescence allows the consumer to satisfy their desire for change. Consumers get tired of the old goods and want a new look in fashion or a new design in cars.

    Difficulty: 2   Page: 563

99. List and discuss each of the social criticisms of marketing's impact on society as a whole.

    Answer:
    The American marketing system has been accused of adding to several societal evils including false wants and too much materialism, too few social goods, cultural pollution and too much political power.

    Difficulty: 2   Page: 566-570

100. Define consumerism. Explain how consumerism affects marketing strategies.

    Answer:
    Consumerism is an organized movement of citizens and government agencies to improve the right and powers of buyers in relation to sellers. Marketing strategies often seek to position the company as more consumer-oriented.

    Difficulty: 2   Page: 570

101. Define environmentalism. Explain how environmentalism affects marketing strategies.

    Answer:
    Environmentalism is an organized movement of concerned citizens and government agencies to protect and improve people's living environment. Marketing strategies often seek to position the company as more environmentally responsible.

    Difficulty: 2   Page: 572

102. Explain the philosophy of enlightened marketing. Include in your discussion the five basic principles.

    Answer:
    Enlightened marketing is a marketing philosophy holding that a company's marketing should support the best long-run performance of the marketing system. Its five principles include consumer-oriented marketing, innovative marketing, value marketing, sense-of-mission marketing, and societal marketing.

    Difficulty: 2   Page: 577